Tableau 10 Business Intelligence Cookbook

Create powerful, effective visualizations to help analyze your data with Tableau 10 by your side

Donabel Santos

BIRMINGHAM - MUMBAI

Tableau 10 Business Intelligence Cookbook

First published: November 2016

Production reference: 1241116

Published by Packt Publishing Ltd.
Livery Place
35 Livery Street
Birmingham B3 2PB, UK.

ISBN 978-1-78646-563-4

www.packtpub.com

Credits

Author
Donabel Santos

Reviewer
Sneha Vijay

Commissioning Editor
Veena Pagare

Acquisition Editor
Vinay Argekar

Content Development Editor
Manthan Raja

Technical Editor
Danish Shaikh

Copy Editor
Safis Editing

Project Coordinator
Nidhi Joshi

Proofreader
Safis Editing

Indexer
Aishwarya Gangawane

Graphics
Disha Haria

Production Coordinator
Arvindkumar Gupta

Cover Work
Arvindkumar Gupta

About the Author

Donabel Santos is a self-confessed data geek. She loves working with data, writing queries and developing reports on her SQL Server databases, and exploring and visualizing data with Tableau.

She is the principal and senior Business Intelligence Architect at QueryWorks Solutions, a Tableau Learning and Alliance partner in Vancouver, BC, Canada providing consulting and training services. She has spent years in consulting and has developed a variety of solutions for clients in different verticals—finance, manufacturing, healthcare, legal, higher education, and local government.

Donabel is a multi-year Microsoft Data Platform MVP (previously known as SQL Server MVP) and has extensive experience in SQL Server in different areas, such as development, administration, data warehouse, reporting (SSRS), tuning, troubleshooting, XML, CLR, integration with ERPs and CRMs using PowerShell, C#, SSIS, and Power BI.

One of Donabel's passions is teaching and sharing her love for data. She is a Tableau Certified Professional and a Tableau Accredited Trainer, delivering Tableau public and on-site client training. She is also the lead instructor for a number of courses at British Columbia Institute of Technology (BCIT), including Applied Database Administration and Design (ADAD) and Applied Data Analytics (ADA) programs. She teaches SQL Server Administration, Development, Integration (SSIS), Data Warehouse Foundations, and Visual Analytics with Tableau.

Donabel has also authored three other books with Packt Publishing: *SQL Server 2012 with PowerShell V3 Cookbook*, *PowerShell for SQL Server Essentials*, and *SQL Server 2014 with PowerShell V5 Cookbook*. She also contributed a chapter in Manning Publications' PowerShell Deep Dives. Her blog is located at www.sqlbelle.com and her Twitter handle is @sqlbelle.

Acknowledgements

To Riley, you have made Mama and Dada's lives so much more beautiful, so much more meaningful. We are so very thankful and blessed that you came into our lives. We cannot imagine life without you.

More than anything, we want you to be happy. We want you to follow your dreams and be all that you want to be. We want your journey to be beautiful, meaningful, and full of happiness. Mama and Dada will always be by your side, supporting you, loving you, and giving you the best that we can.

We love you forever. You will always be our baby, and we will always be Mama and Dada.

Let me borrow some of the lyrics of your favorite lullaby, for these words reflect what Mama and Dada feel every time we see you, hold you, think of you:

And at last I see the light

And it's like the fog has lifted

And at last I see the light

And it's like the sky is new

And it's warm and real and bright

And the world has somehow shifted

All at once everything looks different

Now that I see you

To Eric, you are my ray of sunshine. I am so blessed to go through this journey with you. Now we have a little one to share our crazy adventures with, and I am looking forward to each one of them. *I seem to have loved you in numberless forms, numberless times... In life after life, in age after age, forever.*—Rabindranath Tagore

To Papa and Mama, I am forever grateful for everything that you've done and everything that you've sacrificed to give us a better life. I love you both very, very much. To JR and RR, no matter what happens, you will always be my baby brothers, and I will always be your big sis, and I will always be here for you.

To my nieces and nephews—Chiyo, Jayden, Kristina, Tim, and Evan—now that the book is done, Tita/Agim has more time to play! Let's go!

To my in-laws, I am very thankful to be part of your families.

To my BCIT family—Kevin Cudihee, Elsie Au, Joanne Atha, Vaani Nadhan, Cynthia van Ginkel, Charlie Blattler, Bob Langelaan, Paul Mills—thank you. My special thanks to Kevin Cudihee. Thank you for giving me that first chance to teach at BCIT. More than a decade later, I still love every minute that I teach. And to Elsie Au, for the friendship all these years.

To my UBC family—I am fortunate to work in a great place with great, smart, fun, passionate people who I deeply admire and learn from. To my teammates, co-workers, acquaintances, and friends, especially Joe Xing, Min Zhu, Jason Metcalfe, Tom Yerex, Jing Zhu, George Firican, Shirley Tsui, Lynda Campbell, Cindy Lee, Pat Carew, Stan Tian (our Tableau Server superhero at UBC!), Ana Maria Hobrough, and to my truly wonderful director and mentor, Pradeep Nair: it is a privilege to work with all of you.

To the Packt team, to Vinay Argekar for that e-mail asking if I was interested in authoring a Tableau book, and to Siddhesh Salvi and Manthan Raja, for really supporting me throughout the writing process, thank you. A huge thank you to Sneha Vijay as well for reviewing the book and providing a lot of feedback and nuggets of wisdom. Thank you for helping me make this book better.

To the Tableau family, it is so amazing to be part of your community. So many smart and very passionate professionals—so many data geeks!—how could I not feel at home? Thank you to Dan Murray, who was my instructor when I took my first Tableau course and who encouraged me to attend my very first Tableau conference. You've truly helped change the direction of my career. To Jonathan Drummey and Joe Mako—whom I met at that first TC conference (and who probably don't remember me), who have been so gracious and helpful—I didn't even realize they were THE rockstars! To George Gorczynski—Tableau Picasso—whom I have had the privilege of meeting in Vancouver—I owe you for helping me with my course. To Ramon Martinez, whose visualizations set the bar for healthcare (which I showcase a lot, especially for healthcare training). Special thanks to Molly Monsey for giving me the opportunity to teach the Tableau courses for Tableau (I love teaching Tableau!), and to Meagan Corbett for your constant and very timely help on the TFT (Tableau for Teaching) side—my students appreciate your help a lot!

I have learned so much from so many, and this space simply isn't enough. Thank you to everyone who has helped me, taught me, and inspired me.

And most importantly, thank you Lord for all the miracles and blessings in my life.

About the Reviewer

Sneha has a well-rounded consulting background in domains of Data and Analytics with specialization in Tableau. Having over 4 years of experience and successful track record in Consulting, Analytics, Building sophisticated reporting technologies, Data Mining and Tableau visualizations, she provide users with the ability to examine information and uncover hidden trends and anomalies. Currently, Sneha works at Deloitte US Consulting based out of Gurgaon, India. Sneha's passions are spending time with his family, swimming and enjoying music to the fullest.

www.PacktPub.com

eBooks, discount offers, and more

Did you know that Packt offers eBook versions of every book published, with PDF and ePub files available? You can upgrade to the eBook version at www.PacktPub.com and as a print book customer, you are entitled to a discount on the eBook copy. Get in touch with us at customercare@packtpub.com for more details.

At www.PacktPub.com, you can also read a collection of free technical articles, sign up for a range of free newsletters and receive exclusive discounts and offers on Packt books and eBooks.

https://www.packtpub.com/mapt

Get the most in-demand software skills with Mapt. Mapt gives you full access to all Packt books and video courses, as well as industry-leading tools to help you plan your personal development and advance your career.

Why Subscribe?

- ▸ Fully searchable across every book published by Packt
- ▸ Copy and paste, print, and bookmark content
- ▸ On demand and accessible via a web browser

Table of Contents

Preface

Data viz, visualization, analytics, visual analytics – these are some of the words that you probably hear more often these days. With the explosion of data, we try to find ways to better analyze and represent them to facilitate understanding and communication.

Tableau is a software package that helps explore, visualize, analyze, and make sense of data. It helps us see different kinds of data in a different light. Tableau makes it easy to connect to different kinds of data sets and understand it more and see what kinds of stories we can unearth. It doesn't matter if it's business data, social data, maybe your fitness tracker data, or a playlist—it is fascinating to see and learn something about our business, our health, our own social network, our world in general.

When I was first introduced to Tableau a few years ago, I had no idea what I was getting into. I had the privilege of taking the Tableau in-person class with Tableau Zen Master, Dan Murray, with just a day or two of Tableau exposure. I was blown away by how powerful and fun this product was to use. It didn't feel like work at all!

I was, and still am, used to writing a lot of code to generate queries and reports. It was almost surreal for me to see how I can create beautiful charts with a few drag and drops. I thought Tableau was easy and almost questioned why I had to take the class.

True, Tableau is easy to use. It is a compliment to the company and the product, because as Steve Jobs once said, *easy is hard.* To make the product easy to use amounts to a lot of hard work from those who made it happen. I also realize that it was an invaluable experience to take the class from Dan Murray because he was able to share his knowledge, experience, and nuggets of wisdom as he talked about Tableau—something not captured in the workbooks.

Being a bookworm (or book hoarder) though, I wished there were books I could get to supplement what I learned from that two-day workshop. At the time, there were no books on Tableau. Working through the exercises was easy while the instructor was there, but as soon as I left the classroom, I remember scratching my head asking *how did I do that again?*

I found this same conundrum when I started teaching Visual Analytics with Tableau at BCIT's Part Time program. There were no books available. While there were video tutorials and online documentation, I still needed to have more structure in the classroom. I had to write a lot of notes for students so they would have some easy, accessible references on how to do certain things in Tableau.

This cookbook provides step-by-step instructions on how to build different charts and complete different tasks in Tableau. This book aims to provide a foundation in becoming more comfortable with Tableau—to allow you to see and explore other possibilities.

This book is a labor of love. Mixed with technical details, some nuggets of wisdom, some tips and shortcuts, this is the book I wish I had written for me when I first started learning about the product. This is the book I wish I was able to provide students with when they took my first Tableau courses.

Tableau reignited the curiosity in me. I started becoming more aware and started caring a lot more about data round me. I've enjoyed learning Tableau and still enjoy learning and relearning it as new versions come along. I've enjoyed working different kinds of data.

I hope you enjoy this book, and I hope this book helps you with your own Tableau journey. May the force be with you.

What this book covers

Chapter 1, Basic Charts, introduces some of the common charts, what is required to create them, which situations they might be most effective in, and how to create them in Tableau. Some of the charts covered in this chapter include bar charts, line charts, scatter plots, heat maps, cross tabs (or text tables), highlight tables, area charts, pie charts, and histograms.

Chapter 2, Advanced Charts, looks at creating additional charts in Tableau. These charts are classified as advanced because they may require additional or more specific steps to create in Tableau compared to the charts in *Chapter 1, Basic Charts*. This chapter explores shared axis charts, different variations of dual axis charts, bar in bar charts, box and whisker plot charts , bullet charts, and motion charts.

Chapter 3, Interactivity, presents different ways to incorporate interactivity within Tableau charts. Interactivity can keep whoever is consuming your charts more engaged and encourage them to ask questions, answer questions, and ask more questions without breaking the flow of analysis.

Chapter 4, Dashboards and Story Points, covers how to combine different charts in dashboards to provide a consolidated view of the data. Story points are also introduced to provide a more effective way to present information catered to specific audiences and messages.

Chapter 5, Geospatial, showcases Tableau's different mapping support and capabilities. There are recipes to add layers to default maps, create custom territories, use Web Map Service (WMS), and use custom polygons, backgrounds, and geocoding.

Chapter 6, Analytics, explores Tableau's powerful built-in analytics components, which can help provide additional insights into data. This chapter shows how to use constant lines, trend lines, reference lines and bands, cluster analysis, and forecasting. There is also a recipe that integrates Tableau with R to perform linear regression.

Chapter 7, Data Preparation, includes recipes to help clean, transform, or combine data sets to prepare them for data analysis in Tableau. This chapter discusses different data preparation strategies, including using the Data Interpreter, pivot, and schema.ini, as well as comparing operations such as union, join, and blend.

Appendix A, Calculated Fields Primer, presents an introduction to calculated fields in Tableau. Calculated fields are used throughout the book, and this chapter provides a comprehensive introduction to Tableau's calculated fields for anyone who needs a primer.

Appendix B, Resources, offers a list of resources on articles, white papers, websites, data sources for the workbooks, and a list of publicly available data that readers can use to download data sets. This will help readers further the skills they learn from this book by learning more about the best practices for visual analytics and optimization as well as by discovering additional data sets they can use recipes in this book on.

Appendix C, Working with Tableau 10, is a Tableau 10 primer which will provide fundamental working knowledge of Tableau. This chapter also provides some field notes of things to remember when working with Tableau – to help you avoid common gotchas and get you more effective with Tableau right away. Appendix C is an online downloadable resource from Packt Publishing.

What you need for this book

You will need to install Tableau Desktop V10 to follow the recipes in this book. Tableau Desktop can be downloaded from `www.tableau.com`. The trial version of Tableau offers a fully functional version for 14 days.

If you are an educator or student using Tableau for your course, please check out Tableau for Teaching (TFT). You can find more information at `http://www.tableau.com/academic/teaching`. This is a great program for educators who want to integrate visual analytics in their courses.

If you are a journalist, Tableau Desktop is available free for you at `https://public.tableau.com/en-us/s/blog/2013/06/journalists-now-tableau-desktop-free-you`.

You can also use Tableau Public, a free version of the software, to complete many of the recipes. Tableau Public has some limitations, however, which may prevent you from following some of the steps. You can find the comparison and limitations of the different Tableau Desktop versions at `https://public.tableau.com/en-us/s/download`.

While this book covers Tableau V10, many of the concepts and steps still apply to other versions, barring some minor changes in steps or interface.

Who this book is for

This book is for anyone who wants to explore, analyze, and learn more about their data. From university and college students to business analysts and managers to data and analytics professionals, this is for anyone who wants to build rich interactive visualizations using Tableau.

Familiarity with previous versions of Tableau will be helpful but not necessary. This book comes with a supplementary chapter – *Appendix C, Working with Tableau 10*, which aims to help the novice navigate their way and get up to speed with Tableau. This supplementary chapter can be downloaded from the following link:

`https://www.packtpub.com/sites/default/files/downloads/`
`AppendixCWorkingwithTableau10.pdf`

Sections

In this book, you will find several headings that appear frequently (Getting ready, How to do it, How it works, There's more, and See also).

To give clear instructions on how to complete a recipe, we use these sections, as follows:

Getting ready

This section tells you what to expect in the recipe, and describes how to set up any software or any preliminary settings required for the recipe.

How to do it...

This section contains the steps required to follow the recipe.

How it works...

This section usually consists of a detailed explanation of what happened in the previous section.

There's more...

This section consists of additional information about the recipe in order to make the reader more knowledgeable about the recipe.

See also

This section provides helpful links to other useful information for the recipe.

Conventions

In this book, you will find a number of text styles that distinguish between different kinds of information. Here are some examples of these styles and an explanation of their meaning.

Code words in text, database table names, folder names, filenames, file extensions, pathnames, dummy URLs, user input, and Twitter handles are shown as follows: "In the following example you can see the function syntax for DATEDIFF.

A block of code is set as follows:

```
AVG(
    {INCLUDE [Customer Name]: SUM([Profit])}
)
```

New terms and **important words** are shown in bold. Words that you see on the screen, for example, in menus or dialog boxes, appear in the text like this: "Once we add another discrete value, for example, **Category** onto the **Columns** shelf, we are now breaking **SUM(Sales)** down to a subtotal for each **Category**."

Warnings or important notes appear in a box like this.

Tips and tricks appear like this.

Reader feedback

Feedback from our readers is always welcome. Let us know what you think about this book—what you liked or disliked. Reader feedback is important for us as it helps us develop titles that you will really get the most out of.

To send us general feedback, simply e-mail `feedback@packtpub.com`, and mention the book's title in the subject of your message.

If there is a topic that you have expertise in and you are interested in either writing or contributing to a book, see our author guide at `www.packtpub.com/authors`.

Customer support

Now that you are the proud owner of a Packt book, we have a number of things to help you to get the most from your purchase.

Downloading the workbook starters

You can download the workbook starters and select sample data sets for this book from your account at `http://www.packtpub.com`. If you purchased this book elsewhere, you can visit `http://www.packtpub.com/support` and register to have the files e-mailed directly to you.

You can download the code files by following these steps:

1. Log in or register to our website using your e-mail address and password.
2. Hover the mouse pointer on the **SUPPORT** tab at the top.
3. Click on **Code Downloads & Errata**.
4. Enter the name of the book in the **Search** box.
5. Select the book for which you're looking to download the code files.
6. Choose from the drop-down menu where you purchased this book from.
7. Click on **Code Download**.

Once the file is downloaded, please make sure that you unzip or extract the folder using the latest version of:

▸ WinRAR / 7-Zip for Windows
▸ Zipeg / iZip / UnRarX for Mac
▸ 7-Zip / PeaZip for Linux

The code bundle for the book is also hosted on GitHub at `https://github.com/PacktPublishing/Tableau-10-Business-Intelligence-Cookbook`. We also have other code bundles from our rich catalog of books and videos available at `https://github.com/PacktPublishing/`. Check them out!

Errata

Although we have taken every care to ensure the accuracy of our content, mistakes do happen. If you find a mistake in one of our books—maybe a mistake in the text or the code—we would be grateful if you could report this to us. By doing so, you can save other readers from frustration and help us improve subsequent versions of this book. If you find any errata, please report them by visiting `http://www.packtpub.com/submit-errata`, selecting your book, clicking on the **Errata Submission Form** link, and entering the details of your errata. Once your errata are verified, your submission will be accepted and the errata will be uploaded to our website or added to any list of existing errata under the Errata section of that title.

To view the previously submitted errata, go to `https://www.packtpub.com/books/content/support` and enter the name of the book in the search field. The required information will appear under the **Errata** section.

Piracy

Piracy of copyrighted material on the Internet is an ongoing problem across all media. At Packt, we take the protection of our copyright and licenses very seriously. If you come across any illegal copies of our works in any form on the Internet, please provide us with the location address or website name immediately so that we can pursue a remedy.

Please contact us at `copyright@packtpub.com` with a link to the suspected pirated material.

We appreciate your help in protecting our authors and our ability to bring you valuable content.

Questions

If you have a problem with any aspect of this book, you can contact us at `questions@packtpub.com`, and we will do our best to address the problem.

1
Basic Charts

In this chapter, we will cover:

- Creating a bar chart
- Creating a stacked bar chart
- Creating a line chart
- Creating a scatter plot
- Creating a heat map
- Creating a text table (crosstab)
- Creating a highlight table
- Creating an area chart
- Creating a pie chart
- Creating a bubble chart
- Creating a word cloud
- Creating a tree map

Introduction

You are about to embark on a wonderful journey with Tableau! We will classify charts that are easily created in Tableau without much customization as basic. Charts that might be less commonly used, or ones that require more steps and configurations, will be tackled in the next chapter as advanced charts.

In this chapter, we will start with the basic charts that you can create with Tableau. Each recipe will demonstrate the steps required to create different graphs. You will also find nuggets of formatting and annotation options in select recipes that will enhance the charts.

Although the recipes are presented in a specific sequence of steps, more often than not, you can re-create the same visualization even if the steps are in a different order. You can start experimenting with these once you are more comfortable with Tableau.

Ready to start your Tableau adventure? If so, proceed with gusto!

Creating a bar chart

Bar charts represent numeric values as bars, split across clear categories. Bar charts are very effective charts for comparing magnitudes, and spotting highs and lows in the data.

In this recipe, we will create a bar chart that shows the top 15 movies in 2007-2011 by Average Rotten Tomatoes Score.

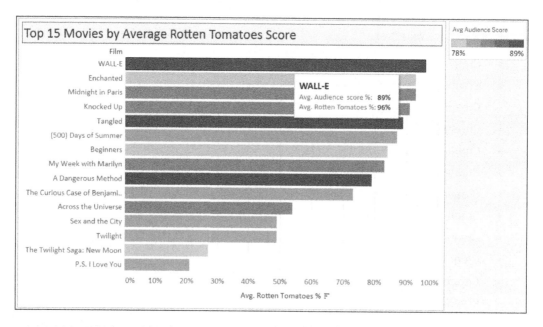

Getting ready

To follow this recipe, open B05527_01 - STARTER.twbx file. Use the worksheet called Bar, and connect to the HollywoodMostProfitableStories data source.

How to do it...

The following are the steps to create the top 15 movies bar chart:

1. From **Dimensions**, drag **Film** to **Rows**.

2. From **Measures**, drag **Rotten Tomatoes** % to **Columns**.

3. Change the aggregation of **Rotten Tomatoes** % from **Sum** to **Average**. You can do this by clicking on the drop-down icon in the **Rotten Tomatoes** % pill, or by right-clicking it:

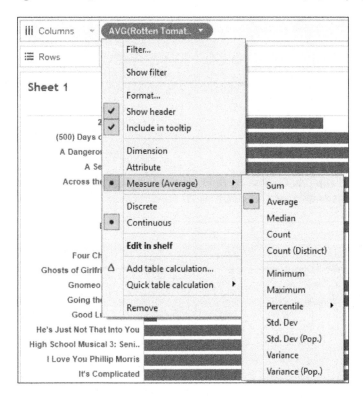

4. Hover your mouse pointer over the **Avg. Rotten Tomatoes** % axis and click on the sort icon that appears. This will sort the bars in descending order:

Note that once the bars are sorted, you will find the descending sort icon appears beside the axis name, even without hovering over it.

5. From **Dimensions**, drag **Film** to the **Filters** shelf. This will open a menu for filters:

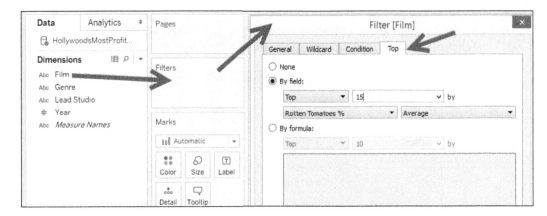

6. Select the **Top** tab. Choose **By field:** and specify **Top**, 15, **Rotten Tomatoes** %, and **Average** as shown next. Click **OK** when done:

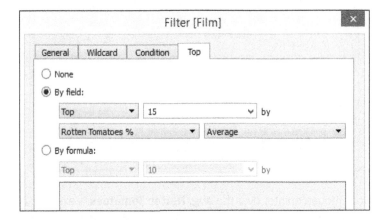

7. Adjust the width and height of the film titles. You can do this by moving your mouse pointer to the column or row edge of a film until you see a double-headed arrow. The left-right double-headed arrow allows you to adjust the width, and the up-down double-headed arrow allows you to adjust the height.

8. From **Measures**, drag **Audience Score** % to the **Color** in the **Marks** card. Change the **Aggregation** from **Sum** to **Average**:

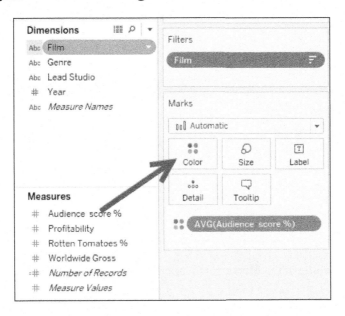

9. Click on the drop-down arrow beside the color legend and choose **Edit title...**. Change the title to `Avg Audience Score`. You can get to this option by clicking on the drop-down arrow on the color legend's top-right corner.

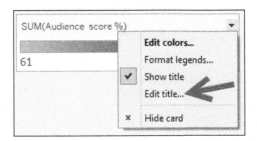

10. Click on the drop-down arrow beside the color legend again. This time choose **Edit colors...**.

11. Choose the **Blue 10.0** palette. Select the **Stepped Color**, and specify 5 steps:

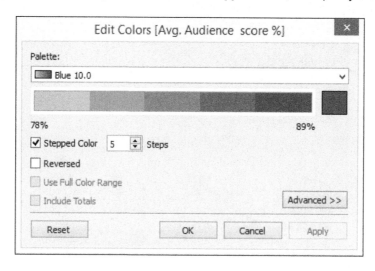

12. Click on **Tooltip** in the **Marks** cards, and add the following tooltip:

 Note that only fields you have used in the sheet can be added in the tooltip via the **Insert** dropdown. You can also add some predefined values such as **Data Source Name**, **Sheet Name**, or **Page Count**.

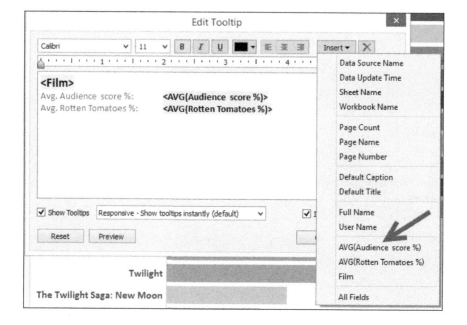

How it works...

Bar charts are probably one of the most common, if not the most common, type of chart that is used to visualize data. Bar charts are best used when you are comparing numeric data that is clearly split between different items or categories. These charts are an easy favorite among the chart types because it allows us to easily look at the edges, and see approximately how much longer one bar is than another, even if the difference is very slight. Bars are also often sorted to make it easy to spot top or bottom items.

Bar charts can be presented either vertically or horizontally. The decision sometimes depends on the number of items being represented. If you have many items, labels can become less readable with vertical bar charts. In Tableau, there is an easy way to switch between vertical and horizontal bar charts. There is a swap icon in the Tableau toolbar that swaps the pills from **Rows** to **Columns** and vice versa.

In this recipe, we simply dragged the **Film** dimension to **Columns** and the **Avg. Rotten Tomatoes** % measure to **Rows**, and Tableau already knew what to do. When you check out your **Marks** card, you will see that the selection is still set to **Automatic**, but the actual icon beside it is bars:

To help the reader understand the bar chart better, we can also sort the bars in either ascending or descending fashion. A quick way to sort items in Tableau is by hovering over a column header or an axis, until you see a sort icon appear. In an axis, the first click on the icon sorts the marks in descending fashion. The second click sorts ascending, and the third click sorts it back to data source order. With a column header, which is produced by discrete fields, the fields will be sorted alphabetically in ascending order on the first click, descending on the second click, and then back to data source order on the third click.

Discrete and continuous fields are discussed in more detail in *Appendix C, Working with Tableau 10*. This book comes with a supplementary chapter – *Appendix C, Working with Tableau 10*, which aims to help the novice navigate their way and get up to speed with Tableau. This supplementary chapter can be downloaded from the following link:

```
https://www.packtpub.com/sites/default/files/
downloads/AppendixCWorkingwithTableau10.pdf
```

In our recipe, we also picked the top 15 highest rated films from our data source. We are setting the expectation that as the reader sees the movies from top to bottom, the ratings also are lower. Tableau makes it easy to pick the top n items on some measure. You can simply right-click on the dimension you want to filter, and select **Filter...** to open the filter window for more options. Tableau provides a tab called **Top**, which allows you to keep only the top or bottom *n* items, based on a measure you specify.

One enhancement we can do with bar charts that Tableau allows us to do very easily is to overlay another measure. In this recipe, we used color to show the **Avg Audience Score** %. You will notice that although the length of the bars are in descending fashion, the color density doesn't follow the same pattern. This indicates that the audience may not necessarily agree with the **Rotten Tomatoes** % ratings.

There's more...

Bar charts can also be created using Tableau's **Show Me** tool, which by default appears in the top-right corner of your Tableau design area. You simply need to select the fields from your side bar that you wish to visualize, and the possible charts from this combination are enabled in the **Show Me** tool. The **Show Me** tool is introduced and discussed in more detail in *Appendix C, Working with Tableau 10*.

See also

▸ Please refer to the *Creating a stacked bar chart* recipe in this chapter

Creating a stacked bar chart

Stacked bar charts, like regular bar charts, represent numeric values as segmented bars, and each bar is a specific, distinct category. The segments in the bar that are stacked on top of each other represent related values, and the total length of the bar represents the cumulative total of the related values for that category.

In this recipe, we will create a stacked bar chart that represents the top movies by year, further segmented by genre.

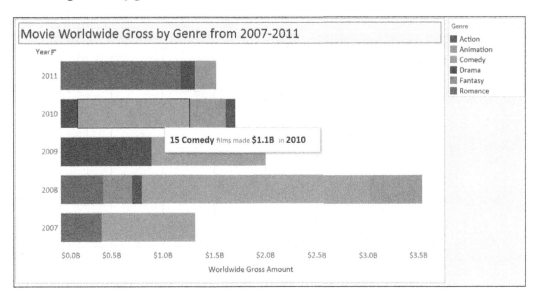

Getting ready

To follow this recipe, open `B05527_01 - STARTER.twbx`. Use the worksheet called **Stacked Bar**, and connect to the **HollywoodMostProfitableStories** data source.

How to do it...

The following are the steps to create the stacked bar chart:

1. From **Dimensions**, drag **Year** to **Rows**.

2. From **Measures**, drag **Worldwide Gross Amount** to **Columns**.

3. Right-click on the **Worldwide Gross Amount** axis and select **Format...**. The original data side bar will now be replaced by the format side bar for the axis.

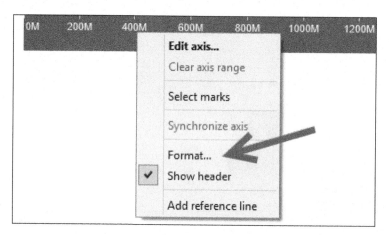

4. Under the **Scale** section, change the **Numbers** format to **Currency (Custom)**, with 1 decimal place, and unit in **Billions (B)**.

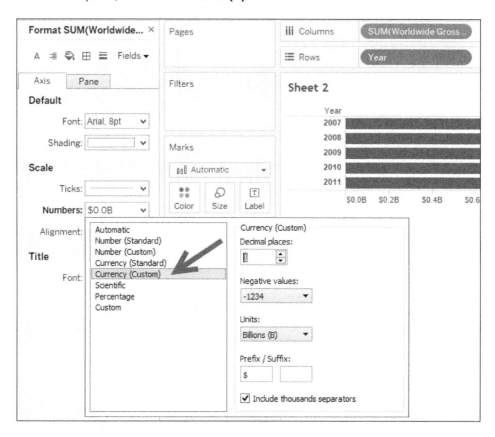

5. Hover your mouse pointer over the **Year** column header, and click twice on the sort icon that appears. The first click sorts the years in ascending order. The second click will sort the years in descending order, with the latest year at the top and earliest year at the bottom.

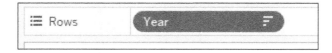

 Note that the **Year** pill in the **Rows** shelf will now have an icon that indicates it is sorted in descending order.

6. Right-click on the **Worldwide Gross Amount** axis and select **Edit Axis**.

7. Under the **Tick Marks** tab in the **Major tick marks** section, select **Fixed** and set it for every **500,000,000** units.

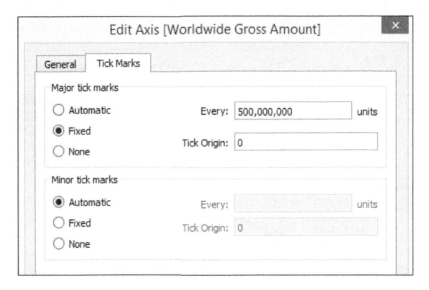

8. From **Dimensions**, drag **Genre** to **Color** in the **Marks** card. This will create the stacked bar.

9. Click on the drop-down arrow beside the color legend and choose **Edit Colors...**.

10. Choose the **Color Blind 10** palette and click on **Assign Palette**. Click on **OK** when done.

11. Adjust the width and height of the bars. You can do this by moving your mouse pointer to the column or row edge of a year until you see a double-headed arrow. The left-right double-headed arrow allows you to adjust the width, and the up-down double-headed arrow allows you to adjust the height.

12. From **Dimensions**, right-click and drag **Film** to **Detail** in the **Marks** card. This will open a window providing options on what exact detail needs to be added to the card.

13. Choose **CNTD(Film)**, which means the number of unique films. **CNTD** is the Count Distinct function.

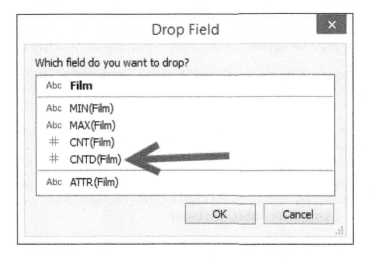

14. Click on **Tooltip** in the **Marks** cards, and add the following tooltip. Note that data points that you have already used in your worksheet (or viz) can be inserted into the tooltip.

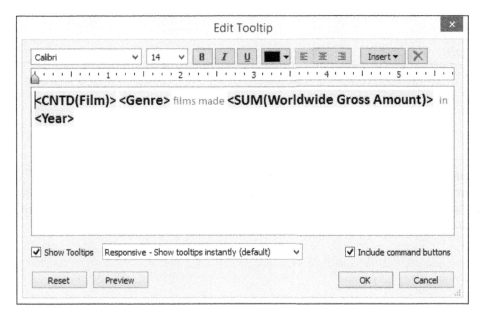

How it works...

A stacked bar chart is simply a bar chart that has bars that are further segmented or split based on some criteria. Stacked bar charts have related values *stacked* on top of each other, and are best used when we want to see cumulative totals instead of individual values.

To create a stacked bar chart, you simply need to drop a discrete field onto a formatting card in your **Marks** card.

 Discrete and continuous fields are discussed in more detail in *Appendix C, Working with Tableau 10*.

The **Marks** card contains additional properties, and depending on the type of mark, there may be a sixth property that appears. To create segments in a bar, we can add the discrete field in any of the following: **Color, Size, Label**, and **Detail**.

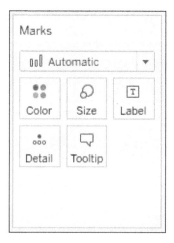

The **Color** tool is often used in stacked bar charts as this splits the bar into different, discernible colors. In this recipe, we started by using a bar chart that represents the top grossing films in 2007-2011. We placed the dimension **Genre** onto **Color**, which created the color partitions in our graph based on **Genre**.

However, depending on what you're displaying, you may also consider using **Size**:

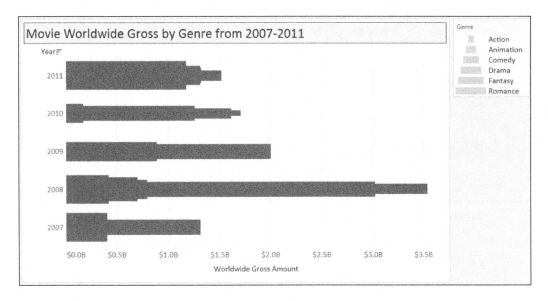

You can also segment the bars by **Label**:

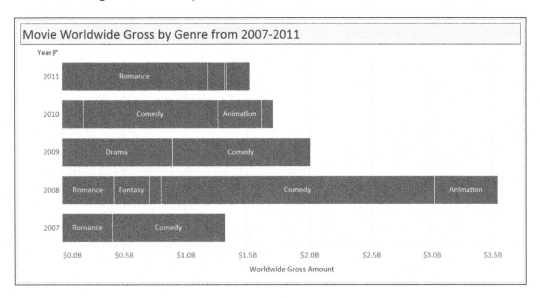

You could also use the combination of **Color**, **Size**, and **Label**:

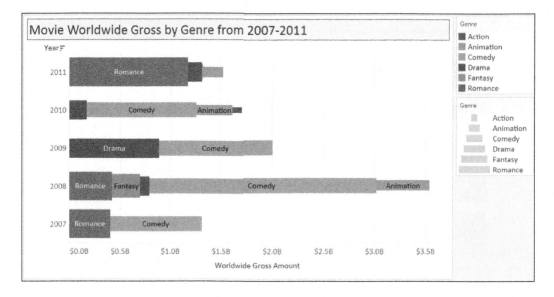

The **Detail** property will also work, but this does not make the segmentation obvious. It simply creates the very thin borders around the segment—which can be easily overlooked.

I encourage you to be adventurous—see what's possible! Tableau allows you to explore possibilities with ease, which is one thing I really love about the tool. I may not necessarily use that combination, but seeing the combination might open up possibilities for me, or see data in a different light, or it might help uncover insights that were previously buried when we were analyzing using a single formatting card.

There's more...

It might be tricky to use **Show Me** to generate a stacked bar chart because the fields placed in **Rows**, **Columns**, and **Headers** are automatically assigned. After the initial chart is generated from **Show Me**, you may need to swap axes, or move pills around.

In addition, be careful when using stacked bar charts. Stacked bar charts are great when you still want to see that cumulative number. However if you wanted to see and compare each individual segment, it will make your analysis hard because the not all of the segments have the same starting point.

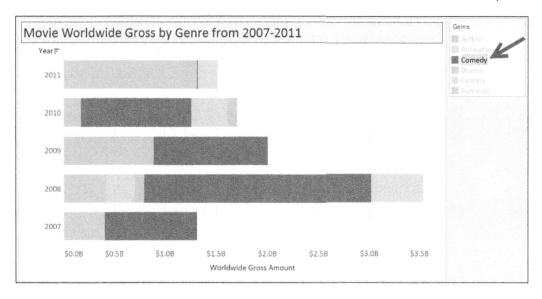

In the previous screenshot, if you highlight just Comedy, you will see that the bars in each year don't start at the same point, therefore it is harder to compare them. For example, can we easily tell that the **Worldwide Gross Amount** for **Comedy** is greater for 2010 compared to 2009? It is hard to tell from this graph.

See also

▸ Please refer to the *Creating a bar chart* recipe in this chapter

Creating a line chart

A line chart often represents trend over time, and typically requires numeric values plotted as lines over date-related fields.

In this recipe, we will create a time series graph (or line chart) that shows the number of floods over time. In addition, we will show the number of fatalities and represent this as the width of the line graph. This will enable us to see more obviously when the most flood-related fatalities occurred.

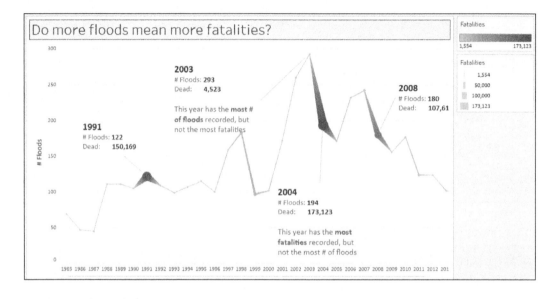

Getting ready

To follow this recipe, open B05527_01 - STARTER.twbx. Use the worksheet called Line, and connect to the MasterTable (FlooddataMasterListrev) data source.

How to do it...

The following are the steps to create a time series graph in Tableau:

1. From **Dimensions**, drag **Began** to **Rows**. Tableau will automatically choose the **YEAR** level for this date field.

2. Right-click on the **Null** column heading in **YEAR(Began)**, and select **Exclude**.

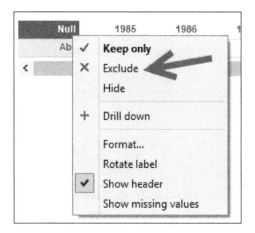

3. From **Measures**, drag **Number of Records** to **Columns**.

4. From **Measures**, drag **Dead** to **Size** in the **Marks** card.

5. Click on the top-right drop-down arrow of the size legend and choose **Edit title...**.

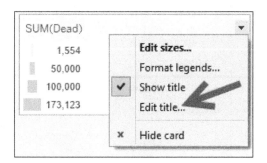

6. Edit the title of the size legend to display **Fatalities**.

7. From **Measures**, drag **Dead** to **Color** in the **Marks** card.

8. Click on the top-right drop-down arrow of the color legend and choose **Edit title...**.

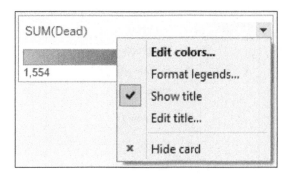

9. Edit the title of the color legend to display **Fatalities**.

10. Click on **Color** in the **Marks** card. Under the **Effects** section, select the middle marker.

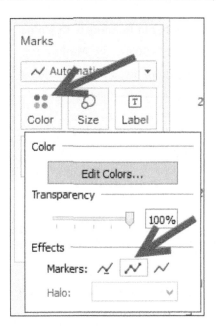

11. Click on **Size** in the **Marks** card. Drag the size control to the right to make the marks in your chart bigger.

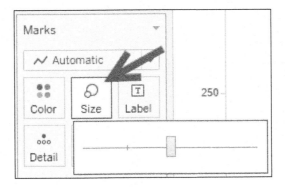

12. Annotate your marks. In this sample, I have chosen to annotate 2003 (the year with the highest number of floods) and 1991, 2004, and 2008 (the years with the highest numbers of fatalities). To annotate the marks, you can right-click on the mark in your chart and select **Annotate**, and then **Mark**.

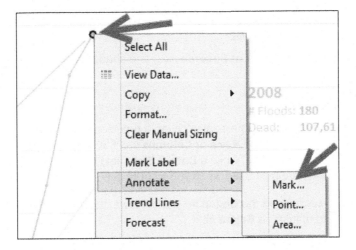

The annotation for the year 2003 looks like the following:

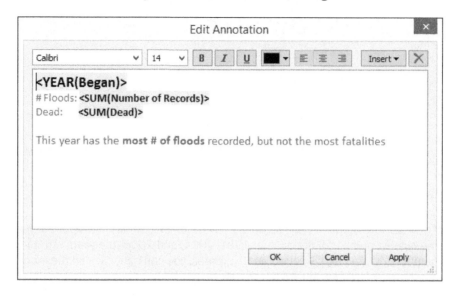

13. Hide the **Began** field label at the top of the chart by right-clicking it, and selecting **Hide field label for columns**.

14. Right-click on the **Number of Records** axis, and change the title to **# Floods**.

How it works...

By default, Tableau creates a line chart—also called a time series chart—when a **Date** (or **Date & Time**) field is placed in either the **Rows** or **Columns** shelf. A **Date** field is presented in the side bar with a small calendar icon, while a **Date & Time** field will be a small calendar icon with a clock. Line charts are best used when you want to see patterns over time.

In this recipe, when we dragged the **Began** field onto **Rows**, the field showed up as **YEAR(Began)** instead of just the **Began** field.

Date fields in Tableau have a natural hierarchy—meaning you can roll up to a higher date level like **YEAR**, or drill down to a lower level like **DAY**. In this case, we see a blue **YEAR(Began)** pill, which indicates Tableau presented the years as a series of discrete headers.

Discrete and continuous fields are discussed in more detail
in *Appendix C, Working with Tableau 10*.

When the year field was rendered, the first column value that appeared was **Null**. A **Null** means there is no value, that is, this data is missing for some records. One way to remove it is to right-click the column header and select **Exclude**. Exclude creates a filter, but it is a negation filter. Whatever is checked will be excluded. When you investigate the settings for this filter, you will find that **Null** is checked, but the bottom checkbox for **Exclude** is checked.

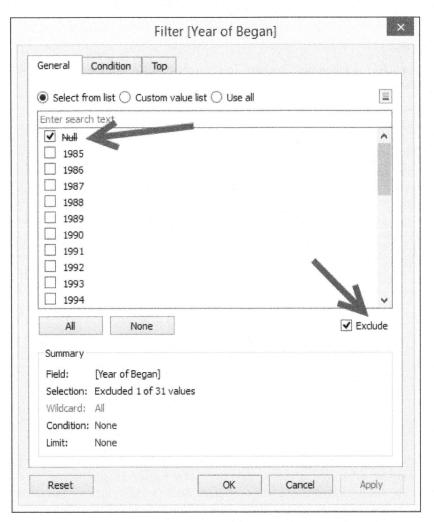

In this recipe, we also used **SUM(Dead)** to be presented both in **Color** and **Size**. The darker the color and the thicker the line indicates the more fatalities. Adding this visual cue in the line graph allows us to easily identify when the most fatalities occurred, without having to hover over each point in the graph and look at the details.

There's more...

Tableau is a great visualization tool that gives us a lot of flexibility over how we want to display our graphs. However, it can also be a double-edged sword. Nothing stops us from creating all kinds of chart just because we can. However, we shouldn't. Just because we can does not mean we should. We should identify first our data points, and evaluate the best (or most effective) way to represent them.

Take, for example, the following line chart. The line chart has a vertical sales axis. At the bottom of the graph, we can find the discrete categories.

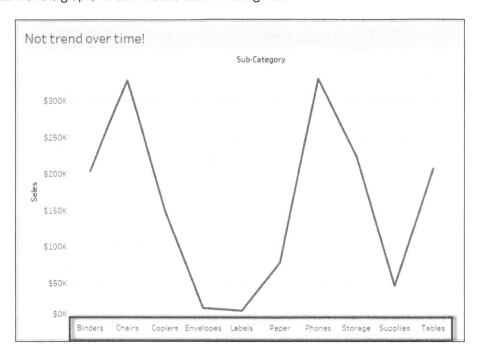

Is the line chart the best way to represent this information? No. In fact, this is incorrect and grossly misleading. When your audience first looks at this graph, the initial perception is that we are showing the fluctuations of sales over time. There is also a notion of *relatedness*, that is, that the category headers are somehow related. This isn't true. Categories are nominal. There is no inherent order in these classifications. When we move the category labels around, it shouldn't affect the message that is being relayed by the graph. This particular graph can be best represented as a bar chart.

See also

▸ Please refer to the *Creating a bar chart* recipe in this chapter

Creating a scatter plot

A scatter plot is technically a collection of *scattered* points. Scatter plots require measures (numeric values) on both the vertical and horizontal axes. Scatter plots allow us to see the relationship between two variables, and are great for visualizing clusters, showing possible correlations, and spotting outliers.

In this recipe, we will use a data source that compiled the highest-paid players in 2014. We will create a scatter plot to see whether there is a general correlation between the earnings of a top player, and the value of their endorsement deals.

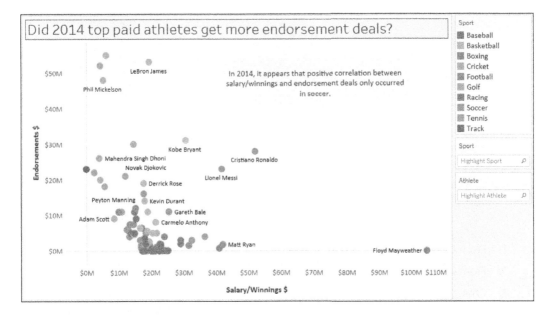

Getting ready

To follow this recipe, open B05527_01 - STARTER.twbx. Use the worksheet called **Scatter Plot**, and connect to the **Top Athlete Salaries (Global Sport Finances)** data source.

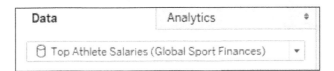

How to do it...

The following are the steps to create the scatter plot presented in this recipe:

1. From **Measures**, drag **Salary/Winnings $** to **Columns**.

2. From **Measures**, drag **Endorsements $** to **Rows**.

3. Change **Mark** to **Circle**.

4. From **Dimensions**, drag **Sport** to **Color** in the **Marks** card.

5. From **Dimensions**, drag **Athlete** to **Label** in the **Marks** card.

6. Change the default number format of **Endorsements $**. You can do this by right-clicking the **Endorsements $** field in the **Measures** section of the side bar, selecting **Default properties** and then **Number Format...**. In the window that shows up, set the following:

    □ **Currency (Custom)**

    □ **Decimal places:** 0

    □ **Prefix $**

    □ **Suffix M**

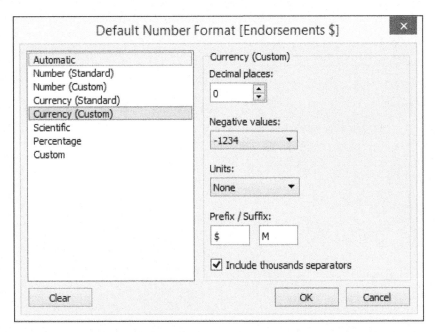

7. Click on the drop-down arrow beside the color legend and choose **Edit colors...**.

8. Choose the **Superfishel Stone** palette and click on **Assign Palette**. Click on **OK** when done.

9. Right-click on the **Sport** pill in the **Marks** card, and select **Show highlighter**. This will show the data highlighter control, a new feature in Tableau 10 that allows you to search and highlight all points on hover.

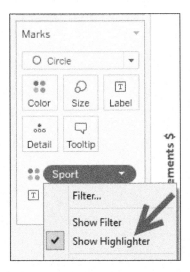

10. Right-click on an empty area in your chart and select **Annotate**, and then **Area**.

11. Add the following text in your area annotation:

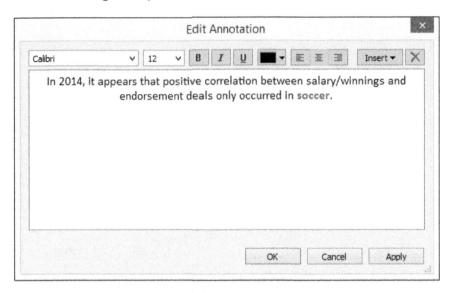

12. Test the data highlighter. Hover each of the options and notice that as you hover over a sports name, only the players (represented by circles) who belong to that sport are highlighted. Note that in this data set, it seems only soccer has a positive correlation between **Salary/Winnings $** and **Endorsements $**.

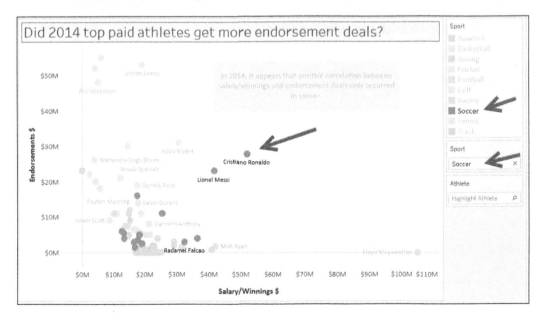

How it works...

Scatter plots are great for determining clusters, correlations, and outliers. Scatter plots require a continuous field in **Rows** (which produces the vertical or *Y* axis) and another continuous field in **Columns** (which produces the horizontal or *X* axis).

 Discrete and continuous fields are discussed in more detail in *Appendix C, Working with Tableau 10*.

When you first plot the continuous measure fields in the **Rows** and **Columns**, you will see a single mark on your canvas.

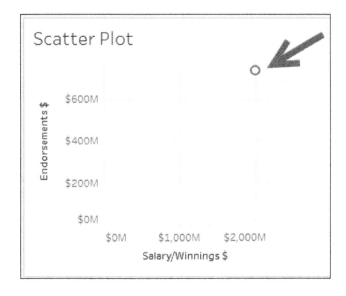

You may be scratching your head and thinking this is not a scatter plot. You are correct, it is not, because it is missing the *scatter*. However, at this point, Tableau is simply following your instructions, which is to display the aggregate of one measure in Rows and the aggregate of another measure in Columns. In our recipe, it is the **SUM(Salary/Winnings $)** and the **SUM(Endorsement $)**. This is really just an *X* and *Y* coordinate.

To create the scatter plot, this one point needs to be scattered. This can be done by adding dimensions in the **Marks** card that can force the scatter. For example, adding the **Player** field to **Detail** in the **Marks** card will make Tableau represent one mark per player, and each mark is the **SUM(Salary/Winnings $)** and **SUM(Endorsements $)** for that player.

If you want each record from the data source to be presented as a mark in your graph, you can drag the unique identifier for that row into **Detail**, and that will force the scatter. Alternatively, you can go to the **Analysis** menu and uncheck **Aggregate Measures**.

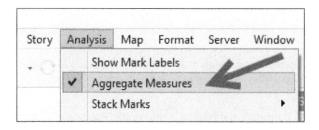

Notice that when you uncheck **Aggregate Measures**, the measure pills in your **Rows** and **Columns** will now be in disaggregated format, that is, **Salary/Winnings $** instead of **SUM(Salary/Winnings $)**.

In this recipe, we also added **Sport** to **Color** in the **Marks** card, so that we can visually identify which points belong to which **Sport**. Tableau 10 also introduces the data highlighter, which you can activate by right-clicking on a pill you have used in your view and selecting **Show Highlighter**.

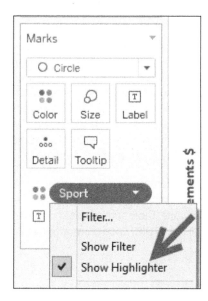

In previous versions, the color legend allows you to highlight the points in the view, based on the color you select from the legend. The data highlighter is an improvement to this, and allows you to highlight the points interactively on hover, based on values you specify, or values that match a pattern, on the highlighter card.

For example, when you click on the **Highlight Sport** field, the list of values will appear. As you hover over the values, the corresponding **Sport** in the **Color** property is highlighted, as well as all the points in the scatter plot that belong to that sport.

The highlighter, however, can also work with the other dimensions you have used in your canvas, not just the pill that is in **Color**. For example, you can show the highlighter for player. This allows you to search for players, and highlight them in the scatter plot.

Creating a heat map

Heat maps are graphs that display information using a matrix of colors. Often the density of color in the matrix represents the concentration of information, or the relative magnitude of the values. Heat maps are great for spotting patterns based on the concentration or density of information.

In this recipe, we will create a heat map that can easily show which flood caused the most fatalities, and in which year it occurred.

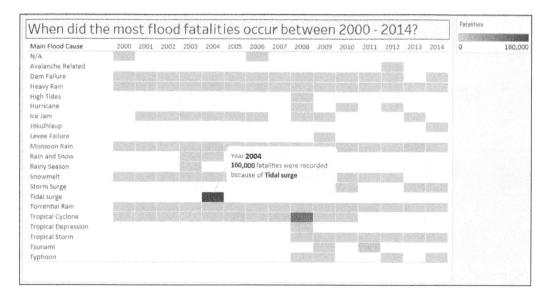

Getting ready

To follow this recipe, open B05527_01 - STARTER.twbx. Use the worksheet called Heat Map, and connect to the MasterTable (FlooddataMasterListrev) data source.

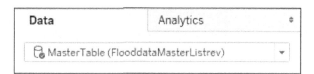

How to do it...

The following are the steps to create the heat map:

1. From **Dimensions**, drag **Began** to **Rows**. Tableau will automatically choose the **YEAR** level for this date field.

2. Right-click on the **Null** column heading produced by the **YEAR(Began)** pill in **Rows**, and select **Exclude**.

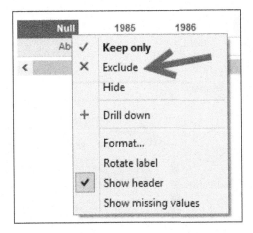

3. From **Dimensions**, drag **Main Flood Cause** to **Columns**.

4. From **Measures**, drag **Dead** to **Color** in the **Marks** card.

5. Click on the top-right drop-down arrow of the color legend and choose **Edit title...**.

6. Edit the title of the color legend to display **Fatalities**.

7. Click on the drop-down arrow beside the color legend and choose **Edit colors...**.

8. Choose the **Gray Warm 10.0** palette and click on **Assign Palette**. Click on **OK** when done.

9. Adjust the width and height of the columns. You can do this by moving your mouse pointer to the column or row edge of a film until you see a double-headed arrow. The left-right double-headed arrow allows you to adjust the width, and the up-down double-headed arrow allows you to adjust the height.

10. Add the grid borders. You can do this by selecting the **Format** menu item, and selecting **Borders....** The format sidebar will replace the original data sidebar. In this **Format borders** side bar, under the **Sheet** tab **Default** section, add borders to the **Cell**, **Pane**, and **Header**.

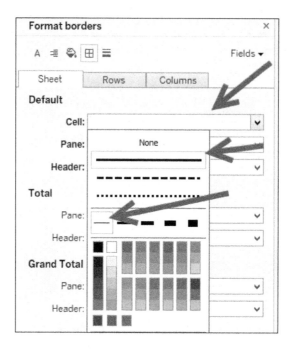

11. Right-click on the column with the darkest color—the column that represents the year **2004** and the main cause of **Tidal Surge**. Select Annotate and then Mark. Add the following annotation:

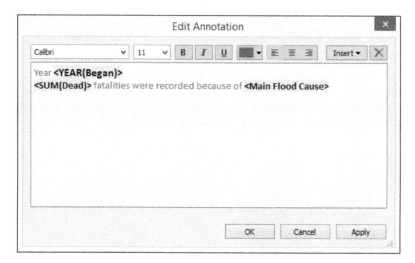

How it works...

Heat maps allow us to easily see values that stand out based on the color density. In our recipe, we created a grid of colors based on the number of fatalities caused by floods. Where the color is darkest is when the number of fatalities was the highest.

To create a heat map in Tableau, we simply need to identify the dimensions we want and place them into our **Rows** and/or **Columns**. We also need to place a measure onto the **Color** in the **Marks** card, and this determines the density of the color for that intersection or column.

There's more...

By default, measures, when dropped onto **Color** in the **Marks** card, will produce a gradient of colors. While pretty, sometimes the color differences are not so discernible. To make the colors more easily identifiable, we can elect to step the colors.

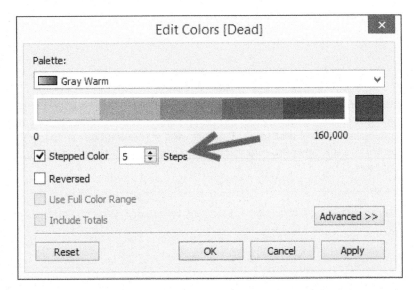

Stepping the color means there will be a finite number of colors used, instead of a gradient of colors that has all the color progression from the palette. The challenge with gradient is it is not easy to see how different one light blue is from another light blue, for example.

Another common variation for heat maps is adding another measure to **Size** in the **Marks** card. When you do this, the heat map will now have a series of different sized squares, instead of having a uniform size grid. For example, the following chart is what we will get if we place the measure **Displaced** onto **Size**.

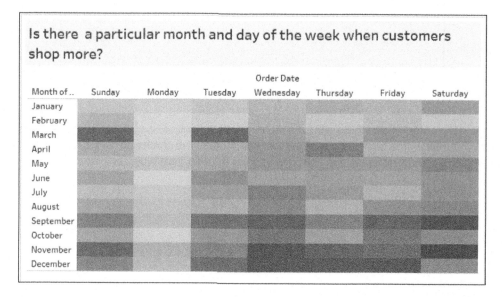

What other use cases can benefit from a heat map? Heat maps can be used to spot trends in different verticals—to spot when students register, promotions are redeemed, profit increases, traffic is light/heavy and so on. The following screenshot can help identify shopper behavior—whether there is any particular month and day combination that seems to be most popular to shoppers.

See also

▸ Please refer to the *Creating a text table (crosstab)* recipe in this chapter

▸ Please refer to the *Creating a highlight table* recipe in this chapter

Creating a text table (crosstab)

A text table is also often referred to as a crosstab, a shortened term for cross tabulation. Another common term that can be used to describe text tables is a spreadsheet. A text table is a series of rows and columns that have headers and numeric values. Text tables are great when the audience requires to see the individual values. A limitation of text tables is that it requires attentive processing—whoever is using the text table needs to focus on reading and comparing the numbers because any patterns or insights are not very easy to spot.

In this recipe, we will create a text table that shows the top 20 movies from 2007-2011, based on the worldwide gross amount.

Top 20 Movies from 2007-2011 based on Worldwide Gross

Film	Year	Worldwide Gross Amount ⤵	Audience score %	Avg. Rotten Tomatoes %	Avg. Profitability
The Twilight Saga: New Moon	2009	$709,820,000	78%	27%	14
Twilight: Breaking Dawn	2011	$702,170,000	68%	26%	6
Mamma Mia!	2008	$609,473,955	76%	53%	9
WALL-E	2008	$521,283,432	89%	96%	3
Sex and the City	2008	$415,253,258	81%	49%	7
Twilight	2008	$376,661,000	82%	49%	10
Tangled	2010	$355,080,000	88%	89%	1
Enchanted	2007	$340,487,652	80%	93%	4
The Proposal	2009	$314,700,000	74%	43%	8
Sex and the City 2	2010	$288,350,000	49%	15%	3
The Curious Case of Benjamin Button	2008	$285,431,000	81%	73%	2
High School Musical 3: Senior Year	2008	$252,044,501	76%	65%	23
It's Complicated	2009	$224,600,000	63%	56%	3
What Happens in Vegas	2008	$219,367,646	72%	28%	6
Knocked Up	2007	$219,001,261	83%	91%	7
Valentine's Day	2010	$217,570,000	54%	17%	4
Marley and Me	2008	$206,073,000	77%	63%	4
The Ugly Truth	2009	$205,300,000	68%	14%	5
Gnomeo and Juliet	2011	$193,967,000	52%	56%	5
He's Just Not That Into You	2009	$178,840,000	60%	42%	7
Grand Total		$6,835,473,705	1,451%	52%	7

Getting ready

To follow this recipe, open `B05527_01 - STARTER.twbx`. Use the worksheet called `Text Table`, and connect to the `HollywoodMostProfitableStories` data source.

How to do it...

The following are the steps to create the crosstab:

1. Change the default number format of **Audience score %**. You can do this by right-clicking the field **Audience score %** in the **Measures** section of the side bar, selecting **Default properties** and then **Number Format....** In the window that shows up, set the following:

    ❑ **Number (Custom)**

    ❑ **Decimal places:** 0

    ❑ **Suffix %**

2. From **Dimensions**, drag **Film** to **Rows**.

3. From **Dimensions**, drag **Year** to **Rows**.

4. From **Dimensions**, drag **Film** to **Filters**. This will open a window with several options for filtering the **Film** field.

5. Select the **Top** tab. Choose **By field:** and specify **Top 20** by **Average Rotten Tomatoes %**, as shown here:

6. From **Measures**, drag **Worldwide Gross Amount** to **Text** in the **Marks** card.

7. Right-click on the **Worldwide Gross Amount** pill in the **Marks** card, and choose **Format**.

8. Format the **Pane** tab to use:

    ❑ **Currency (Custom)**

    ❑ **Decimal places:** 0

    ❑ **Prefix:** $

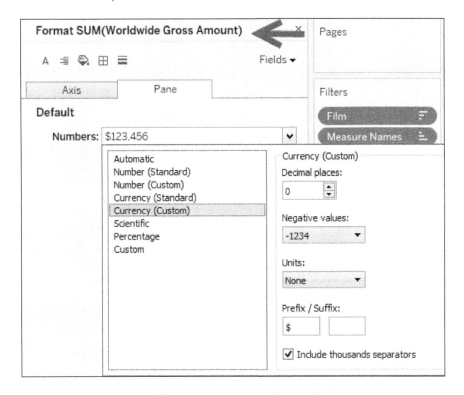

9. Double-click on **Audience score %** in the **Measures** pane. This adds this measure to the text table. This also introduces a new **Measure Values** shelf in your canvas.

10. From **Measures**, double-click on **Rotten Tomatoes %** to add this to the text table.

11. Change the **Rotten Tomatoes %** aggregation to **Average**. You can do this by right-clicking on this pill in the **Measure Values** shelf, going to **Measure (Sum)**, and changing this to **Average**.

12. From **Measures**, double-click on **Audience Score %** to add this to the text table.

13. Change the aggregation of **Audience Score %** to Average.

14. From **Measures**, double-click on **Profitability** to add this to the text table.

15. Rearrange the pills in the **Measure Values** shelf by dragging them manually to have the following order:

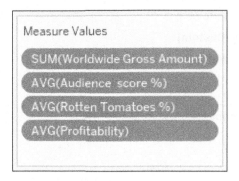

16. Right-click the **Film** pill in **Rows**, and click on **Sort...**.

17. In the **Sort** window, select:

  ❑ **Sort order Descending**

  ❑ **Sort by** field **Worldwide Gross Amount** using **Aggregation** of **Sum**

How it works...

A text table is simply a series of text values and numbers in a grid. This is a pretty common request for organizations that are very numbers-oriented, and have just started transitioning to a more visual culture.

To create a text table in Tableau, usually you identify the dimensions you want to place in your **Rows** and/or **Columns**. There are a couple ways to create the text table:

▸ Drag the measures onto the middle canvas until you see the **Show Me** icon, and then let go of the mouse

▸ Drag the first measure onto **Text** in the **Marks** card, and double-click on the rest of the measures you want to add

Both of these actions introduce the **Measure Names** and **Measure Values** pills in your visualization.

 Measure Names and **Measure Values** are discussed in more detail in *Appendix C, Working with Tableau 10*.

Measure Names, which is discrete, gets placed in your **Rows** or **Columns** as a header, and **Measure Values** gets placed onto the **Text** property in your **Marks** card:

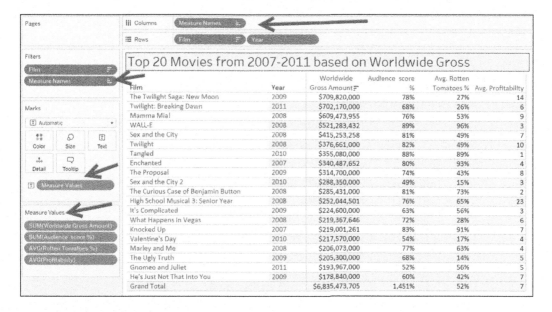

There's more...

Tableau places limitations on creating text tables. By default, for example, only six columns will display properly. If you have more than six columns, the leftmost columns get concatenated.

To adjust this, you need to go to the **Analysis** menu, then **Table Layout**, then **Advanced**. There you can adjust the number of rows and column labels.

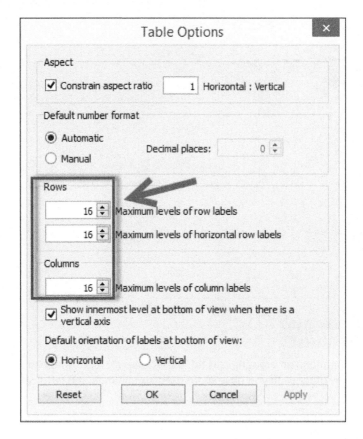

Tableau still, however, restricts this number. The maximum you can use is sixteen (16). Ultimately, if you need more columns and want to display all the numbers in the table, but not necessarily support visual analysis, then perhaps Tableau isn't the tool that is meant to do that job. Tableau is a great tool for visual analysis and exploration, so it is best to use it as such.

See also

> ▸ Please refer to the *Creating a highlight table* recipe in this chapter

Creating a highlight table

Highlight tables represent tabular information in a color-coded grid. The background color of the individual cells corresponds to the relative magnitude of the value it represents. Highlight tables are great when displaying the actual numeric values are important, but you also want the visual emphasis by adding the background colors on the cells.

In this recipe, we will modify the text table created in the *Creating a text table (crosstab)* recipe to create a text table with colored background, based on a film's worldwide gross amount:

| | | Worldwide Gross | Avg. Audience | Avg. Rotten | |
Film	Year	Amount	score %	Tomatoes %	Avg. Profitability
Enchanted	2007	$340,487,652	80%	93%	4
Gnomeo and Juliet	2011	$193,967,000	52%	56%	5
He's Just Not That Into You	2009	$178,840,000	60%	42%	7
High School Musical 3: Senior Year	2008	$252,044,501	76%	65%	23
It's Complicated	2009	$224,600,000	63%	56%	3
Knocked Up	2007	$219,001,261	83%	91%	7
Mamma Mia!	2008	$609,473,955	76%	53%	9
Marley and Me	2008	$206,073,000	77%	63%	4
Sex and the City	2008	$415,253,258	81%	49%	7
Sex and the City 2	2010	$288,350,000	49%	15%	3
Tangled	2010	$355,080,000	88%	89%	1
The Curious Case of Benjamin Button	2008	$285,431,000	81%	73%	2
The Proposal	2009	$314,700,000	74%	43%	8
The Twilight Saga: New Moon	2009	$709,820,000	78%	27%	14
The Ugly Truth	2009	$205,300,000	68%	14%	5
Twilight	2008	$376,661,000	82%	49%	10
Twilight: Breaking Dawn	2011	$702,170,000	68%	26%	6
Valentine's Day	2010	$217,570,000	54%	17%	4
WALL-E	2008	$521,283,432	89%	96%	3
What Happens in Vegas	2008	$219,367,646	72%	28%	6
Grand Total		$6,835,473,705	73%	52%	7

Top 20 Movies from 2007-2011 based on Worldwide Gross

Worldwide Gross
179M   710M

Getting ready

To follow this recipe, open `B05527_01 - STARTER.twbx`. Use the worksheet called `Highlight Table`, and connect to the `HollywoodMostProfitableStories` data source.

Data	Analytics	⬍
🗄 HollywoodsMostProfitableStories		⌃

In addition, this recipe requires the text table in the *Creating a text table (Crosstab)* recipe to be created. This text table is the starting point of this recipe.

How to do it...

The following are the steps to creating a highlight table:

1. If you haven't already done so, follow the steps in the recipe *Creating a text table (crosstab)* to create the starting text table.

2. From **Measures**, drag **Worldwide Gross Amount** to **Color** in the **Marks** card.

3. Change the mark in the **Marks** card to **Square**.

4. Click on the drop-down arrow beside the color legend and choose **Edit colors...**.

5. Choose the **Orange-Blue Light Diverging** palette. Select the **Stepped Color**, and specify 5 steps.

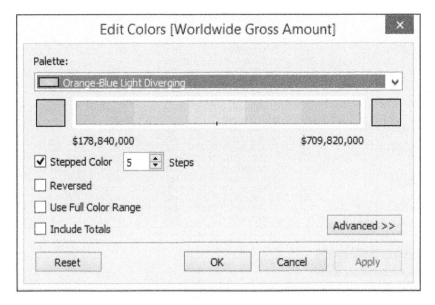

6. Click on the drop-down arrow beside the color legend and choose **Edit title...**.

7. Edit the title of the color legend to display **Worldwide Gross**.

How it works...

You might like the heat map because it emphasizes the items that have the darkest or lightest colors, but don't like the fact that it doesn't have the numbers.

Film	Year	Worldwide Gross Amount
Enchanted	2007	
Gnomeo and Juliet	2011	
He's Just Not That Into You	2009	
High School Musical 3: Senior Year	2008	
It's Complicated	2009	
Knocked Up	2007	
Mamma Mia!	2008	
Marley and Me	2008	
Sex and the City	2008	
Sex and the City 2	2010	
Tangled	2010	
The Curious Case of Benjamin Button	2008	
The Proposal	2009	
The Twilight Saga: New Moon	2009	
The Ugly Truth	2009	
Twilight	2008	
Twilight: Breaking Dawn	2011	
Valentine's Day	2010	
WALL-E	2008	
What Happens in Vegas	2008	

You might like text tables, but it requires that you look at the numbers closely and focus before you can make sense of it.

Film	Year	Worldwide Gross Amount
Enchanted	2007	$340,487,652
Gnomeo and Juliet	2011	$193,967,000
He's Just Not That Into You	2009	$178,840,000
High School Musical 3: Senior Year	2008	$252,044,501
It's Complicated	2009	$224,600,000
Knocked Up	2007	$219,001,261
Mamma Mia!	2008	$609,473,955
Marley and Me	2008	$206,073,000
Sex and the City	2008	$415,253,258
Sex and the City 2	2010	$288,350,000
Tangled	2010	$355,080,000
The Curious Case of Benjamin Button	2008	$285,431,000
The Proposal	2009	$314,700,000
The Twilight Saga: New Moon	2009	$709,820,000
The Ugly Truth	2009	$205,300,000
Twilight	2008	$376,661,000
Twilight: Breaking Dawn	2011	$702,170,000
Valentine's Day	2010	$217,570,000
WALL-E	2008	$521,283,432
What Happens in Vegas	2008	$219,367,646

You're in luck, you can create a *hybrid* table. You can have the text table, and color the grids according to your selected measure. This hybrid table is called the highlight table.

There is a trick to creating highlight tables in Tableau. The first is to create a text table. See the *Creating a text table* recipe in this chapter for the steps. Once you have the text table, you can drop a measure onto **Colors** in the **Marks** card. This colors your text table with a gradient of colors, which honestly will make your text table very hard to read.

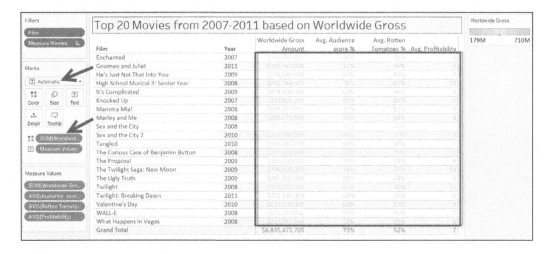

Once your table already has the gradient-colored text, the final step is to change the mark to a **Square**. This is the magic sauce that creates your highlight table.

See also

▶   Please refer to the *Creating a text table* recipe in this chapter

Creating an area chart

An area chart is very similar to a line chart (time series graph) with the area between the axis and the line shaded. A stacked area chart segregates the area, based on related categories. Area charts may allow trends to be more easily spotted because the eye focuses on a bigger area rather than comparing lines.

In this recipe, we will create an area chart that will show the results of restaurant re-inspections in New York City from June 2012 to June 2016.

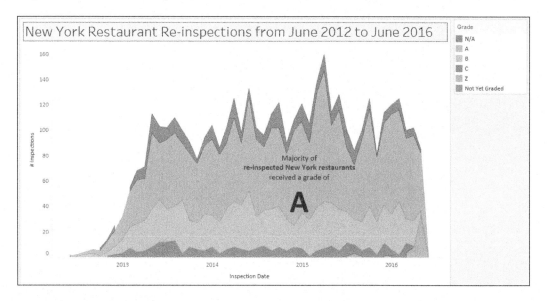

Getting ready

To follow this recipe, open `B05527_01 - STARTER.twbx`. Use the worksheet called **Area**, and connect to the **DOHMH New York City Restaurant** data source.

How to do it...

The following are the steps to create the area chart for re-inspections:

1. Change the mark type to **Area** in the **Marks** card.

2. From **Measures**, drag **Number of Records** to **Rows**.

3. From **Dimensions**, right-click and drag **Inspection Date** to **Columns**. This will open a window asking for the specific value to place.

4. Choose continuous month. This is the **MONTH(Inspection Date)** option in the fourth section, with a green calendar icon to its left.

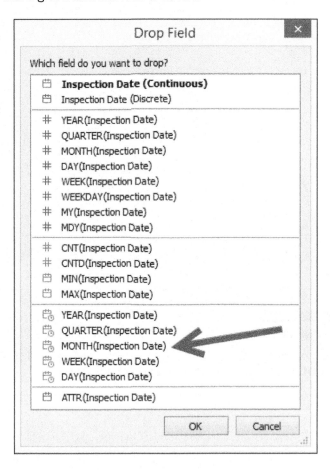

5. From **Dimensions**, right-click drag **Inspection Date** to **Filter**. This will open a window that shows the possible variation of values that can be used.

6. Choose to filter by discrete year, which is the third option called **Years** with a blue **#** beside it, and then click **Next >**.

7. Under the **General** tab, choose all years except for **1900**.

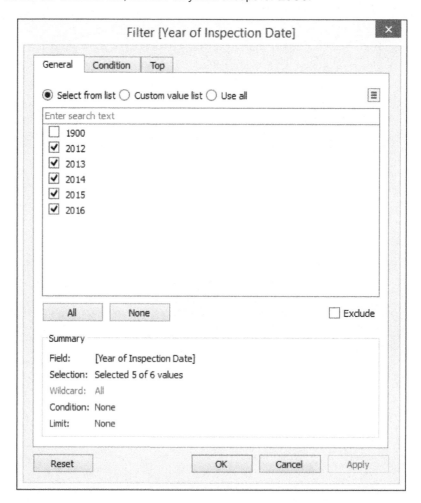

8. Under the **Wildcard** tab:

- Type the keyword **Re-inspection** in the **Match value:** text box
- Choose **Contains** in the radio button options

❑   Leave the checkbox to **Include all values when empty** checked

9. From **Dimensions**, right-click and drag **Grade** to **Color** in the **Marks** card.

10. Click on the drop-down arrow beside the color legend and choose **Edit colors…**

11. Choose the **Color Blind 10** palette and click on **Assign Palette**. Click on OK when done.

12. Right-click on an empty area in your chart and select **Annotate**, and then **Area**.

13. Add the following annotation, and place it on top of the area that represents the A grades.

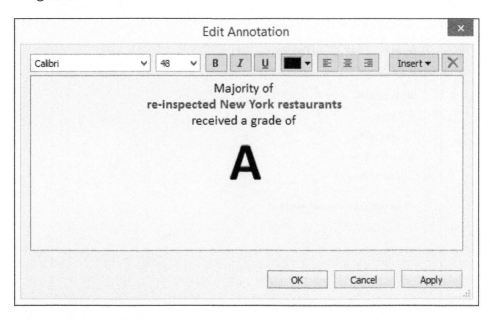

How it works...

Area charts look like line charts (or time series graphs) that have shaded areas. Area charts are also similar to stacked bar charts, where the areas are cumulative. It is best used when you want to show the cumulative value of the measures you are using. Area charts, however, bear the same risks as the stacked bar chart. Because individual areas are stacked, it is hard to compare the different areas because they don't all start in the same level.

Creating an area chart is similar to creating your line chart and your stacked bar chart. You create a time series graph first. By default, Tableau will create a time series graph (or line graph) first when you put a **Date** or **Date & Time** field in either **Rows** or **Columns**, and a **Measure** in the other.

Once you have the time series graph, you can change the mark to **Area**, and drop a dimension in **Color** in the **Marks** card to create the different colored areas.

There's more...

I've often asked students in my training classes when they would usually use area charts, and majority of the time students mention budgeting. With budgeting, they care about what proportion over time goes to which categories, but they also care about the cumulative value of the budget.

See also

▸ Please refer to the _Creating a stacked bar chart_ recipe in this chapter

Creating a pie chart

A pie chart is a circle—or pie—that is sliced. Each slice is identified using a different color and/or label. The size or angle of the slice represents that item or category's proportion to the whole. Pie charts are best at showing part-to-whole relationships when there aren't too many slices. Bar charts are great and popular alternatives to pie charts.

In this recipe, we will create a pie chart that shows the top five endorsements in 2014, sliced by sport.

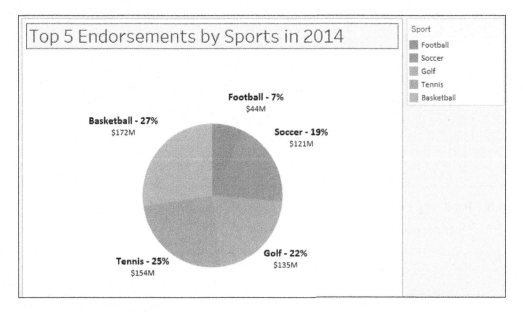

Getting ready

To follow this recipe, open `B05527_01 - STARTER.twbx`. Use the worksheet called **Pie**, and connect to the **Top Athlete Salaries (Global Sport Finances)** data source.

How to do it...

The following are the steps to create a pie chart:

1. Change the mark type to **Pie** in the **Marks** card.

2. From **Measures**, drag **Endorsements $** to **Angle** in the **Marks** card.

3. From **Dimensions**, drag **Sport** to **Color** in the **Marks** card.

4. Right-click on **Sport** pill in the **Color** property in the **Marks** card and select **Filter....**

5. In the **Top** tab, select **By field: Top** and 5 by **Sum of Endorsement $**.

6. Right-click on **Sport** pill in the **Color** in the **Marks** card and select **Sort**.

7. Filter **Ascending** by **Sum** of **Endorsement $**.

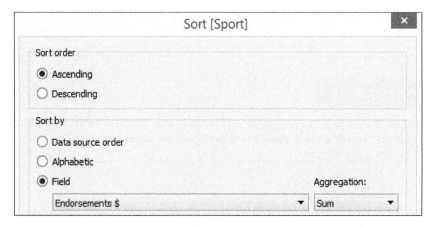

8. From **Measures**, drag **Endorsements $** to **Label** in the **Marks** card.

9. Right-click on **SUM(Endorsements $)** pill in the **Label** property in the **Marks** card. Select **Quick table calculation**, and then **Percent of total**.

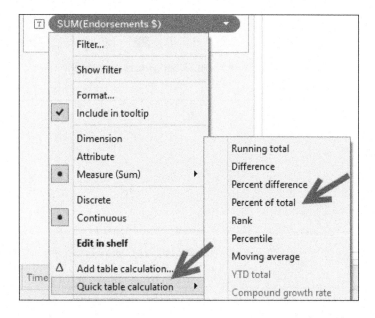

10. From **Measures**, drag **Endorsements $** again to the **Label** in the **Marks** card.

11. Click on **Label** in the **Marks** card, and select the ellipsis button under **Label Appearance** to modify the style of the text.

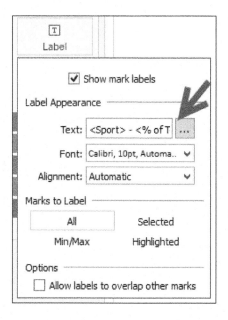

12. Change the format of the label to show the following, and click **OK** when done.

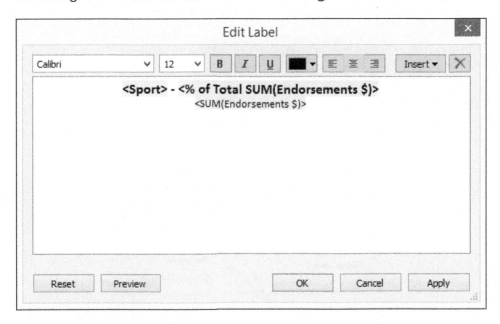

How it works...

Tableau comes with a built-in mark called **Pie**. When you switch the mark to a **Pie**, a new property appears under the **Marks** card called **Angle**.

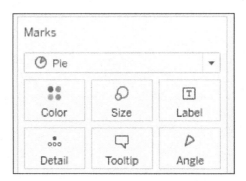

To create a pie chart, simply change the mark to a **Pie**. Drag a measure to **Angle**, and a discrete field to **Color**.

Often a pie chart is accompanied by a label containing what the pie is, and what percentage of the pie that slice is. **Percent of Total** is a readily available **Quick Table Calculation**.

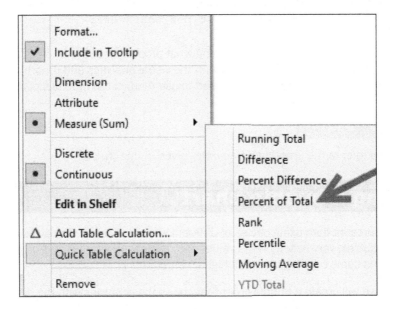

To add this as a label, you need to add a measure to the **Label** in **Marks** card first. This will initially display the actual values of that measure. Once added, you can right-click on this measure and select **Quick Table Calculation**. This should expand the readily available quick table calculations, which would include **Percent of Total**.

There's more...

Pie charts often get a bad reputation in the visual analytics world. One reason is because humans can't naturally compare angles (or pie slices) easily, especially if the pie slices are pretty close in size. Bar charts are often more effective in showing the difference in magnitudes, because all we need to look at are the edges.

 If you are interested, you can check out the world's most accurate pie chart. Word of warning however, you have to have humor to continue (*credit to Damien Foley's blog site*): `http://bit.ly/accuratepiechart`.

I think part of the issue is also abuse. Sometimes there is a tendency to overuse pie charts in presentations—especially the 3D tilted, exploded ones. Comparing angles is hard enough, tilting and exploding the pies do not help clarify the numbers.

Word of wisdom: the slices of the pie in a pie chart must sum up to 100%. Wisdom is learning from other's mistakes `http://bit.ly/best-pie-chart-ever`.

However, pie charts can be effective in showing what proportion of the whole is allocated to something. I think pie charts have their place in the visual analytics and reporting world. Just like any other tools in your toolset, we just need to use them in the right place, right time.

See also

▸ Please refer to the *Creating a tree map* recipe in this chapter

Creating a bubble chart

Bubble charts present data using circles of different sizes and colors. The sizes and colors of circles, or bubbles, vary based on the values they represent. A larger and/or darker circle often represents items or categories with higher values.

In this recipe, we will create a bubble chart that shows the countries with the highest populations in 2015.

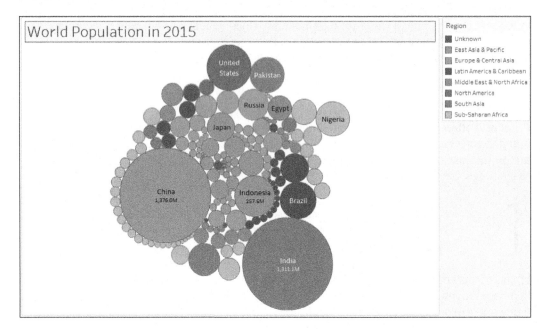

Getting ready

To follow this recipe, open B05527_01 - STARTER.twbx. Use the worksheet called Bubble, and connect to the Data (Modified Gapminder Population) data source.

How to do it...

The following are the steps to create a bubble chart:

1. Change the mark type to **Circle** in the **Marks** card.

2. From **Dimensions**, drag **Year** to the **Filter** shelf. This will open a new window for the filtering options.

3. Under the **General** tab, while **Select from list** radio button option is selected, type in **2015** in the search text box to find this value from the list of years, and check it.

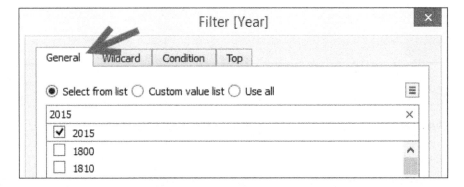

4. From **Measures**, drag **Population** to **Size** in the **Marks** card.

5. From **Dimensions**, drag **Region** to **Color** in the **Marks** card.

6. From **Dimensions**, drag **Country** to **Label** in the **Marks** card.

7. From **Measures**, drag **Population** to **Label** in the **Marks** card.

8. Right-click on the **SUM(Population)** pill in the **Label** card, and select **Format**. This will open a format pane that temporarily replaces your data side bar.

9. In the **Format** side pane, under the **Pane** tab in **Defaults** section, choose **Number (Custom)** with 1 decimal place, and **Millions (M)** as unit.

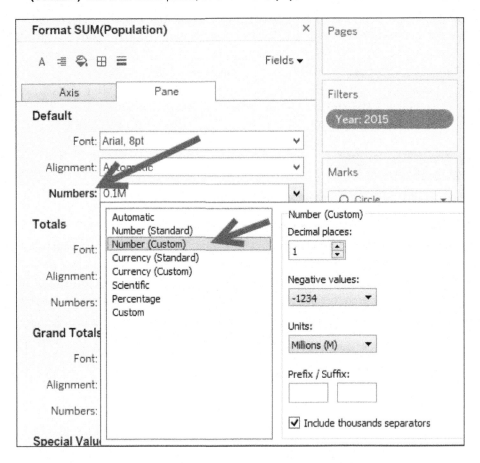

10. Right-click on the **Country** pill in the **Label** card and select **Sort**.

11. Choose an **Ascending** sort order by **Sum** of **Population**.

12. Click on **Label** in the **Marks** card, and select the ellipsis button under **Label Appearance** to modify the style of the text.

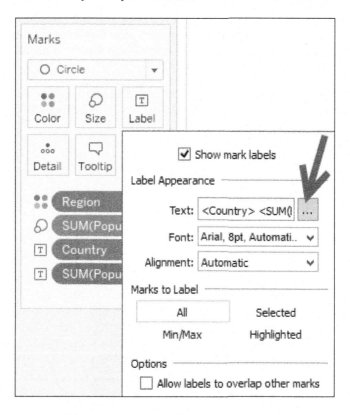

13. Adjust the label so Country is shown with a larger font, and population appears underneath it with a smaller font.

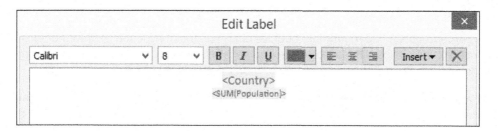

14. Click on the drop-down arrow beside the color legend again. This time choose **Edit colors...**.

15. Choose the **Color Blind 10** palette.

How it works...

A bubble chart typically shows information in circles of varying colors and sizes. Creating a bubble chart in Tableau requires changing the mark type to **Circle**. A measure is typically placed in **Size**, as well as another dimension in either **Color**, **Label**, or **Detail** (or any combination thereof).

In this recipe, we placed the **Population** measure onto **Size**, created different bubbles for every country by placing **Country** in **Label**, and color the circles by **Region**.

There's more...

If the pie chart gets a bad reputation, bubbles charts do too (maybe more). If we humans cannot compare angles with ease, we are also generally not very good at comparing diameter and circumference. *Is that circle 15% bigger than the previous circle?*

Most would argue that bar charts would be more effective than bubble charts, and I mostly agree. However, as with the pie chart, I think bubble charts can be effective—depending on the intent and audience.

In my courses, I ask students to present their work to the rest of the class. The goals of the presentation are to present their findings, as well as to engage the audience. One of the charts that frequently captures the attention of the audience is the bubble chart. Sometimes this chart also garners the most questions—therefore more engagement.

I would also argue that typically a single chart is not a be-all and end-all—typically we complement this with other charts, dashboards, and storytelling. There is nothing that stops us from starting our story with a bubble chart to get the audience's initial attention, and once we have their attention, proceed to more details using dependable bar and line charts.

The storytelling piece is also key. We have to be effective storytellers—our charts are simply our props. With effective storytelling, any chart can be effective and exciting.

If you haven't seen Hans Rosling's TED talk on *The best stats you've ever seen* yet, you are missing out. He is using bubbles that move—aka dancing bubbles!

```
https://www.ted.com/talks/hans_rosling_shows_the_best_
stats_you_ve_ever_seen?language=en
```

However, it's not the chart that makes the presentation, it's the storyteller that makes this presentation impactful and unforgettable.

See also

▸ Please refer to the *Creating a pie chart* recipe in this chapter

Creating a word cloud

A word cloud, also called a tag cloud, is typically a collection of keywords or text data visualized using size and color. Often, the goal of a word cloud is to represent the relative importance or prevalence of the keywords. Word clouds are not meant to allow the audience to clearly and accurately compare the underlying values of each keyword.

In this recipe, we will create a viz that shows the most popular baby names from 1910-2012. *Note that viz is a slang word for visualization.*

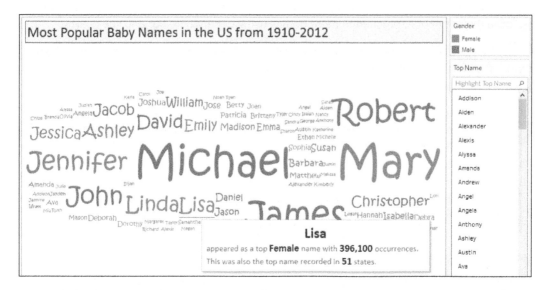

To follow this recipe, open `B05527_01 - STARTER.twbx`. Use the worksheet called `Word Cloud`, and connect to the `TopBabyNamesByState` data source.

How to do it...

The following are the steps to create a word cloud:

1. Change the mark type to **Text** in the **Marks** card.
2. From **Measures**, drag **Occurences** to **Size** in the **Marks** card.
3. From **Dimensions**, drag **Gender** to **Color** in the **Marks** card.
4. From **Dimensions**, drag **Top Name** to **Text** in the **Marks** card.
5. From **Dimensions**, right-click and drag **State** to **Text** in the **Marks** card.
6. Select **CNTD(State)**.

7. Click on **Tooltip** in the **Marks** card to format the tooltip with the following information:

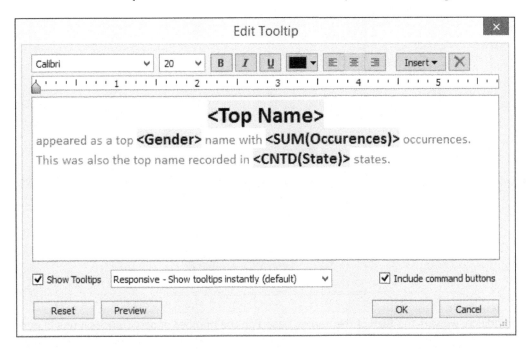

8. Click on the drop-down arrow beside the color legend and choose **Edit colors...**.

9. Choose the **Superfishel Stone** palette and click on **Assign Palette**. Click on **OK** when done.

10. Right-click on the **Top Name** pill in the **Marks** card, and select **Show highlighter**. This will show the data highlighter control, a new feature in Tableau 10, which allows you to search and highlight all points on hover.

11. Change the font style of the names to a font style of your choice. To do this, click on **Label** in the **Marks** card, and select the ellipsis button under **Label Appearance** to modify the style of the text.

How it works...

A word cloud can be created in Tableau if you have a field that contains the keywords or values you want displayed in the word cloud, as well as a measure that determines the size of that keyword.

In this recipe, we change the mark to **Text**, and display the **Top Name** in **Text**.

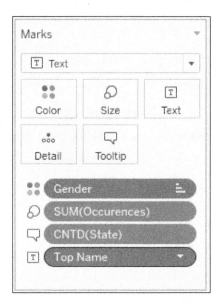

In addition, we vary the **Size** of the names based on the number of occurrences it has in our data source. We also color the names differently based on **Gender** which is recorded from our data source.

In our tooltip, we also display in how many states this name was recorded as a **Top Name**. Since we don't use **State** anywhere in the visualization, but want to use it in our tooltip, we can make this data field available either by dragging it to **Tooltip** or **Detail**.

When you right-click and drag a data field onto **Rows**, **Columns**, or any of the other shelves, a window with different options for values comes up. When you right-click and drag **State**, you are going to be prompted with exactly what about **State** you want to display.

In our recipe, we chose **CNTD(State)**, which is the numeric value for the unique number of states related to the **Top Name**.

There's more...

You have probably seen some word clouds in some of the websites or blog sites you visit. Although it is hard to measure just by looking at the word cloud how many more times a keyword occurs compared to another keyword, this may be an effective chart depending on the context, intent, and audience. Arguably, bar charts would be more effective if you want to clearly state the difference in magnitude. However, in some cases, the intent is to simply illustrate and highlight which keywords are often used or mentioned. Sometimes, the relative comparison may be sufficient.

See also

▶ Please refer to the *Creating a bubble chart* recipe in this chapter

Creating a tree map

Tree maps represent part-to-whole and hierarchical relationships using a series of rectangles. The sizes and colors of rectangles will vary based on the values they represent. Typically, the larger rectangles, or rectangles with most concentrated colors, depict the highest values.

In this recipe, we will represent the 2015 world population as a tree map.

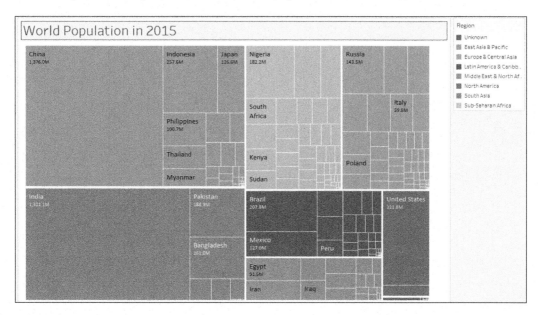

Getting ready

To follow this recipe, open `B05527_01 - STARTER.twbx`. Use the worksheet called `Tree Map`, and connect to the `Data (Modified Gapminder Population)` data source.

How to do it...

The following are the steps to create the population tree map:

1. From **Dimensions**, drag **Year** to the **Filter** shelf. This will open a new window for the filtering options.

2. Under the **General** tab, while **Select from list** radio button option is selected, type **2015** in the search text box to find this value from the list of years, and check it.

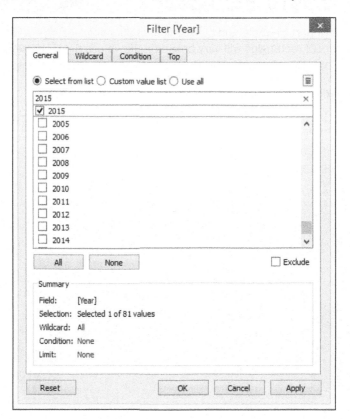

3. From **Measures**, drag **Population** to **Size** in the **Marks** card.

4. From **Dimensions**, drag **Region** to **Color** in the **Marks** card.

5. From **Dimensions**, drag **Country** to **Text** in the **Marks** card.

6. From **Measures**, drag **Population** to **Text** in the **Marks** card.

7. Click on the drop-down arrow beside the color legend card and choose **Edit colors...**.

8. Choose the **Color Blind 10** palette and click on **Assign Palette**. Click on **OK** when done.

9. Click on **Label** in the **Marks** card, and select the ellipsis button under **Label Appearance** to modify the style of the text.

10. Adjust the label so **Country** is shown with a larger font, and population appears underneath it with a smaller font.

How it works...

A tree map allows us to present a part-to-whole relationship, just like a pie chart, but by subdividing a rectangle into smaller areas rather than subdividing a circle into different angled slices.

In Tableau, when you place a measure onto **Size** and a dimension onto either **Color**, **Label**, or **Detail**—or any combination thereof—the rectangle is broken down into smaller rectangles.

In this scenario, Tableau actually automatically assigns the **Square** mark. Although under **Marks** you will see **Automatic**, the icon refers to a **Square**. If you leave this as **Automatic**, or change the **Mark** explicitly to **Square**, you will get the same tree map.

There's more...

Pie charts get a bad reputation because angles and slices are not easy to compare. Bubble charts are also hard to compare, because it is also hard to compare diameters and circumferences. Guess what, tree maps also fall into this same category. It is also not easy nor natural for us humans to discern and compare one area to another. Can we tell how much bigger or smaller one rectangle is compared to another? However, as with the other charts, with the right intent, audience, and story, this could be an effective chart—either by itself, or as a complementary chart to another.

See also

▸   Please refer to the *Creating a Pie Chart* recipe in this chapter

2

Advanced Charts

In this chapter, we will cover:

- ▶ Creating a histogram
- ▶ Creating a small multiple chart
- ▶ Creating a shared axis chart
- ▶ Creating a combo chart (dual axis chart)
- ▶ Creating a bullet chart
- ▶ Creating a bar in bar chart
- ▶ Creating a donut chart
- ▶ Creating a unit chart
- ▶ Creating a box and whisker plot
- ▶ Creating a sparkline with indicators
- ▶ Creating a KPI text table
- ▶ Creating a waterfall chart
- ▶ Creating a population pyramid

Introduction

In this chapter, we will explore additional techniques for creating more advanced charts in Tableau. Some of the charts introduced in this chapter are quite effective for specific use cases, for example the waterfall chart for showing cumulative changes to a measure and the population pyramid for showing population over time. However, this should not discourage you from exploring and testing your data set with different charts! Sometimes different types of chart can help uncover insights in ways we don't expect, or they may surprisingly convey information much more clearly than the chart we had originally intended to use.

Some of the charts covered in this chapter may well just be starting points to even more charts you may want to explore and experiment on your own. Be not afraid—explore, explore, explore!

 Make sure to check out *Appendix A, Calculated Fields Primer*, as this chapter starts using more calculated fields.

Creating a histogram

Histograms are graphs that plot frequency distribution of data.

In this recipe, we will create a histogram that will visualize what the most common heights and weights are of NBA players, based on a 2014 NBA player's stats data source.

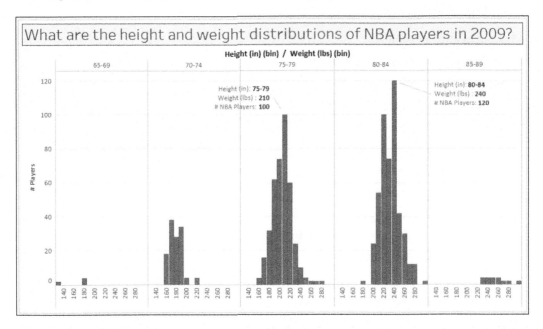

Getting ready

To follow this recipe, open `B05527_02 - STARTER.twbx`. Use the worksheet called `Histogram`, and connect to the `Player Stats (NBA Players Regular Season 2009)` data source.

How to do it...

The following are the steps to create the histogram in this recipe:

1. Under **Measures**, right-click on **Height (in)** and select **Create** and then **Bins....**

2. Set the bin size to 5, and click **OK** when done. This will create a new discrete field called **Height (in) (bin)** under the **Dimensions** section of the side bar.

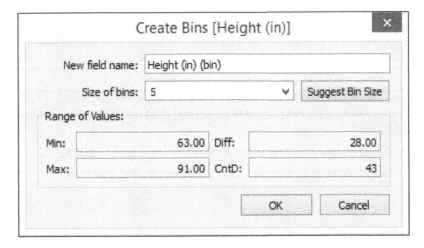

3. Under **Dimensions**, right-click on **Height (in) (bin)** and select **Aliases....**

4. Change the alias values of the **Member** items to the following. To edit the alias, simply click on the **Value (Alias)** field and that field will become editable.

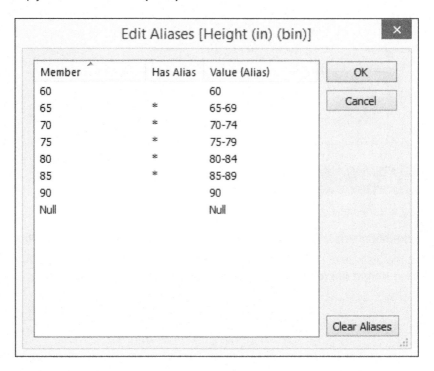

5. Create another bin for **Weight (lbs)** under **Measures**. Set this size to 10. This will create a new discrete field called **Weight (lbs) (bin)** under the **Dimensions** section of the side bar.

6. From **Dimensions**, drag **Year** to the **Filters** shelf and filter to **2009**.

7. From **Dimensions**, drag **League** to the **Filters** shelf, and filter to **N**.

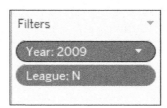

8. From **Dimensions**, drag **Height (in) (bin)** to **Columns**.

9. From **Dimensions**, drag **Weight (lbs) (bin)** to **Columns**, to the right of **Height (in) (bin)**.

10. From **Dimensions**, right-click and drag **Player ID** to **Rows**. This will open up a new window showing all possible values that can be added.

11. Choose **CNTD(Player ID)**, which means the number of unique players.

12. Right-click on the highest marks in the **75-79** lbs and **80-84** lbs bins, and choose **Annotate** and then **Mark**. Display the height, weight, and # of NBA players in these highest marks, as show here:

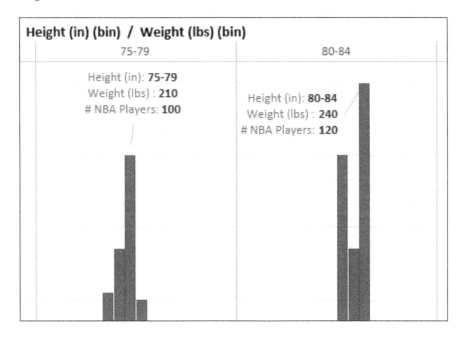

How it works...

Tableau supports the creation of histograms. Histograms are charts that show frequency distribution of data and are best when data can be broken down into clear groups.

The first step is typically to create the bin first. This can be done by right-clicking the measure you want to bin, and selecting **Create** and then **Bins...**. When you do this, Tableau will suggest a bin size based on your data set.

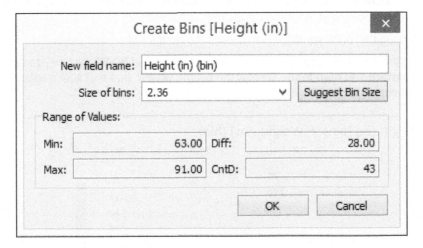

Once you click **OK**, a new dimension field gets created. This field also gets its own icon that looks like a small histogram with normal distribution to signify a bin data type.

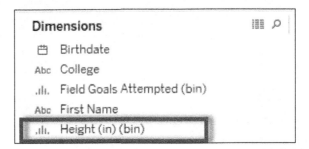

Once the bin is created, this bin field can be placed in either **Rows** or **Columns**. To display the frequency distribution, typically we place a count or a count distinct of another dimension in the other shelf.

However, we can definitely place other aggregations and these may give us different insights about our data. For example, in the following screenshot, I have placed **AVG(Points)** and **AVG(Three Pts Made)** alongside **CNT(Player ID)**.

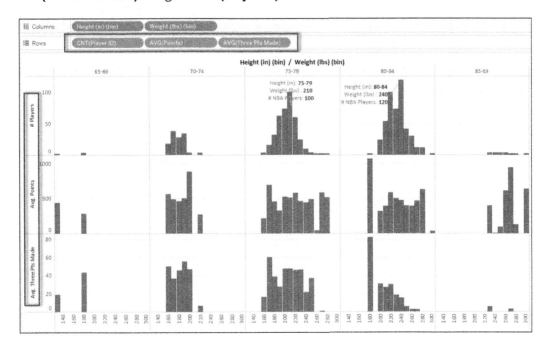

At a glance, this tells me that taller players tend to not make as many successful three-point shots compared to shorter players. We are measuring not just the number of players based on their height and weight buckets, but also the average points and three points they make.

There's more...

When you do a quick Google search on histogram, the images that you find will look a little bit different than the histogram we create in Tableau by default. Histograms from the search engine typically have the bars touching. This is because histograms use continuous variables in the axis. Tableau implements histograms a little bit differently. Notice that when you created the bin, the new bin field gets placed in the dimension, and the icon is blue—meaning it is discrete. Because it is discrete, in Tableau, it produces headers, not a continuous axis, when placed onto either **Rows** or **Columns**. This also means that, by default, there will be gaps between the bars. You can however make your Tableau histogram look similar to a typical histogram, by altering the size of the bars manually and making them wider until the edges touch.

Creating a small multiple chart

A small multiple is a series of smaller charts that share the same type and scale. This chart is typically used when you want to have multiple values (or categories) to be compared side by side.

In this recipe, we will create a small multiple area chart that shows the world population sliced by region and income group.

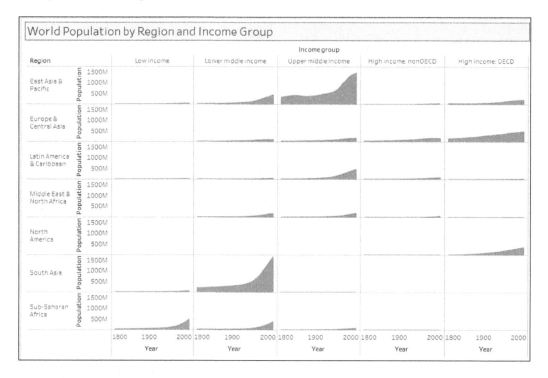

Getting ready

To follow this recipe, open `B05527_02 - STARTER.twbx`. Use the worksheet called `Small Multiple`, and connect to the `Data (Modified Gapminder Population)` data source.

How to do it...

The following are the steps to create a small multiple chart:

1. From **Dimensions**, drag **Year** to the **Columns** shelf.

2. Right-click on the **Year** field in the **Columns** shelf, and select **Continuous**. You should notice that the pill color changes from blue to green.

3. From **Measures**, drag **Population** to the **Rows** shelf.

4. In the **Marks** card, click on the dropdown to change the mark from **Automatic** to **Area**.

5. From **Dimensions**, drag **Income Group** to the **Columns** shelf.

6. Right-click on the first column produced by **Income Group** with value of **Null**, and choose **Exclude**.

7. Manually drag the **Income Group** headers to order the values as follows:

	Income group			
Low income	Lower middle income	Upper middle income	High income: nonOECD	High income: OECD

8. From **Dimensions**, drag **Region** to the **Rows** shelf.

9. Go to the **Format** menu, and choose **Lines**. This will show a formatting side bar.

10. Under the tabs **Sheet**, **Rows** and **Columns**, set the **Grid Lines** to **None**. Close the formatting side bar when done.

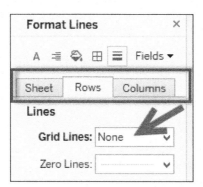

How it works...

A small multiple chart is simply a collection of the smaller version of the same type of chart. For example, it could be a series of line charts or bar charts or area charts, instead of having one big chart.

To create a small multiples chart, we can start with a single chart, just like the charts introduced in *Chapter 1, Basic Charts*. Creating the small multiples requires that additional dimensions are placed in the **Rows** or **Columns** shelves, or both. In this recipe, we created an area chart, and then placed the **Income Group** dimension to **Columns**, and the **Region** dimension to **Rows**.

With small multiples, because we are looking at many small graphs, having axes and gridlines for all the small charts can sometimes distract the readers. Depending on how many charts there are, it may be best to remove these repetitive lines and headers. In the recipe, we simply chose to remove the grid lines, but leave the axes headers for reference.

There's more...

Small multiples are also referred to as Trellis charts, or panel charts, and sometimes sparklines. There are a few other names that refer to small multiples depending on which literature you read.

The big question about small multiples is why you would ever want many small graphs and sacrifice detail. If we can keep a graph big, bold, and beautiful, why not leave it in that state and simply add additional details or filters?

Small multiples are great if you want to be able to compare multiple instances side by side. The trouble with adding filter, for example, is that we are forced to remember what the previous ones looked like. By nature, we cannot remember different versions of a graph once they've left our sight.

If, however, we add more details to one big graph, we risk adding too much detail and it may make the graph too busy and unwieldy. For example, this is what the small multiple could have looked like if we chose to put the details in the same graph instead of slicing them into multiples:

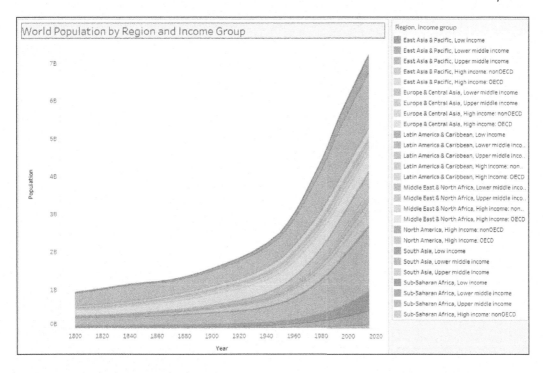

See also

▸ Please refer to the *Creating a sparkline with indicators* recipe in this chapter

▸ Please refer to the *Creating a dynamic column/row trellis chart* recipe in *Chapter 3, Interactivity*

Creating a shared axis chart

A shared axis chart in Tableau is a chart that shares one axis among multiple measures. This chart can be used when the measures have similarly ranged values, and can be presented using one mark and one scale.

In this recipe, we will compare field goals made vs field goals attempted by Phoenix Suns players in the NBA 2009 season by using a shared axis chart.

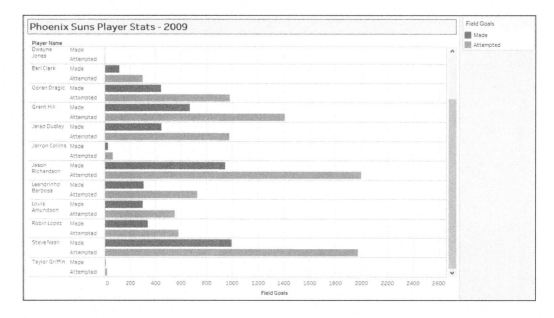

Getting ready

To follow this recipe, open B05527_02 – STARTER.twbx. Use the worksheet called Shared Axis, and connect to the Player Stats (NBA Players Regular Season 2009) data source.

How to do it...

The following are the steps to create a shared axis chart:

1. From **Dimensions**, drag **Team Name** to the **Filters** shelf.
2. Under the **General** tab, check **Suns**.
3. From **Dimensions**, drag **Year** to the **Filters** shelf.
4. Under the **General** tab, choose **2009**.
5. From **Dimensions**, drag **League** to the **Filters** shelf.

6. Under the **General** tab, check **N** for NBA.

7. If it doesn't exist yet, create a calculated field called `Player Name`, and provide the following formula that concatenates `[First Name]` and `[Last Name]`:

8. From **Dimensions**, drag **Player Name** to the **Rows** shelf.

9. From **Measures**, drag **Field Goals Made** to the **Columns** shelf. This creates a horizontal axis for your view.

10. From **Measures**, drag **Field Goals Attempted** to the horizontal axis created by the **Field Goals Made** measure. Do not let go of the mouse until you see the double ruler icon appear on top of the axis.

11. Right-click on the **Field Goals Attempted** field header in your view, and **Edit alias**. Change the alias to **Attempted**.

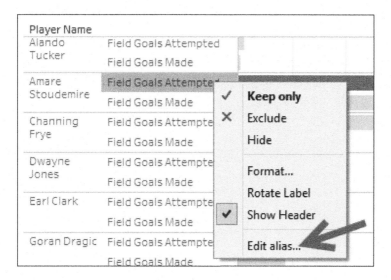

12. Right-click on the **Field Goals Made** field header in your view, and **Edit alias**. Change the alias to **Made**.

13. Manually drag the **Made** field header and move it to before the **Attempted** field.

14. Control drag the **Measure Names** field in your **Rows** shelf to the **Color** shelf.

15. Click on the drop-down arrow beside the color legend and choose **Edit colors....**

16. Change the colors of your bar. Assign a red color to **Made**, and gray to **Attempted**. Close the edit box when done.

How it works...

A shared axis chart, as the name implies, is a chart that shares the same axis with multiple measures. One way to do this in Tableau is by dragging another measure to an existing measure's axis.

In this recipe, we started by creating a bar chart with the measure **Field Goals Made**. **Field Goals Made** is a continuous measure, thus creates an axis when placed onto the **Columns** shelf.

To share the axis this field has created with other measures, the other measures simply need to be dropped on top of the existing axis. When another measure is dragged on top of the existing axis, a faint double ruler icon appears on the axis. When you see this, release the mouse button and drop the field onto the view.

Once a second measure is added to the chart, there are a few things that happen:

▸ The original measure field gets replaced with **Measure Values** (green pill).

▸ **Measure Names** (blue pill) gets placed on the opposite shelf. This provides a column that shows the actual measure the mark represents.

▸ **Measure Names** (blue pill) gets placed in the **Filters** shelf. This would select the measures that have been dragged onto the same axis.

▸ A **Measure Values** shelf appears, which contains the measures that have been dragged onto the same axis.

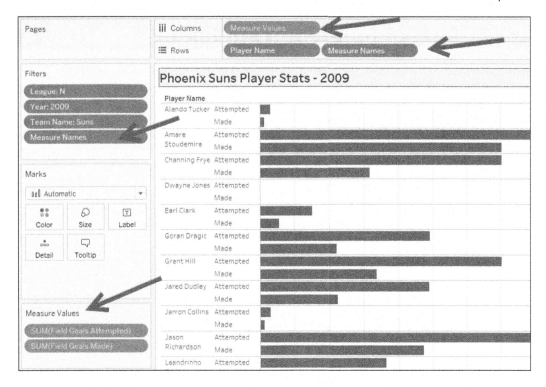

If you want more than two measures to share the same axis, simply keep on dragging the measures onto the existing axis, or add the measures directly to the **Measure Values** shelf.

There's more...

A shared axis chart is useful when you want to show multiple measures in the same graph. You can use a shared axis chart when you want to display the different measures using the same mark, and using the same range in axis. This is important to note, because when you change the mark in a shared axis chart, you change the mark for all the measures. A change in axis (range, size, and format) also affects all the measures in the graph.

See also

▶ Please refer to the *Creating a combo chart (dual axis chart)* recipe in this chapter

Creating a combo chart (dual axis chart)

A dual axis chart is a chart that uses two axes for two different measures. This chart is useful when two measures have different types or ranges (for example, monetary value and percentage), or if the two measures need to be displayed differently (for example, one as a bar and one as a line).

In this recipe, we will create a dual axis chart, also often referred to as a combo chart.

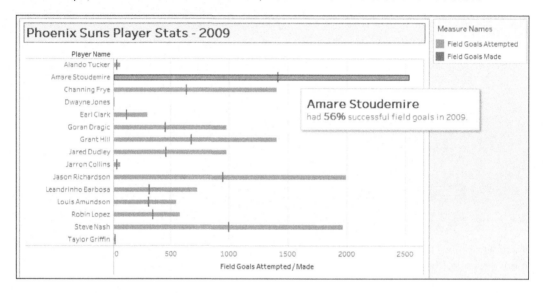

Getting ready

To follow this recipe, open `B05527_02 - STARTER.twbx`. Use the worksheet called `Combo Chart Dual Axis`, and connect to the `Player Stats (NBA Players Regular Season 2009)` data source.

How to do it...

The following are the steps to create a combo chart (dual axis chart):

1. From **Dimensions**, drag **Team Name** to the **Filters** shelf.

2. Under the **General** tab, check **Suns**.

3. From **Dimensions**, drag **Year** to the **Filters** shelf.

4. Under the **General** tab, choose **2009**.

5. From **Dimensions**, drag **League** to the **Filters** shelf.

6. Under the **General** tab, check **N** for NBA.

7. If it doesn't exist yet, create a calculated field called `Player Name`, and provide the following formula that concatenates `[First Name]` and `[Last Name]`:

Player Name   ☐ Player Stats (NBA Players Regular Season 2009)

```
[First Name] + " " + [Last Name]
```

8. From **Dimensions**, drag **Player Name** to the **Rows** shelf.

9. From **Measures**, drag **Field Goals Attempted** to the **Columns** shelf. This creates a horizontal axis for your view.

10. From **Measures**, drag **Field Goals Made** to the opposite side of the **Field Goals Attempted** axis. Do not let go of the mouse until you see the dashed line or the arrow icon.

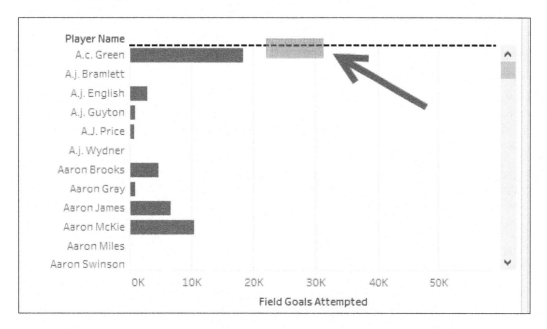

11. This creates another axis opposite to the **Field Goals Attempted** axis.

12. Click on the **SUM(Field Goals Attempted)** field in the **Columns** shelf to activate its **Marks** card. Change the mark for this field to **Bar**.

13. Adjust the **Bar** size that represents **SUM(Field Goals Attempted)** so that it is narrower.

14. Click on the **SUM(Field Goals Made)** field in the **Columns** shelf to activate its **Marks** card. Change the mark for this field to **Gantt**.

15. Right-click on the **Field Goals Made** axis, and select **Synchronize Axis**.

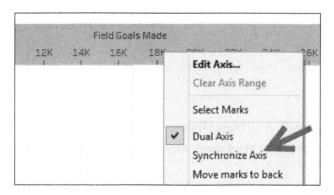

16. Right-click on the **Field Goals Made** axis, and uncheck **Show Header**.

17. Right-click on the **Field Goals Attempted** axis and choose **Edit Axis**. Change the **Title** to Field Goals Attempted. Close the window when done.

How it works...

Dual axis charts, as the name implies, allow for two axes in the chart. In Tableau, this can be done by dragging a second measure to the opposite of the first measure's axis. You will know when to release the field when you see the dashed line on the opposite side of the existing axis appear.

In this recipe, we started with the **Field Goals Attempted** measure. With one measure, Tableau creates a bar chart by default. When placed in the **Columns** shelf, Tableau creates a horizontal axis at the bottom of the view.

To create a dual axis chart, the second measure, in this case the **Field Goals Made**, is dragged onto the top of the view until the dashed line visual cue appears. When the field is dropped, the second axis is added.

With dual axis, Tableau maintains each measure's individual **Marks** card. In addition to this, another **Marks** card called **All** is introduced, which will affect all the marks in the view. Since the measures have their own **Marks** cards, each measure can use a different mark, a different color, a different sizing scheme, and so on. Dual axis charts can be very powerful charts because of their flexibility.

From a visual perspective, a dual axis chart will exhibit a fused pill appearance. Instead of two individual pills, a dual axis chart will be fused at the center—the center has straight edges instead of rounded ends.

There's more...

The dual axis chart is a *premium* chart. This chart is powerful because it allows you to have two different mark types, as well as different axis ranges and different sizing configuration if you so need it. If you want to have one measure as a bar, another as a line, dual axis can help. If you want a percentage and an absolute in the same graph, a dual axis can help. A shared axis may make the mark for the percentage unit look like a flat line because of the discrepancy in values, but the dual axis will preserve the relative comparison.

When comparing measures that have comparable values, like sales and profit, you may want to consider synchronizing the axes. Otherwise, the view may give the perception that there are very high profits (sometimes higher than sales!), and this would be misleading.

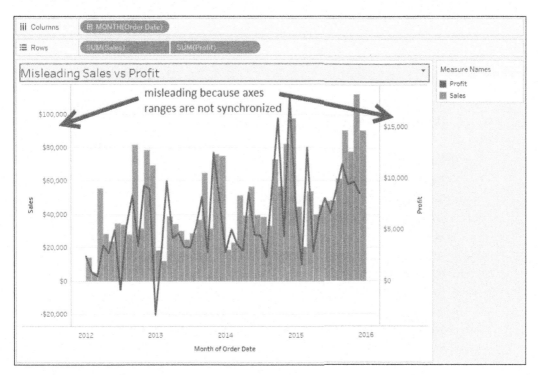

Another thing to note is that in Tableau, every green pill beside a non-dual axis field will have a dual axis menu option.

See also

▸ Please refer to the *Creating a shared axis chart* recipe in this chapter

▸ Please refer to the *Creating a bar in bar chart* recipe in this chapter

Creating a bullet chart

A bullet chart allows us to visualize progress in a small, concise graph. This chart borrows from thermometers and progress bars, and is typically used to show goals vs actuals.

In this recipe, we will create a bullet chart that shows the comparison between field goals attempted and field goals made by Phoenix Suns players in the NBA 2009 season.

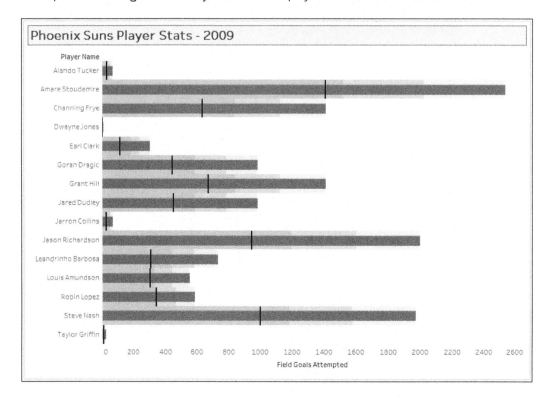

Getting ready

To follow this recipe, open `B05527_02 - STARTER.twbx`. Use the worksheet called `Bullet Chart`, and connect to the `Player Stats (NBA Players Regular Season 2009)` data source.

How to do it...

The following are the steps to create a bullet chart:

1. From **Dimensions**, drag **Team Name** to the **Filters** shelf.
2. Under the **General** tab, check **Suns**.
3. From **Dimensions**, drag **Year** to the **Filters** shelf.
4. Under the **General** tab, choose **2009**.
5. From **Dimensions**, drag **League** to the **Filters** shelf.
6. Under the **General** tab, check **N** for NBA.
7. If it doesn't exist yet, create a calculated field called **Player Name**, and provide the following formula that concatenates **First Name** and **Last Name**:

> See Appendix A, Calculated Fields Primer for more details on creating calculated fields

8. From **Dimensions**, drag **Player Name** to the **Rows** shelf.
9. From **Measures**, drag **Field Goals Attempted** to the **Columns** shelf. This creates a bar chart by default.
10. From **Measures**, drag **Field Goals Made** to **Details** in the **Marks** card.
11. Click on the **Analytics** tab in the side bar to activate it.

12. Drag the **Reference Line** onto your view, and choose Cell.

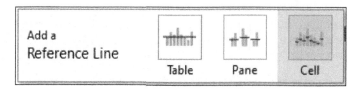

13. In the **Line** section, for **Value:** choose **SUM(Field Goals Made)** and use the default aggregation of **Average**. Set **Label:** to **None**.

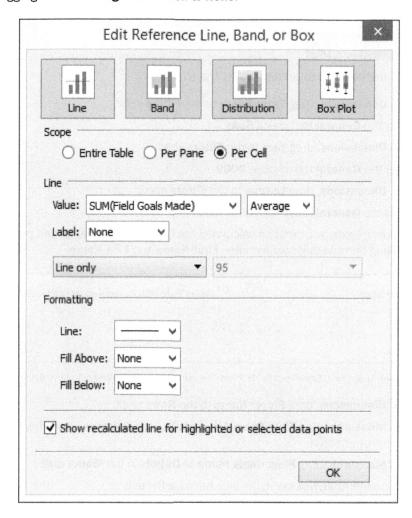

14. Click on **Size** in the **Marks** card to adjust the bar chart to be narrower so that the reference line stands out more. Slide the control to the left to make the bar narrower.

15. From the **Analytics** tab, drag **Distribution Band** to your view and choose **Cell**.

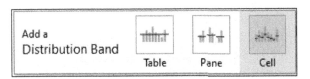

16. Set the following values for the distribution band:

   ❑ For **Computation Value**, use **Percentages**, and provide the values 60, 80, 100

   ❑ For **Formatting**, use **Gray Very Light** for **Fill**, and check the **Fill Below** checkbox

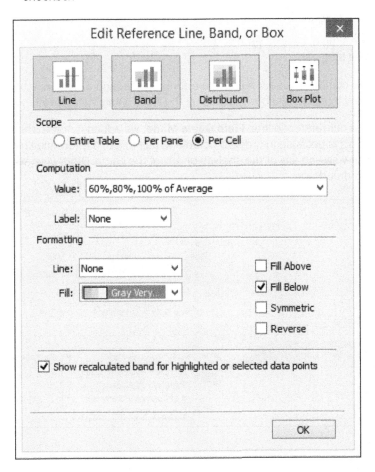

17. Go to the **Format** menu, and choose Lines. This will show a formatting side bar.

18. Under the tabs **Sheet**, **Rows** and **Columns**, set the **Grid Lines** to **None**. Close the formatting side bar when done.

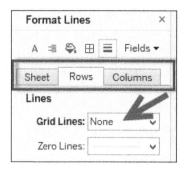

How it works...

Bullet charts are simple, concise graphs that are packed with information. These charts are great for tracking progress.

Bullet charts are composed of a bar chart, a reference line, and a reference band. In this recipe, we started by creating a bar chart using the **Field Goals Attempted** measure.

Before we added our reference line, **Field Goals Made**, we added it first to the **Details** card. The reason for this is because in order to be able to use this in a reference line, it needed to already be in our view—on any of the shelves or any of the cards. Otherwise, you will not see this in the **Value** dropdown.

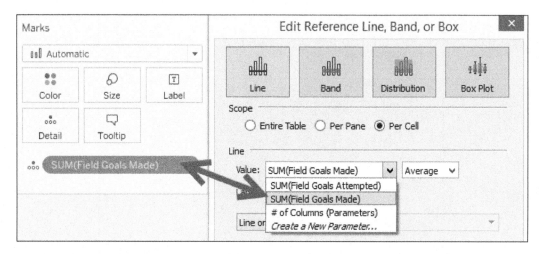

The final piece is the distribution band. Although it looks like it is simply an aesthetic addition, it does in fact display additional information. Stephen Few calls this the *Quantitative Scale*, which typically color codes certain sections or ranges in the bullet chart. In our case, we used this to indicate 60%, 80%, and 100% of the average sum of goals.

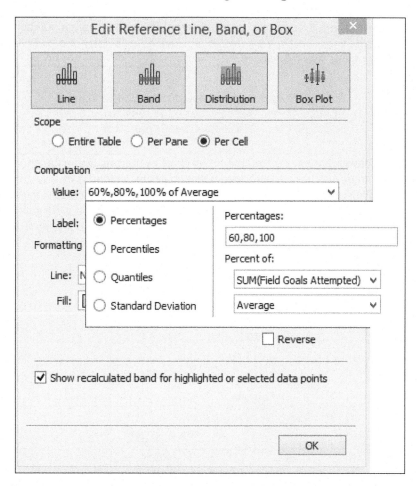

The additional options are **Percentiles**, **Quantiles**, and **Standard Deviation**. In the configuration box, you can also choose the type of aggregation to use with the measure.

There's more...

There was a time when radial gauges in dashboards were all the rage. The inherent problem with these dashboards was gauges took up a lot of space, and they weren't very clear in communicating the information. Stephen Few mentioned this in his books and blogs.

Check out this article called *Business Gauges—BI vendors just don't get it:*
`https://www.perceptualedge.com/blog/?p=102`

Stephen Few coined the word bullet chart as an alternative graph to these gauges. It is meant to be a very compact chart, and every element is meant to communicate a number. Stephen Few mentions that *its linear and no-frills design provides a rich display of data in a small space, which is essential on a dashboard.*

 Stephen Few's bullet chart specification can be found at
`https://www.perceptualedge.com/articles/`
`misc/Bullet_Graph_Design_Spec.pdf.`

In this recipe, we have manually created the bullet chart by starting with a bar chart, and then adding reference lines. Another way to create bullet charts in Tableau is by selecting all the dimensions and measures you want to graph, and selecting the bullet chart icon in **Show Me**. The only challenge with this approach is that Tableau will pick which measure goes on the bar and which measure goes on the reference line. If the selection turned out to be the incorrect selection, you can simply right-click on the axis and choose to swap the reference lines.

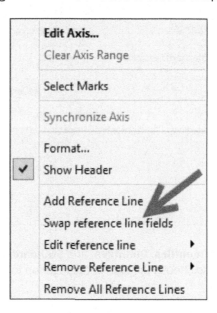

If you need to remove any reference lines, you can right-click on the axis as well, and choose to remove the reference line.

- ▸ Please refer to the *Creating a bullet chart* recipe in this chapter
- ▸ Please refer to the *Creating a combo chart (dual axis)* recipe in this chapter

Creating a bar in bar chart

A bar in bar chart stacks one bar chart on top of the other. Typically the two bars will have different colors and widths. Bar in bar charts can be effective in showing progress to a goal, or any two measures from the same starting point. In this recipe, we will compare the field goals made and attempted by the Phoenix Suns players in 2009 using a bar in bar chart.

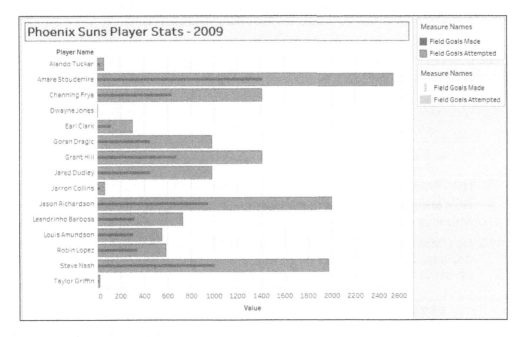

Getting ready

To follow this recipe, open `B05527_02 - STARTER.twbx`. Use the worksheet called `Bar in Bar`, and connect to the `Player Stats (NBA Players Regular Season 2009)` data source.

How to do it...

The following are the steps to create a bar in bar chart:

1. From **Dimensions**, drag **Team Name** to the **Filters** shelf.

2. Under the **General** tab, check **Suns**.

3. From **Dimensions**, drag **Year** to the **Filters** shelf.

4. Under the **General** tab, choose **2009**.

5. From **Dimensions**, drag **League** to the **Filters** shelf.

6. Under the **General** tab, check **N** for NBA.

7. If it doesn't exist yet, create a calculated field called **Player Name**, and provide the following formula that concatenates **First Name** and **Last Name**:

See Appendix A, Calculated Fields Primer for more details on creating calculated fields

8. From **Dimensions**, drag **Player Name** to the **Rows** shelf.

9. From **Measures**, drag **Field Goals Made** to the **Columns** shelf. This creates a horizontal axis for your view.

10. From **Measures**, drag **Field Goals Attempted** to the horizontal axis created by **Field Goals Made**. Do not let go of the mouse until you see the double ruler icon appear on top of the axis.

11. Change the mark from **Automatic** to **Bar** in the **Marks** card.

12. Move the **Measure Names** pill from the **Rows** shelf to **Color** in the **Marks** card. Ensure that **Measure Names** does not exist in the **Rows** shelf after this step.

13. Control drag the **Measure Names** pill in **Color** to **Size** in the **Marks** card. This creates a copy of the **Measure Names** pill in the **Marks** card, but this time to **Size**.

14. Go to the **Analysis** top menu item, then **Stack Marks** and choose **Off**. This unstacks the marks.

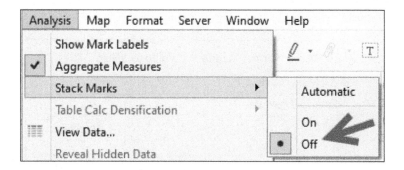

15. Rearrange the measures in the **Measure Values** shelf so that **SUM(Field Goals Made)** is placed on top of **SUM(Field Goals Attempted)**. This reverses the size and makes **SUM(Field Goals Attempted)** the wider bar.

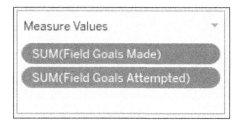

16. Click on the drop-down arrow beside the color legend card and choose **Edit colors...**

17. Change the colors of your bar. Assign a red color to **Made**, and gray to **Attempted**. Close the edit box when done.

How it works...

In this recipe, we started by creating a bar chart. A simple bar chart will typically have a dimension in either **Rows** or **Columns**, and a measure on the other shelf. Here we started with the **Player Name** dimension on **Rows**, and the **Field Goals Made** measure on **Columns**. When you drag another measure to the axis initially created by the measure, the original measure in the shelf gets replaced with **Measure Values**. This means that there are now multiple measures that are sharing the same axis.

By default when we have a shared axis chart, the bars are stacked on top of each other. The total length of the bar is cumulative total of both bars. This is great if we only care about the cumulative total. However, if you want to compare the two bars, it becomes tricky because the bars don't both start at the same starting point. The bar in bar chart can help in this case.

To create a bar in bar, we can start with the stacked bar chart, and then unstack the bars so instead of having the bars on top of each other, the bars now will start at the same point (which is zero). In Tableau, this can be done by going to the **Analysis** menu, and under **Stack Marks**, checking **Off**.

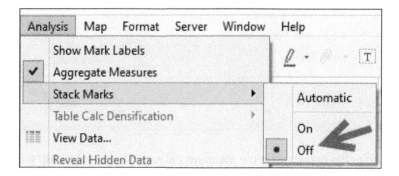

When we first unstack the bar, one bar may completely mask another bar, which still makes comparing the bars difficult. A key technique here is to differentiate the bars by color and by size—this makes the bars easier to compare.

There's more...

A bar in bar can be used to compare two measures, and can be used to track actual to goal or target. A bullet chart can also track actual to target by using a mark (bar) and a reference line. Dual axis charts can also be used for this purpose.

See also

▸ Please refer to the *Creating a bullet chart* recipe in this chapter

▸ Please refer to the *Creating a combo chart (dual axis)* recipe in this chapter

Creating a donut chart

A donut chart, like a pie chart, shows part-to-whole relationships. And like a traditional donut (the sweet, edible kind), it has a hole in the middle.

In this recipe, we will create a donut chart that shows the breakdown of Hollywood's top movies from 2007-2011 by genre.

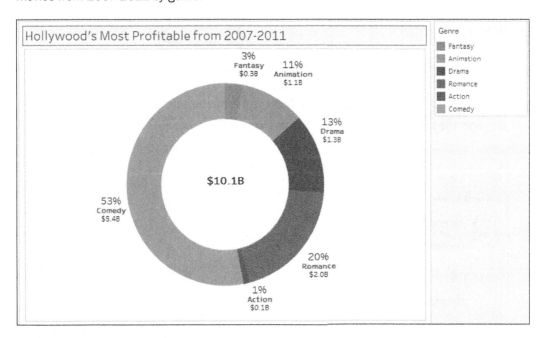

Getting ready

To follow this recipe, open B05527_02 - STARTER.twbx. Use the worksheet called Donut, and connect to the HollywoodMostProfitableStories data source.

How to do it...

The following are the steps to create a donut chart:

1. Change the mark type to **Pie** in the **Marks** card.

2. From **Measures**, drag **Worldwide Gross Amount** to **Angle** in the **Marks** card.

3. From **Dimensions**, drag **Genre** to **Color** in the **Marks** card.

4. To make the pie easier to view, set the chart to show as **Entire View** from the toolbar.

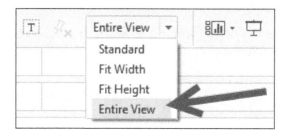

5. Right-click on the **Genre** pill in the **Color** in the **Marks** card and select **Sort...**.

6. Sort the slices by the **Sum** of the **Worldwide Gross Amount** in **Ascending** order.

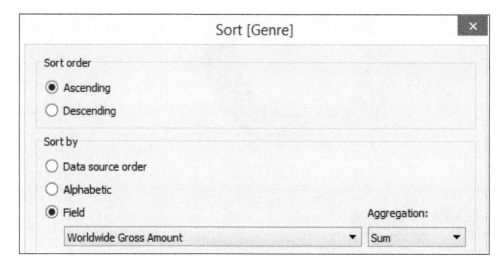

7. From **Dimensions**, drag **Genre** to **Label** in the **Marks** card.

8. From **Measures**, drag **Worldwide Gross Amount** to **Label** in the **Marks** card.

9. Right-click on the **SUM(Worldwide Gross Amount)** pill in the **Label** property in the **Marks** card. Select **Quick table calculation**, and then **Percent of total**.

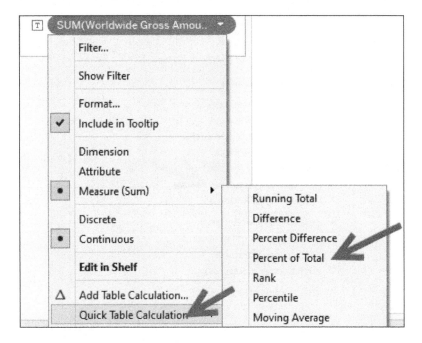

10. From **Measures**, drag **Worldwide Gross Amount** again to the **Label** in the **Marks** card.

11. Click on **Label** in the **Marks** card, and select the ellipsis button under **Label Appearance** to modify the style of the text.

12. Change the format of the label to show the following, and click **OK** when done.

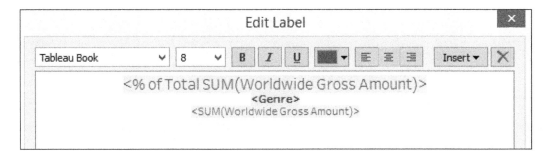

13. Right-click and drag **Number of Records** from **Measures** onto the **Rows** shelf, and choose **MIN(Number of Records)**.

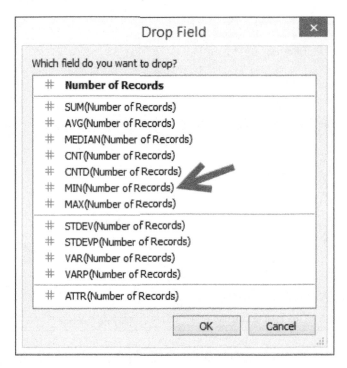

14. Right-click and drag **Number of Records** again from **Measures** onto the **Rows** shelf, and choose **MIN(Number of Records)**. Note this should be the second instance of this pill in the **Rows** shelf.

15. Right-click on the second **MIN(Number of Records)** in the **Rows** shelf, and select **Dual Axis**.

16. Select the second **MIN(Number of Records)** pill in **Rows** to activate its **Marks** card.

17. Click on the **Size** in the **Marks** card and adjust to make the pie smaller.

18. Remove **Genre** from the **Color** in the **Marks** card. This creates just a whole circle and leaves the total **Worldwide Gross Amount** as a label in the center of the circle.

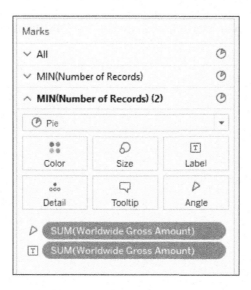

19. Right-click on both **MIN(Number of Records)** pills in **Rows** and uncheck **Show Header** for both.

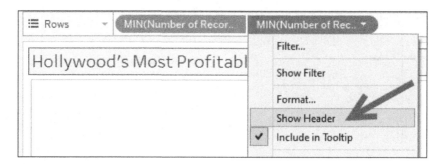

How it works...

Donut charts are not available natively in Tableau. Donut charts, however, can be simulated by overlapping two pies together. One of the pies will be the regular pie chart, and the other pie will be a smaller version of it without the slices.

To create a donut chart in Tableau, we can start by creating a regular pie chart in Tableau. After this is created, we have to force an axis on the pie chart (I know this doesn't make sense, but bear with me for a little bit). We can use the **Number of Records** measure to create this axis, which is a Tableau auto-generated measure field. When you right-click and drag this measure on any of the shelves, we can choose any of the aggregated measures presented. We choose **MIN**, for minimum, in our recipe.

Once we have one axis, we can create our dual axis chart. We can simply duplicate the existing axis by copying the **MIN(Number of Records)** a second time in the Rows shelf. From here, we can choose the **Dual Axis** option on the second **MIN(Number of Records)** pill.

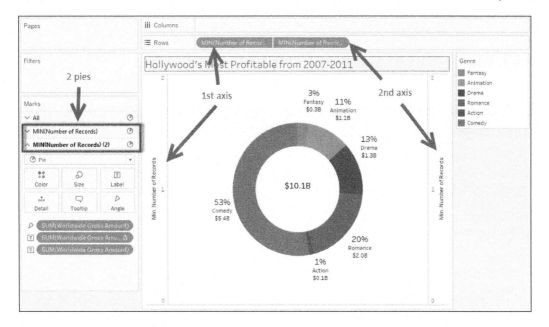

Once we have the two axes, these are the next steps:

1. Make one of the pies smaller so that the outer slices will be more evident
2. Remove the slices from the smaller pie so it appears as a solid circle
3. Add a label to the smaller pie, such as the total value of the measure

There's more...

Donut charts could technically be layered, that is, have a donut inside a donut if you wanted to show multiple series of data. For our purposes, we are sticking with a pie on the outside and a hole on the inside since this can be achieved in Tableau using a dual axis graph. Layered donut charts can also be quite confusing to look at and understand.

If you have read Stephen Few's books, you may be scratching your head as to why you would even bother with a donut chart. Stephen Few considers donut charts as one of the no-no charts, and for good reason. If we cannot easily tell angles, how much better will we be at telling it if we take out the center hole? We will be worse, and it will be a much harder chart to read!

There are definitely better alternatives to donut charts. However, sometimes this is what is asked of us. We can pick our battles. Instead of fighting for the "right" graph every time, we can slowly show the benefits of using different types of charts. The company may or may not eventually appreciate other graphs that convey the message more clearly. Adopting best practices takes time, and sometimes also requires a culture shift.

See also

▶ Please refer to the *Creating a pie chart* recipe in *Chapter 1, Basic Charts*

▶ Please refer to the *Creating a combo chart (dual axis)* recipe in this chapter

Creating a unit chart

Unit charts, also referred to as pictogram charts, display each unit of measure as a single mark or symbol. While other types of charts may be more effective and less cluttered, unit charts may create more engagement because of the images and visuals used.

In this recipe, we will create a unit chart that shows all the medals that were won by Canada in the Summer Olympics from 1896-2008.

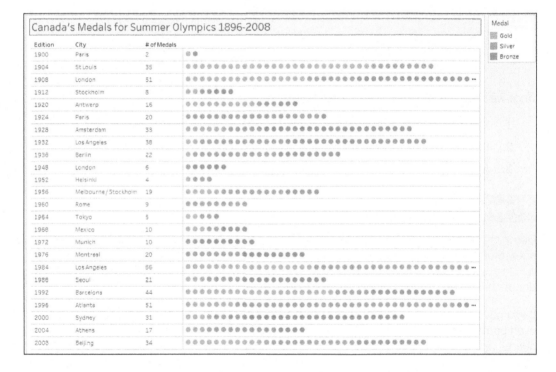

Getting ready

To follow this recipe, open B05527_02 - STARTER.twbx. Use the worksheet called Unit Chart, and connect to the ALL MEDALISTS (Summer_Olympic_ medallists_1896-2008) data source.

How to do it...

The following are the steps to create a unit chart:

1. From **Dimensions**, drag **NOC** to the **Filters** shelf and filter to **CAN**.

2. From **Dimensions**, drag **Edition** to **Rows**.

3. From **Dimensions**, drag **City** to **Rows**, to the right of **Edition**.

4. Create a calculated field called **# of Medals**. This field should be fixed to **Edition** and **NOC** so that it is not affected by the data fields (pills) used in the view.

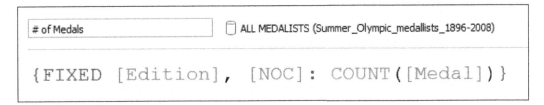

5. From **Dimensions**, drag **# of Medals** to **Rows**, to the right of **City**. By default, this creates a bar chart.

6. Right-click on the **SUM(# of Medals)** in **Rows**, and select **Discrete** to display it as text instead of a bar chart.

7. Change the mark of the view to **Circle**.

8. From **Dimensions**, drag **Athlete** to **Details**. This will create a circle for each athlete who won a medal.

9. Click the **Analysis** menu and uncheck **Aggregate Measures**.

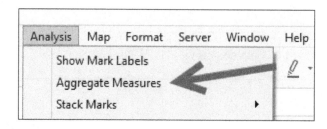

10. From **Dimensions**, drag **Medal** to **Color**.

11. Click on the drop-down arrow beside the color legend again. This time choose **Edit colors...**.

12. Choose colors that closely resemble **Gold**, **Silver**, and **Bronze**. Click OK when done.

13. Using the **Color** property in the **Marks** card, manually re-order the medal colors by dragging the names in the correct order. **Gold** should be at the top, followed by **Silver**, and then **Bronze**.

How it works...

To create a unit chart in Tableau, there are a couple of crucial steps. First, the mark has to be something that can represent distinct, discrete units—a shape, a circle, a square. Second, the marks have to be disaggregated. This can be done by going to the **Analysis** top menu and unchecking **Aggregate Measures**.

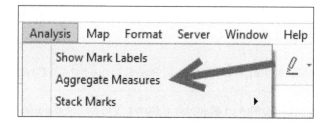

In this recipe, we are displaying Canada's medals for the Summer Olympics. To do this, we started off by displaying all the dimensions we want displayed as text columns—**Edition**, **City**, and **Number of Medals**. **Number of Medals** by default produces a bar chart with an axis. To convert this to a text field, we can simply select **Discrete**.

The main step involve changing the mark type to **Circle** so that each discrete unit can be represented as a circle mark. We also added **Athlete** to **Detail**, which forces each athlete to have their own circle mark. When we disaggregate the measures, each athlete will be represented multiple times if that athlete has won more than one medal.

Other mark types can technically work, for example a bar, but this mark has to be further broken down by placing something in Detail, as well as disaggregating the measure.

There's more...

Each mark in a unit chart can also represent a number of individual units. In Tableau, we can use the table calculation function `INDEX()` in combination with integer division based on the number of units you want represented to help *chunk* the items.

In this recipe, for example, if we wanted to display one circle for units of five medals, we can use the following formula:

```
# of Medals (Unit)                    ALL MEDALISTS (Summer_Olympic_medallists_1896-2008)

Results are computed along Table (across).
IF INDEX()-1 <= INT(WINDOW_SUM(SUM([Number of Records])))/5)
THEN INDEX()*5
END
```

The `INDEX()` function creates a sequential number for each item in the window. The formula uses `INDEX()` computed across the table, and checks if this number is within five before it returns a number divisible by five.

Let's walk through this. For example if there are six medals, we expect two circles—one for the first five, the other for the remaining one. `INT(WINDOW_SUM(SUM([Number of Records])))/5)` is `INT(6/5)`, therefore 1.

INDEX()	INDEX() - 1	Condition	Result	Resulting Value
1	0	0 <= (6/5)?	True	Circle for value 5
2	1	1 <= (6/5)?	True	Circle for value 10
3	2	2 <= (6/5)?	False	
4	3	3 <= (6/5)?	False	
5	4	4 <= (6/5)?	False	
6	5	5 <= (6/5)?	False	

To change this to *n* units, where *n* is your preferred unit number, you simply need to replace the denominator with *n* in the `IF` statement, and the multiplier with *n* in the action block.

We will need to display the result of this calculated field in the **Columns** shelf, and still need to disaggregate the measures. What you will get will be similar to the following:

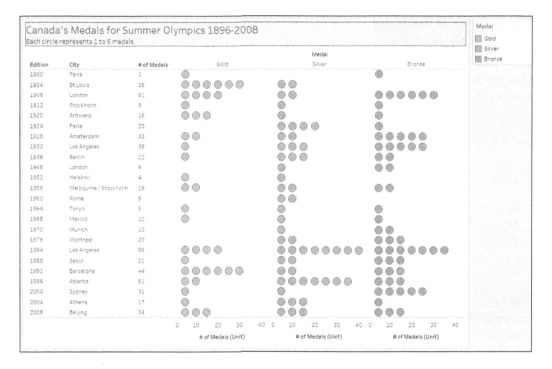

What we have is a chart that has a circle for every 1-5 medals. Of course you can make adjustments if you want to have different marks or icons showing half units, quarter units, and so on.

There may be other charts that may convey information more clearly than unit charts. The trouble with unit charts is that you cannot tell the measures right away. Attentive processing— or focus—is required to fully understand and compare. Unit charts, however, may be effective charts depending on the audience and purpose. These charts may be used to pique the interest or engage an audience. To help increase the clarity of the charts, we can use common, understandable symbols and label the units each symbol represents.

Creating a box and whisker chart

Box and whisker plots, also called box plots, are charts that divide their data points into quartiles. Box plots are great at comparing distributions of data for different groups or categories side by side.

In this recipe, we will create a box and whisker plot that shows the spread of points garnered by NBA teams from 2000-2009.

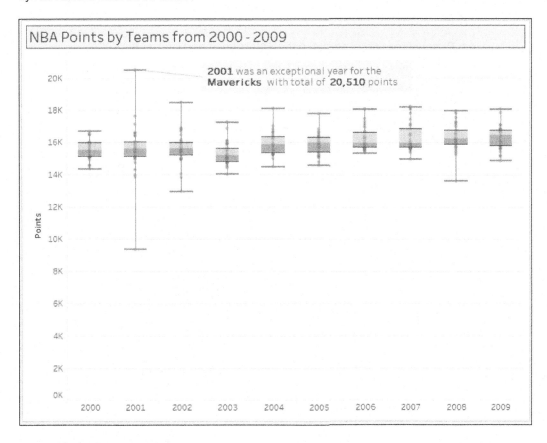

Getting ready

To follow this recipe, open B05527_02 - STARTER.twbx. Use the worksheet called Box and Whisker, and connect to the Player Stats (NBA Players Regular Season 2009) data source.

How to do it...

The following are the steps to create a box and whisker plot:

1. From **Dimensions**, drag **League** to the **Filters** shelf and filter to **N** for NBA.

2. From **Dimensions**, drag **Year** to the **Filters** shelf and choose years 2000-2009.

3. *Ctrl* + click **Year** from **Dimensions** and **Points** from **Measures** to select both data fields from the side bar.

4. While **Year** and **Points** are still selected, expand **Show Me**.

5. Select the Box and Whisker plot icon in **Show Me**, as shown in the following screenshot. This will place **Year** in the **Details** property in the **Marks** card, and **SUM(Points)** in the **Rows** shelf.

6. Move **Year** from the **Details** in the **Marks** card to the **Columns** shelf.

7. From **Dimensions**, drag **Team Name** to **Details** in the **Marks** card.

8. Click on **Size** in the **Marks** card to make the **Circle** marks smaller.

9. Right-click on the box and whisker plot that gets created, and select **Edit...**.

10. Under **Plot Options**, choose **Maximum extent of the data** option for the **Whiskers extend to** setting. Click **OK** when done.

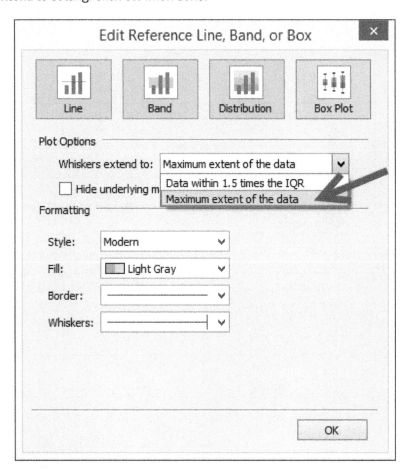

How it works...

Box and whisker plots allow you to show the spread of your data, and can easily show where 50% of your data is.

This recipe is probably one of the few recipes that start with **Show Me**. This is because in this case, we select a dimension, **Year**, and a measure, **Points**, first and then click on the box and whisker plot in **Show Me**. The following is what **Show Me** creates. Each circle represents the points in a specific field.

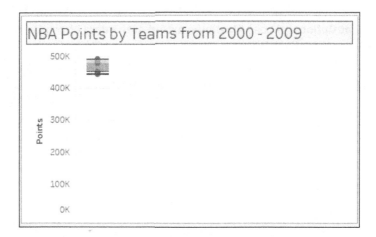

If we want to show this by year, then we can move Year from **Details** to the **Columns** shelf, which will give us the following viz.

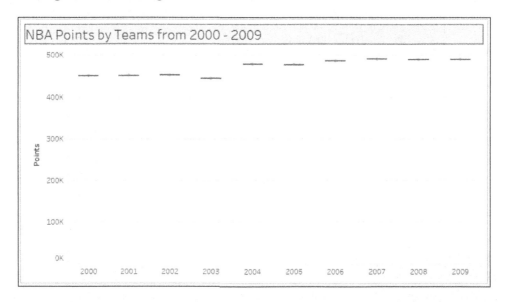

What's missing in this box and whisker plot is the scatter. We need to see the individual teams' points as individual points. To do this, we can add the team name onto **Details** in the **Marks** card. Remember that adding a field onto **Detail** changes the level of detail of the visualization; in this case each point is now the sum of points for **Year** and **Team**.

Once team name is added, we can see the variation in team points from year to year, and we can note that the box is where 50% of the points lie (thus where 50% of the teams are for that year).

As for the whisker, the default option is to plot the lines based on points that are within 1.5 times the IQR (interquartile range).

There is another option to extend the whiskers to the maximum extent of the points. This extends the whiskers even to the outliers, making outliers even more prominent. However this will skew your boxes.

There's more...

Box and whisker plots can be shown whenever you want to see how the variations compare. Here is a box-and-whisker plot for the same data set used in this recipe, but this time narrowed down to the Phoenix Suns players who played for the Phoenix Suns for at least 3 years between 2000 and 2009. Each point represents that player's points for a year. The smaller box may mean that the player is more consistently producing points per year. The longer the box means the more variation—in some years the player does very well, and other years not so much.

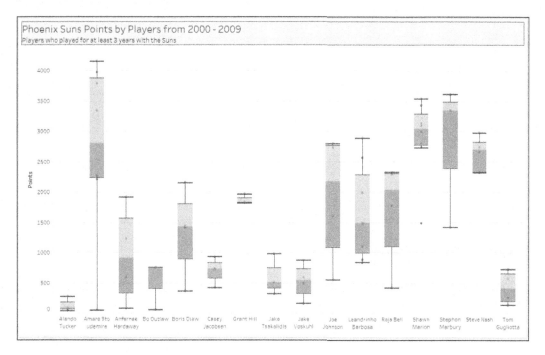

See also

▶ Please refer to the *Creating a scatter plot* recipe in *Chapter 1, Basic Charts*.

Creating a sparkline with indicators

Sparklines are really small, compressed charts that are good for showing a high level volatility or trends in data.

In this recipe, we will create a sparkline with additional indicators at the line end.

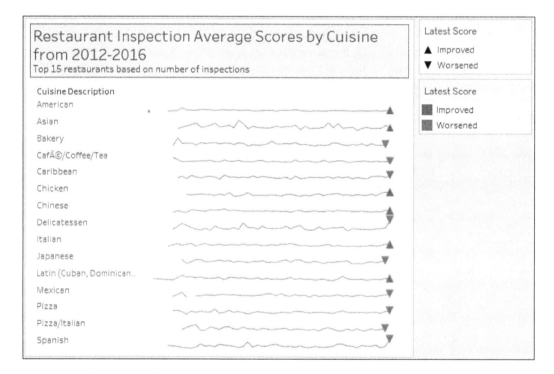

Getting ready

To follow this recipe, open `B05527_02 - STARTER.twbx`. Use the worksheet called `Sparkline with Indicators`, and connect to the `DOHMH New York City Restaurant` data source.

How to do it...

The following are the steps to create a sparkline with indicators at the end:

1. From **Dimensions**, drag **Inspection Date** to the **Filters** shelf.
2. When prompted on what to filter, choose **Years**.

3. In the next window, under the **General** tab, select all years except 1900.

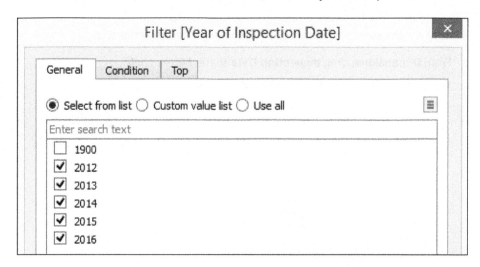

4. From **Dimensions**, drag **Cuisine Description** to the **Filters** shelf and under the **Top** tab, select **Top** and 15 by **Sum** of **Number of Records**.

5. From **Dimensions**, drag **Cuisine Description** to the **Rows** shelf.

6. From **Dimensions**, right-click drag **Inspection Date** to the **Columns** shelf, and choose continuous month. This is the fourth field from the bottom of the list.

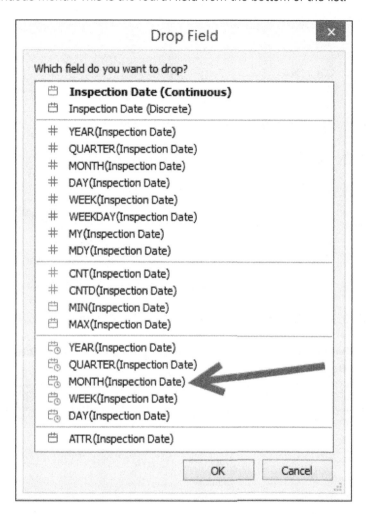

7. From **Measures**, drag **Score** to the **Rows** shelf to the right of **Cuisine Description**.

8. Right-click on **Score** on the **Rows** shelf and change aggregation to **Average**.

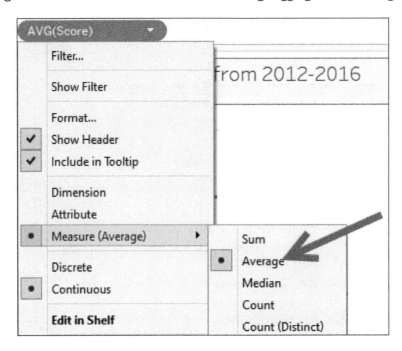

9. Under **Dimensions**, right-click on **Inspection Date** and choose **Create**, and then **Custom Date...**.

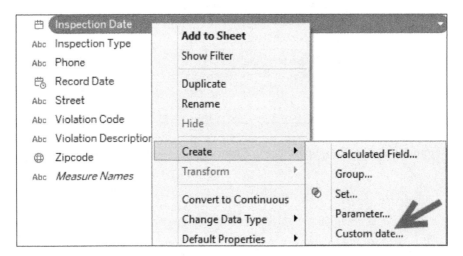

10. Choose **Months** under **Detail** and provide the name **Inspection Date (Cont Months)**.

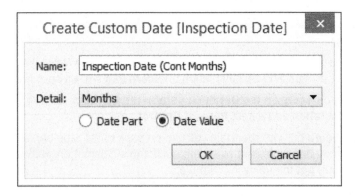

11. Create a calculated field called **Last Inspection Month (Cont)**, which will hold the last inspection done for that particular cuisine family.

```
Last Inspection Month (Cont)          DOHMH New York City Restaurant (DOHMH_New_York_City

{
    FIXED [Cuisine Description]:
    MAX([Inspection Date (Cont Months)])
}
```

12. Create another calculated field called **Last Inspection Avg Score**, which will hold the average score for the last inspection month for that cuisine family. Note that if the inspection date does not fall on the last inspection month, the score is not included in the average calculation.

```
Last Inspection Avg Score          DOHMH New York City Restaurant (DOHMH_New_York_City_Restaurant_Inspection_Results)          X

AVG
(
   IF [Inspection Date (Cont Months)] = [Last Inspection Month (Cont)]
   THEN [Score]
   END
)
```

13. From **Measures**, drag the new calculated field **Last Inspection Avg Score** to the **Rows** shelf, to the right of **AVG(Score)**.

14. Right-click on **Last Inspection Avg Score** pill in the **Rows** shelf and select **Dual Axis**.

15. From **Measures**, drag **Score** to **Detail** of any of the **Marks** cards. We will use this to create a quick table calculation on **Score** that we will save back to the side bar.

16. Right-click on **Score** on the **Detail** property in the **Marks** card. Go to **Quick Table Calculation** and select **Percent Difference**.

17. Drag the **Score** pill with the table calculation back to the side bar, and rename this field to **% Diff**. Note that when the quick table calculation was set, this pill automatically got the following formula:

% Diff   🗇 DOHMH New York City Restaurant (DOHMH_New_York_City_Restaurant_Inspection

Results are computed along Table (across).

```
(ZN(SUM([Score])) - LOOKUP(ZN(SUM([Score])), -1)) /
ABS(LOOKUP(ZN(SUM([Score])), -1))
```

---

18. You can delete the **Score** in the **Detail** in the **Marks** card now. We simply needed this to auto-generate the formula for us.

19. Create another calculated field called **Last Change**, which checks the last change and assign an overall status of **Improved** if the final **% Diff** is positive, **Worsened** if the last **% Diff** is negative, and **No change** if there was no change.

Last Change   🗇 DOHMH New York City Restaurant (DOHMH_New_York

Results are computed along Table (across).

```
IF LOOKUP([% Diff],LAST()) < 0
THEN "Improved"
ELSEIF LOOKUP([% Diff],LAST()) > 0
THEN "Worsened"
ELSE "No change"
END
```

---

20. Select the **AGG(Last Inspection Avg Score)** in the **Rows** shelf to activate its **Marks** card.

21. From **Measures**, drag **Last Change** to **Color** in the **Marks** card.

22. Change the mark type to **Shapes**.

23. From **Measures**, drag **Last Change** to **Color** in the **Shape** property in the **Marks** card, and choose the **Filled Shape Palette**.

24. Choose a filled upwards arrow for **Improved**, and a filled downwards arrow for **Worsened**.

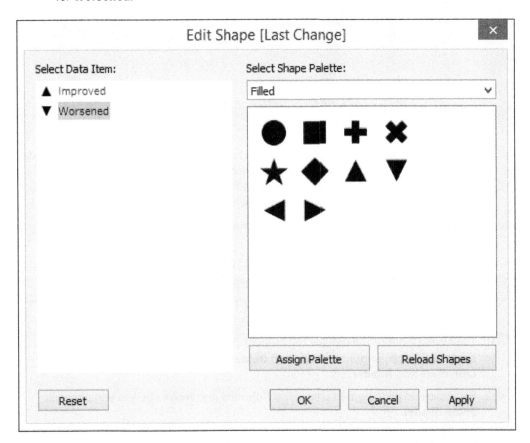

25. Change the titles of the shape and color legends to display **Latest Score**. You can do this by right-clicking on the top-right corner of each legend box, and selecting **Edit Title...**.

26. Adjust the width and height of the rows and columns. You can do this by moving your mouse pointer to the column or row edge of a film until you see a double-headed arrow. The left-right double-headed arrow allows you to adjust the width, and the up-down double-headed arrow allows you to adjust the height.

27. Remove the grid lines. You can do this by selecting **Format** menu item, and select **Lines...**.

28. Under the **Rows** tab, select **Grid Lines** and set it to **None**.

29. Go to **Format** menu again, and this time select **Borders...**.

30. Under the **Sheet** tab, set **Pane** line to **None** for both the **Row Divider** and **Column Divider** section.

31. The format sidebar will replace the original data sidebar. In this **Format borders** side bar, under the **Sheet** tab **Default** section, add borders to the **Cell**, **Pane** and **Header**.

32. Right-click on all the green pills in the **Columns** and **Rows** shelves and uncheck **Show Header**.

How it works...

Sparklines are great for representing a lot of information in a very small space. Creating a sparkline in Tableau requires creating a small multiple and formatting the small multiple so it's smaller and without many of the axis labels.

In this recipe, we started by creating a small multiple of line charts by **Cuisine Description**. We adjusted the formatting so that the rows and columns are smaller than the default style. Overall, these steps are fairly similar to *Creating a small multiple chart* recipe in this chapter.

The enhancement to this chart is the addition of indicators at the end of the line. Since the indicators are a different mark, this means we need to use a dual axis chart to accomplish this visual.

What we need to do is to share the same **Inspection Date** axis with the line chart, and another chart that has a single mark that is color coded depending on whether that last point improved or worsened from the previous period. We can do this by creating a series of calculated fields:

- A calculated field that contains the month/year of the inspection date. We need to use this as axis to both our marks. This field is created using the **Create Custom Date** option for the **Inspection Date** field. We called this **Inspection Date (Cont Months)**.

- A calculated field that calculates the last month/year of inspection. This is because we need to have a second axis to put the second mark, which is a single mark that occurs at the end of the inspection period. This calculated field uses a FIXED LOD (level of detail) expression, which means this will be fairly static and will not be affected by any dimension filters. This calculation is fixed to the cuisine. We called this **Last Inspection Month (Cont)**.

Last Inspection Month (Cont)	DOHMH New York City Restaurant (DOHMH_New_York_City

```
{
    FIXED [Cuisine Description]:
    MAX([Inspection Date (Cont Months)])
}
```

▶ A calculated field that contains the table calculation for percent difference. This calculates the percent difference of the average score from the previous month. We called this % **Diff**.

% Diff   ⬚ DOHMH New York City Restaurant (DOHMH_New_York_City_Restaurant_Inspection

Results are computed along Table (across).

```
(ZN(SUM([Score])) - LOOKUP(ZN(SUM([Score])), -1)) /
ABS(LOOKUP(ZN(SUM([Score])), -1))
```

▶ A calculated field that determines whether the score has improved, worsened, or stayed the same. This will be based on whether the last month's average score is higher or lower than (or the same as) the previous month's. We called this **Last Change**.

Last Change   ⬚ DOHMH New York City Restaurant (DOHMH_New_York

Results are computed along Table (across).

```
IF LOOKUP([% Diff],LAST()) < 0
THEN "Improved"
ELSEIF LOOKUP([% Diff],LAST()) > 0
THEN "Worsened"
ELSE "No change"
END
```

Once the calculated fields are set, the steps are fairly similar to creating a dual axis chart. The first measure will be displayed as line, and the second measure—which is a single value represented by the **Last Change** calculated field—will be represented as **Shape**. A green triangle represents an improvement from second to the last month's average inspection score, and a red inverted triangle represents an increase in score, hence more violations for that particular cuisine compared to the second to the last month.

[*Appendix A, Calculated Fields Primer* provides a primer on calculated fields in Tableau.]

There's more...

When using sparklines, it is important to not get hung up on not having the details. Often labels and axes headers are removed so only the small graphs remain.

Stocks are a great use case for using sparklines. They allow you to see the volatility of the stocks without having to clutter the screen with too many numbers for individual stocks.

The following is an example of stock information with sparklines from `http://finance.yahoo.com/stock-center/`:

Market Movers						U.S. Composite ⌄

Most Actives   % Gainers   % Losers

Symbol	Company Name	Price	Change	% Change	Volume	1-Day
BAC	Bank of America Corp...	13.10	-0.17	-1.28%	88,888,071	
MU	Micron Technology, Inc.	12.50	-1.26	-9.16%	68,847,094	
SIRI	Sirius XM Holdings Inc.	3.97	+0.02	+0.51%	55,401,835	
F	Ford Motor Co.	12.72	+0.15	+1.19%	45,067,772	
RAD	Rite Aid Corporation	7.31	-0.18	-2.40%	43,526,350	
VALE	Vale S.A.	5.16	+0.10	+1.98%	34,514,258	
CHK	Chesapeake Energy C...	4.59	+0.31	+7.24%	33,140,122	
GE	General Electric Com...	31.49	+0.01	+0.03%	32,700,349	
VRX	Valeant Pharmaceutic...	20.44	+0.30	+1.49%	31,070,439	
FCX	Freeport-McMoRan Inc.	11.35	+0.21	+1.89%	27,441,718	

While traditionally sparklines have meant small line graphs, sparklines are now represented using other chart types including bar charts, area charts, and so on.

See also

- ▸ Please refer to the *Creating a small multiple chart* recipe in this chapter.
- ▸ Please refer to the *Creating a dynamic column/row trellis chart* recipe in *Chapter 3, Interactivity*.

Creating a KPI text table

Key performance indicators, or KPIs, are metrics that indicate how well an organization is performing against its objectives. KPIs are typically represented as easily understandable color-coded symbols in a dashboard. For example, a red circle could mean that area is not meeting objectives, while a green circle does.

In this recipe, we will show the top 10 New York restaurant cuisines based on their average inspection scores from 2012-2016 in a text table with KPIs.

Restaurant Inspection Average Scores by Cuisine from 2012-2016
Top 10 restaurants based on average score

			Inspection Date		
Cuisine Description	2012	2013	2014	2015	2016
Chilean			Ⓐ 8.50	Ⓒ 61.00	Ⓑ 22.00
Continental		Ⓑ 21.50	Ⓑ 19.91	Ⓑ 25.45	Ⓑ 23.67
Creole		Ⓒ 29.71	Ⓑ 21.90	Ⓑ 25.50	Ⓑ 19.25
Creole/Cajun		Ⓑ 14.00			Ⓒ 43.50
Ethiopian		Ⓐ 9.00	Ⓑ 19.50	Ⓒ 35.00	Ⓑ 25.50
Korean	Ⓐ 12.00	Ⓑ 21.08	Ⓑ 24.76	Ⓑ 19.33	Ⓒ 27.11
Pakistani	Ⓐ 10.00	Ⓒ 46.33	Ⓒ 36.67	Ⓑ 26.00	Ⓑ 17.80
Scandinavian		Ⓒ 31.00	Ⓒ 39.00		
Soul Food		Ⓑ 19.50	Ⓒ 30.22	Ⓑ 20.73	Ⓑ 19.50
Vietnamese/ Cambodian/Malaysia		Ⓑ 26.44	Ⓒ 30.00	Ⓑ 15.35	Ⓒ 33.29

Getting ready

To follow this recipe, open B05527_02 - STARTER.twbx. Use the worksheet called KPI Text Table, and connect to the DOHMH New York City Restaurant data source.

How to do it...

The following are the steps to create a KPI table:

1. From **Dimensions**, drag **Inspection Date** to the **Filters** shelf.

2. When prompted on what to filter, choose **Years**.

3. In the next window, under the **General** tab, select all years except 1900.

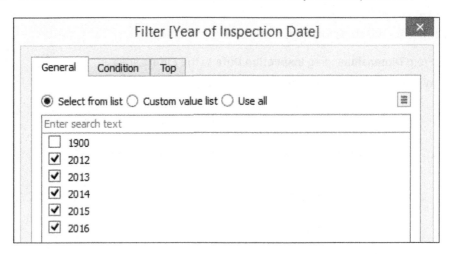

4. From **Dimensions**, drag **Inspection Date** to the **Columns** shelf.

5. From **Dimensions**, drag **Cuisine Description** to the **Filters** shelf and under the **Top** tab, select **Top 10** by **Average** of **Score**.

6. From **Dimensions**, drag **Cuisine Description** to the **Rows** shelf.

7. Create a calculated field called **Cuisine A Grade**. If the average score is between 0 and 13, the score is A. A in this case is a special character that you can copy from `http://www.copypastecharacter.com/alphabetical-order`.

8. The formula for the calculated field is as follows:

Cuisine A Grade   🗇 DOHMH New York City Restaurant (DOHMH_New_York_City_Restaurant

```
IF AVG([Score]) >= 0 AND AVG([Score]) <= 13
THEN "Ⓐ"
END
```

---

9. Create another calculated field called **Cuisine B Grade**, which assigns the special B character if the average score is between 14 and 27.

Cuisine B Grade   🗇 DOHMH New York City Restaurant (DOHMH_New_York_City_Restaurant

```
IF AVG([Score]) >= 14 AND AVG([Score]) <= 27
THEN "Ⓑ"
END
```

---

10. Create another calculated field called **Cuisine C Grade**, which assigns the special C character if the average score is greater than 27.

Cuisine C Grade   🗇 DOHMH New York City Restaurant (DOHMH_New_York_City_Restaurant

```
IF AVG([Score]) > 27
THEN "Ⓒ"
END
```

---

11. Create one more calculated field called **Avg Score String**, which creates a text field that contains the average score. If the average score is a single digit, we pad the text with spaces. We are creating this to ensure that single and double digit scores align when displayed as text.

Avg Score String	⬡ DOHMH New York City Restaurant (DOHMH_New_York_City

```
IF (LEN (STR (ROUND (AVG ([Score]),2))) = 4)
THEN "    " + STR (ROUND (AVG ([Score]),2))
ELSE  STR (ROUND (AVG ([Score]),2))
END
```

12. Drag the newly created calculated fields **Cuisine A Grade**, **Cuisine B Grade**, **Cuisine C Grade**, and **Avg Score String** to **Text** in the **Marks** card.

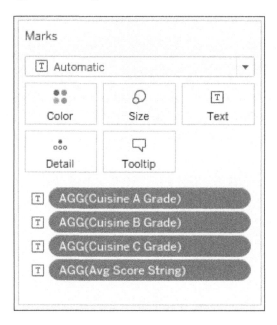

13. In the **Marks** card, click on **Label**.

14. Click on the ellipsis in the **Text** field to change the label to the following. Note that each cuisine grade can be added using the **Insert** dropdown. Each cuisine grade is also colored differently—green for an A grade, orange for a B grade, and red for a C grade. Feel free to change the color to your preference.

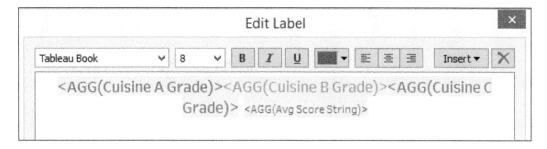

How it works...

In this recipe, we have chosen to display a symbol beside each value in our text table. In many ways this is really just a text table, which is covered in _Creating a text table_ recipe in _Chapter 1, Basic Charts_. How this is different is based on how the text for each cell is created.

We first need to create calculated fields that will determine the grades for the cuisines. According to the Government of New York website, for each inspection:

▶ 0 to 13 points earns an A

▶ 14 to 27 points receives a B

▶ 28 or more is a C

 If you are interested in how New York restaurants are graded, you can read the official guide from http://www1.nyc.gov/assets/doh/downloads/pdf/rii/how-we-score-grade.pdf.

We are just going to use the same criteria for the average scores for each cuisine. Each of these calculations is an If statement. If the value falls within a certain range, the If statement returns a special character:

```
Cuisine A Grade                    DOHMH New York City Restaurant (DOHMH_New_York_City_Restaurant

IF AVG([Score]) >= 0 AND AVG([Score]) <= 13
THEN "Ⓐ"
END
```

The characters are copied from `http://www.copypastecharacter.com/alphabetical-order`.

Once the score fields are created, the text field needs to be created. In this text field, all the previous calculated fields are included—each grade is formatted with a different color.

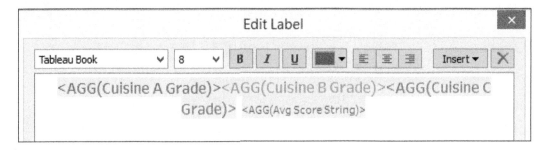

Each of the grades are mutually exclusive. Since the individual grade calculated fields just IF statements and not `If...Else` statements, if the scores are outside of a specific range, there is nothing that gets displayed. This creates the *dynamic* label effect.

Instead of multiple calculated fields, you can also choose to just have a single calculated field. In this case, having multiple calculated fields may be helpful especially if you want to reuse these in tooltips and so on.

There's more...

Another way, and perhaps more common, is to use the shapes to create a KPI table. We will still need a calculated field that will give us the discrete values for the average grade.

Cusine Average Grade	⬭ DOHMH New York City Restaurant (DOHMH_New_York_City_Restaurant_Inspection

```
IF AVG([Score]) >= 0 AND AVG([Score]) <= 13
THEN "A"
ELSEIF AVG([Score]) >= 14 AND AVG([Score]) <= 27
THEN "B"
ELSEIF AVG([Score]) > 27
THEN "C"
END
```

This field can be used in a **Shape** property in the **Marks** card to display common KPI icons.

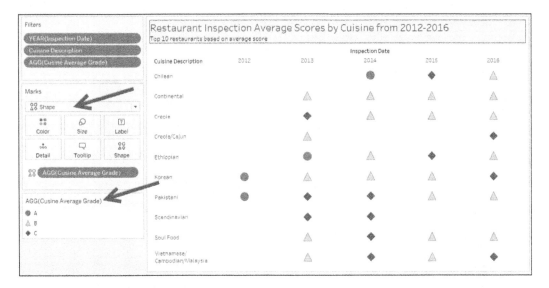

See also

▸   Please refer to the *Creating a text table* recipe in *Chapter 1, Basic Charts*

Creating a waterfall chart

Waterfall charts look like bar charts, but these specifically show the aggregated effect of a series of positive and negative values. The final bar represents the net value of all the preceding values. Waterfall charts can be useful when the history as well as the final net value is important to be shown. This can be applied, for example, to showing beginning and ending inventory numbers, and showing how the ending inventory number came to be.

In this recipe, we will use the waterfall chart to show cumulative changes in profit for **Furniture** in the **Superstore** data set.

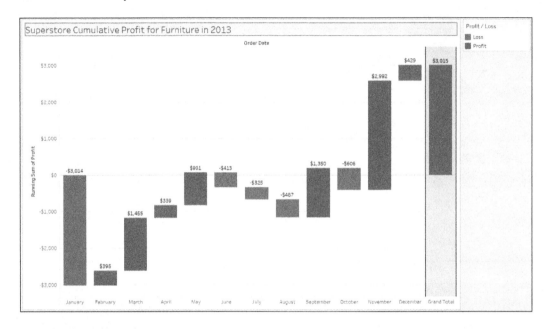

To follow this recipe, open `B05527_02 - STARTER.twbx`. Use the worksheet called `Waterfall`, and connect to the `Orders (Sample - Superstore)` data source.

How to do it...

The following are the steps to create a waterfall chart:

1. From **Dimensions**, drag **Category** to the **Filters** shelf.
2. In the next windows, under the **General** tab, select **Furniture**.
3. From **Dimensions**, drag **Order Date** to the **Filters** shelf.
4. When prompted on what to filter, choose **Years**.
5. In the next windows, under the **General** tab, select 2013.

6. From **Dimensions**, drag **Order Date** to the **Columns** shelf.

7. Right-click on **Order Date** in the **Columns** shelf and choose discrete month. Discrete month is the third menu item after **Show Missing Values**.

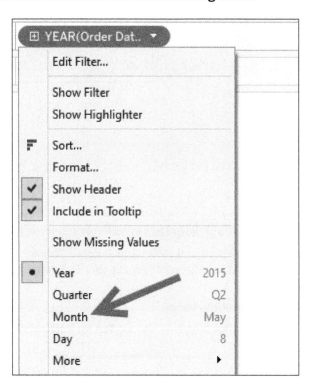

8. Change the mark type to **Gantt**.

9. Create a calculated field called **Negative Profit**, which is just the negative equivalent of the **Profit** field. This is needed to size the Gantt chart.

10. From **Measures**, drag **Profit** to the **Rows** shelf.

11. Right-click on the **Profit** pill in the **Rows** shelf. Go to **Quick Table Calculation** and select **Running Total**.

12. From **Measures**, drag **Negative Profit** to **Size** in the **Marks** card.

13. Create another calculated field called **Profit/Loss**, which will describe the status of a sale based on profit. The formula is as follows:

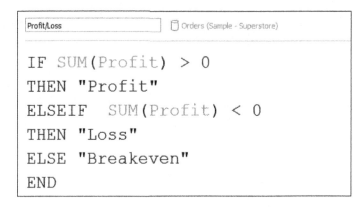

```
IF SUM(Profit) > 0
THEN "Profit"
ELSEIF  SUM(Profit) < 0
THEN "Loss"
ELSE "Breakeven"
END
```

14. Drag the newly created **Profit/Loss** calculated field to **Color** in the **Marks** card.

15. Right-click on the color legend and select **Edit Color...**. Change the color so that red represents loss, and blue represents profit. Feel free to replace this with your color preference.

16. From **Measures**, drag **Profit** to **Label**.

17. Click on **Label** in the **Marks** card, and choose **Top** for **Vertical Alignment**.

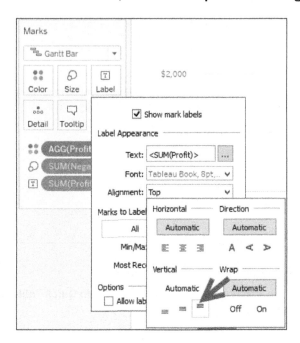

18. Go to the **Analysis** menu item. Expand **Totals** and select **Show Row Grand Totals**.

19. Go to the **Format** menu, and choose **Shading**. This will show a formatting side bar.

20. Under the **Sheet** tab, change the background color for **Grand Total** to be light brown. Feel free to replace this with a color of your choice.

21. Go to the **Format** menu, and choose **Borders**. This will show a formatting side bar.

22. Under the **Sheet** tab, change the border for **Grand Total** to be a thicker, darker line. Feel free to replace this with a line style of your choice. Close the formatting side bar when done.

23. Change title of color legend to show **Profit** or **Loss**. You can do this by right-clicking on the top-right corner of the legend box and selecting **Edit Title...**.

How it works...

A waterfall chart shows the cumulative results of positive and negative values over a series. In our recipe, we are showing how profits for **Furniture** grow or shrink over time.

There is no native waterfall chart in Tableau. We can create this by using a **Gantt** mark.

We start by filtering our view for only 2013. We drag discrete month across the columns, and drag **Profit** measure onto rows. By default, Tableau will create a time series line graph for these fields. We care about the cumulative effects of profit, so we can add the **Quick Table Calculation** for **Running Total**.

Next we change the mark type to **Gantt**, which makes the mark look like a series of underlines. In order to add the actual size of the bar, we use a calculated field called **Negative Profit**, which is simply the negative value of the profit. The reason we need to negate the field is because if we don't, the **Gantt** bar will start at the profit value, and then extend the bar downwards if the value is positive and extend the bar upwards if the value is negative.

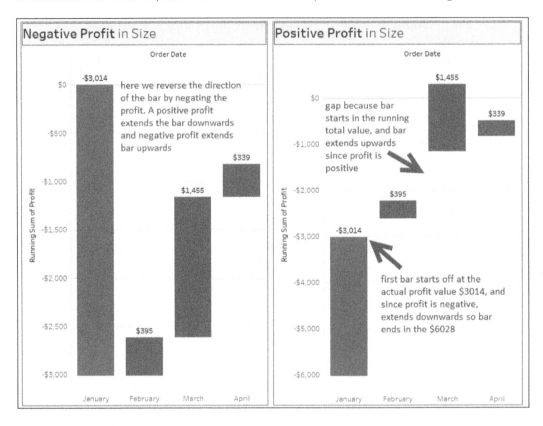

Once all the fields are set up with the **Gantt** mark, the **Running Total** for the **SUM(Profit)** on the column, and Negative Profit for the size of the **Gantt**, you should now see that each succeeding bar show the cumulative effect of all the previous profits.

Lastly, we add the total bar by simply selecting the **Analysis** menu and choosing **Totals** and **Show Row Grand Totals**. By default, this shows as the last column, but you can also choose to show row **Totals to the Left** starting in Tableau v9.2.

There's more...

The **Model Systems Knowledge Translation Center** (**MSKTC**) has a good short document that describes what waterfall charts are, and when they are useful. You can find the document at `http://bit.ly/waterfallcharts`.

Creating a population pyramid

A population pyramid is a chart that shows population distribution by age and gender. Age is typically distributed using five-year age groups. The youngest groups are located at the base and the oldest groups at the top. Population pyramids can indicate how slow or fast the population ages, and can also be used to forecast how the population will change in the future.

In this recipe, we will create British Columbia's population pyramid from 1986 to 2041.

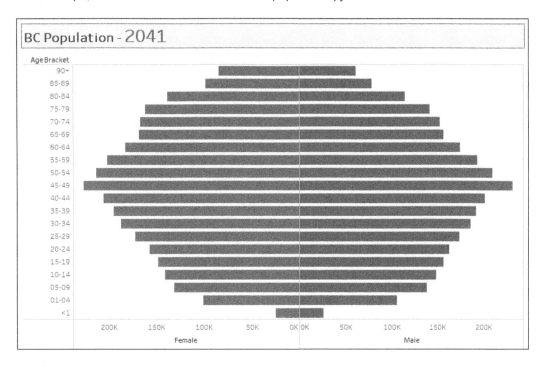

Getting ready

To follow this recipe, open B05527_02 - STARTER.twbx. Use the worksheet called Population Pyramid, and connect to the BC Population Projection data source.

How to do it...

The following are the steps to create a population pyramid:

1. From **Dimensions**, drag **Age Bracket** to the **Rows** shelf.

2. Hover over the **Age Bracket** column header until you see a sort icon, and click on the sort icon. Click on the sort icon twice to sort the **Age Bracket** values descending.

3. Right-click on **Total** value for **Age Bracket** and select **Exclude**.

4. Manually drag the **<1** header for **Age Bracket** so that it is the last value. This should be placed after the value **01-04**.

Age Bracket	
90+	Abc
85-89	Abc
80-84	Abc
75-79	Abc
70-74	Abc
65-69	Abc
60-64	Abc
55-59	Abc
50-54	Abc
45-49	Abc
40-44	Abc
35-39	Abc
30-34	Abc
25-29	Abc
20-24	Abc
15-19	Abc
10-14	Abc
05-09	Abc
01-04	Abc
<1	Abc

5. Create a calculated field called **Female** that returns the **Population** value if the gender is female.

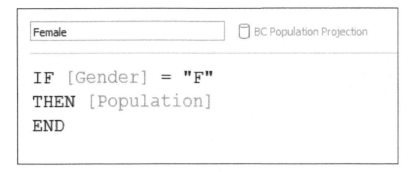

6. From **Measures**, drag the newly created **Female** calculated field to the **Columns** shelf. This creates a bar chart that represents the female population.

7. Using the **Marks** card for **Female**, click on **Color** and change the color of the bars to pink. Feel free to change this color to a color of your choice.

8. Create a calculated field called **Male** that returns the **Population** value if the gender is male. You will need to check the value of **Gender** and return the population if the value is **M**. Use the formula for the **Female** calculated as reference.

9. From **Measures**, drag **Male** to the **Columns** shelf, to the right of the **Female** pill.

10. Using the **Marks** card for **Male**, click on **Color** and change the color of the bars to blue. Feel free to change this color to a color of your choice.

11. Right-click on the axis for the **Female**, and select **Edit Axis**.

12. Under **Scale**, select **Reversed**. Click **OK** when done.

13. Double-click on the worksheet title, and using the Insert dropdown, add the **Page Name** to the worksheet title.

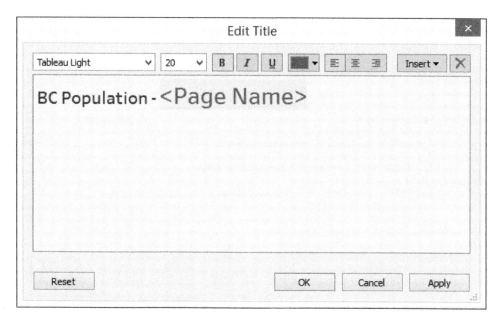

14. From **Dimensions**, drag **Year** to **Pages**.

15. Using the **Year** play control, click on the forward arrow to play.

How it works...

The population pyramid is meant to show the population distribution by gender. It is described in Wikipedia as a back-to-back histogram, where one histogram shows the age distribution for males and the other shows for females.

As far as Tableau is concerned, depending on the data set, this can simply be two bar charts. The first bar chart needs to have its axis reversed, so that the 0 value of the axis touches the zero value of the second axis.

Reversing the axis in Tableau is actually straightforward. You simply need to right-click on the axis to edit the axis, and select **Reversed** under **Scale**.

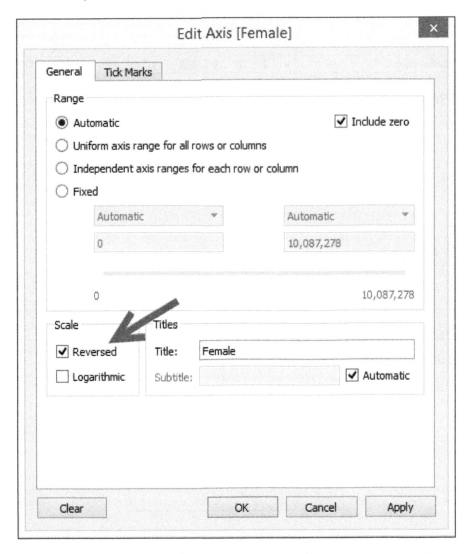

In this chart, we can also take advantage of the **Pages** shelf. When we drop the **Year** dimension onto this shelf, a play control shows up. This allows us to see the animated changes of the population pyramid from 1986-2041.

There's more...

It is interesting to note that a population pyramid, as the name suggests, typically looks like a pyramid. The older age bands at the upper section of the chart exhibit shorter bars than the younger ones. In British Columbia, however, you can see that based on the 2041 projected population, it looks like a pear, not a pyramid, with the longest bars for those in their 40s to 60s. Currently, this shape is indicative of a constrictive population pyramid, which means the population is both aging and shrinking. For BC, what this means is its population is getting older. While lifespan is getting longer, there aren't more births. This definitely has a substantial impact on economy and sustainability, but that discussion is for another book. It's just very interesting to see how population has changed over the years.

Population Education has a good short article on different types of population pyramids at `https://www.populationeducation.org/content/what-are-different-types-population-pyramids`.

If you are interested in seeing how the world population has changed and what the impact is, there is an interesting article called *The World Reshaped* that can be found at `http://www.economist.com/news/21631911-end-population-pyramid-world-reshaped`.

See also

▸ Please refer to the *Creating a bar chart* recipe in *Chapter 1, Basic Charts*

3
Interactivity

In this chapter, we will cover:

- ▸ Creating a motion chart
- ▸ Creating a dynamic column/row trellis chart
- ▸ Creating a top/bottom N filter
- ▸ Comparing one to everything else
- ▸ Dynamically displaying dimensions
- ▸ Dynamically displaying and sorting measures
- ▸ Creating a custom date period filter

Introduction

Tableau can empower its audience by allowing them to interact with the visualization, ask more questions, answer those questions, and maybe even pique their curiosity into what other answers the viz can offer.

In this chapter, we will add a few more interactive components to our views. Interactivity in Tableau can be achieved in many different ways. In this chapter, we focus on using filters, parameters and calculated fields to give the users of our dashboards more control over what is being shown in the charts.

Creating a motion chart

In this recipe, we will create an animated chart that shows how population has changed over the years for a few selected countries.

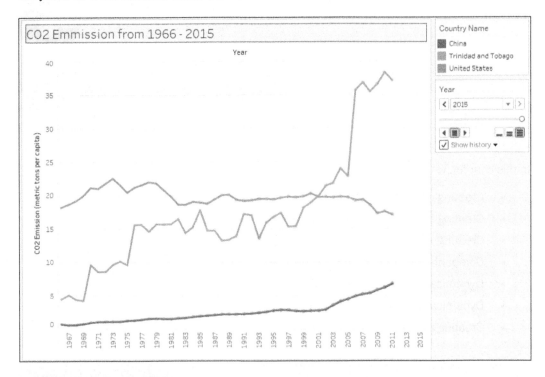

Getting ready

To follow this recipe, open B05527_03 - STARTER.twbx. Use the worksheet called Motion Chart, and connect to the CO2 (Worldbank) data source.

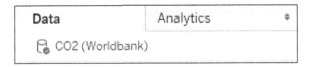

How to do it...

The following are the steps to create a motion chart:

1. From **Dimensions**, drag **Year** to the **Columns** shelf.

2. From **Measures**, drag **CO2 Emission** to the **Rows** shelf.

3. Right-click on the **CO2 Emission** axis, and change the title to CO2 Emission (metric tons per capita).

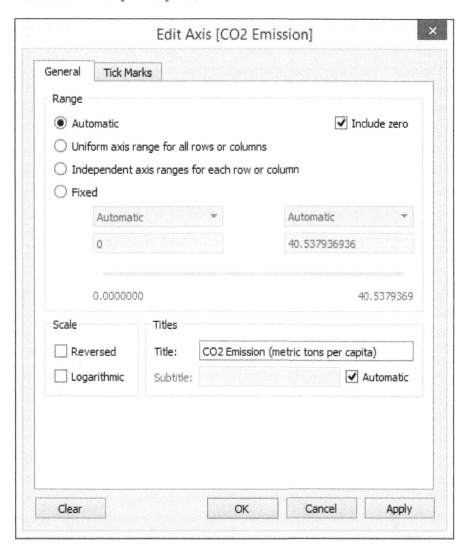

4. In the **Marks** card, click on the dropdown to change the mark from **Automatic** to **Circle**.

5. From **Dimensions**, drag **Country Name** to **Color** in the **Marks** card.

6. From **Dimensions**, drag **Country Name** to the **Filter** shelf.

7. Under the **General** tab of the **Filter** window, while the **Select from list** radio button is selected, select **None**.

8. Select the **Custom value list** radio button, still under the **General** tab, and add **China**, **Trinidad and Tobago**, and **United States**.

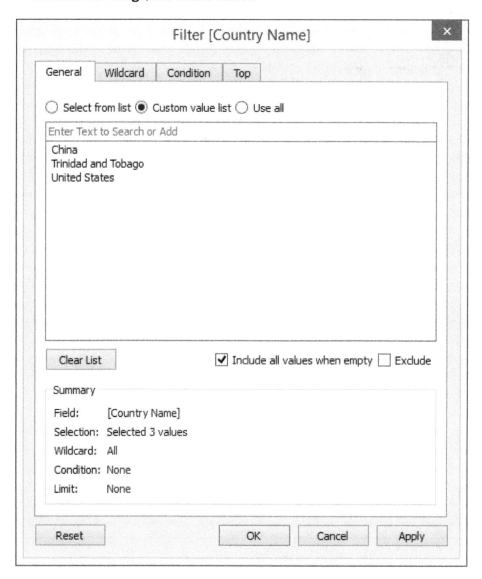

9. Click **OK** when done. This should close the **Filter** window.

10. From **Dimensions**, drag **Year** to **Pages**. This adds a page control to the view.

11. Click on the **Show history** checkbox to select it.

12. Click on the dropdown beside **Show history** and perform the following steps:
    - ❑ Select **All** for **Marks to show history for**
    - ❑ Select **Both** for **Show**

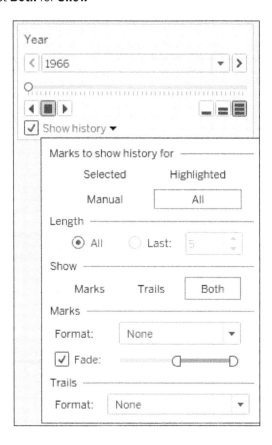

13. Using the **Year** page control, click on the forward arrow to play. This should show how the populations of the three selected countries have changed over the years.

How it works...

Have you ever doodled in your notebook—stick figures, bouncing ball—and flipped the pages to see doodle move and come to life? I've done it when I was a kid, and it's amazing to see it in action using Tableau! It feels like play but it's really work (right?).

It is possible to create motion charts in Tableau using the **Pages** shelf. When you drop a field onto the **Pages** shelf, Tableau creates a series of "pages" that filters the view for each value in that field.

Tableau also presents us with a page control. This is where we can "flip" the pages, enabling our view to come to life. We can control the speed—Tableau offers three predefined speed settings. One bar pertains to the slowest speed, and three bars to the fastest speed. The page control also enables us to further format the marks, and to show the marks or trails or both.

In our viz, we used a *circle* for our marks. Each year is marked by a circle. Each year, the circle moves to the new position, representing the new population value for a specific country. The circles are all connected by trail lines. By setting the mark and trail histories to both show in the page control, we are simulating a moving time series graph.

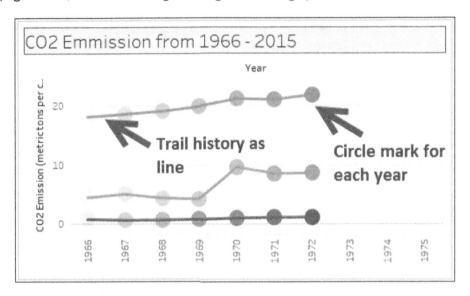

There's more...

If you ever want to loopback the animation, you can click on the dropdown on the top-right of your page control card, and select **Loop Playback**.

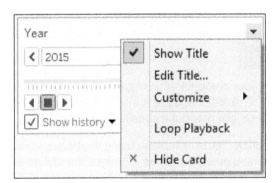

A quick word of caution for motion charts, though. The animation effect that you see when working with motion charts using Tableau Desktop is absent in Tableau Server. Because Tableau wants to have zero footprint when serving the charts and dashboards on server— meaning there is no additional download to enable the functionalities—the play control does not work the same. Fret not, however. You can still click on the slider manually and still have a similar effect.

See also

▸ Please refer to the recipe in *Chapter 2, Creating a Population Pyramid*

Creating a dynamic column/row trellis chart

In this recipe, we will create a parameter that will help us adjust the number of columns—and indirectly rows—for our trellis chart.

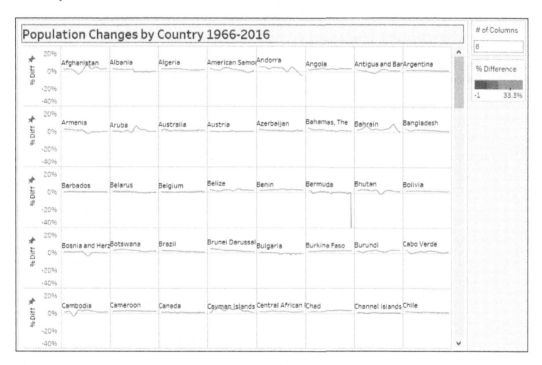

Getting ready

To follow this recipe, open B05527_03 - STARTER.twbx. Use the worksheet called **Trellis**, and connect to the Population (WDI 1966-2016) data source.

Data	Analytics	⬍
🗒 Population (WDI 1966-2016)		▼

How to do it...

The following are the steps to create a dynamic column/row chart:

1. From **Dimensions**, drag **Year** to the **Columns** shelf.

2. Right-click on the **Year** pill in the **Columns** shelf, and select **Continuous**.

3. From **Measures**, drag **Population** to the **Rows** shelf.

4. Right-click on the **SUM(Population)** pill in the **Rows** shelf, and under **Quick Table Calculation**, select **Percent Difference**.

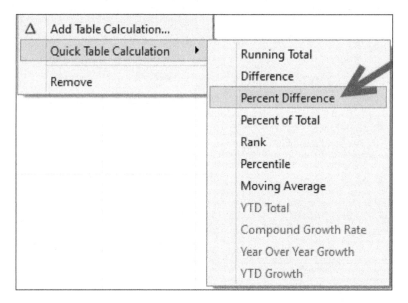

5. Control drag the **SUM(Population)** pill in your **Rows** shelf to the **Color** shelf.

6. Right-click on the color legend and choose **Edit Colors**. Check **Stepped Color**, and enter **4** as the value for **Steps**.

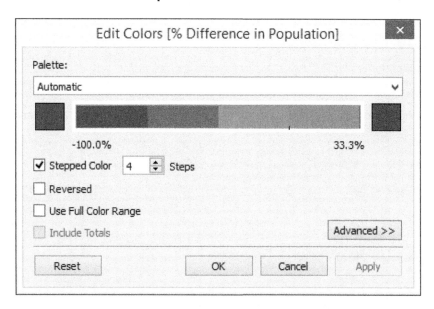

7. Right-click on the color legend and choose **Edit Title**. Change the color legend title to **% Difference**.

8. From **Dimensions**, drag **Country Name** to **Label** in the **Marks** shelf.

9. Right-click on the arrow beside **Dimensions** section in the sidebar, and select **Create Parameter**.

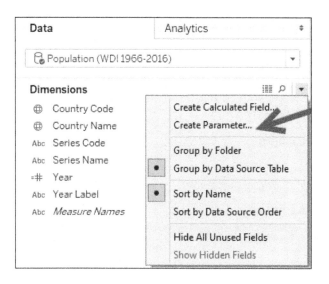

10. Create a parameter called `# of Columns` with the following settings:

   ❑ Data type: **Integer**

   ❑ Current value: 8

   ❑ Allowable values: **All**

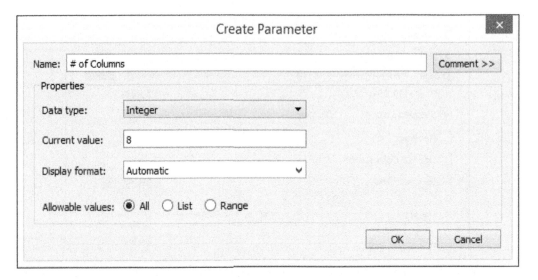

11. Show the parameter control for **# of Columns**. You can do this by right-clicking on the parameter, and selecting **Show Parameter Control**.

12. Create a calculated field called `Index`, with the following formula:

> | Index | 🗂 Population (WDI 1966-2016) |
>
> ```
> INDEX()
> ```

13. Create a calculated field called `Columns`, with the following formula:

> | Columns | 🗂 Population (WDI 1966-2016) |
>
> ```
> IIF([Index]%[# of Columns]==0,
>     [# of Columns],
>     [Index]%[# of Columns]
>   )
> ```

14. Create a calculated field called `Rows`, with the following formula:

> | Rows | 🗂 Population (WDI 1966-2016) |
>
> ```
> (INT(([Index]-1)/[# of Columns])) + 1
> ```

15. From **Measures**, drag the calculated field **Columns** to the **Columns** shelf, to the left of **Year**.

16. Right-click on the **Columns** pill in the **Columns** shelf, and select **Compute Using** and then **Country Name**.

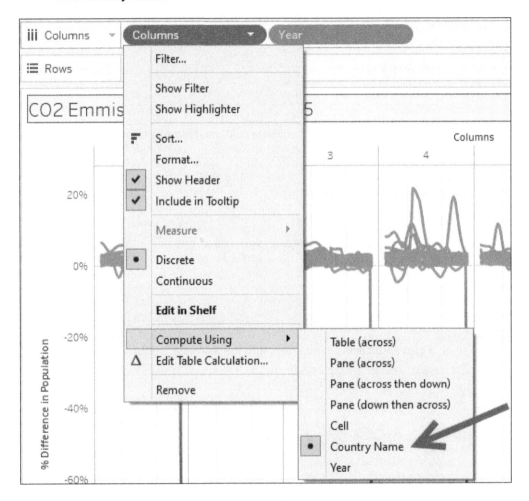

17. Change the **Columns** pill to discrete by right-clicking on this pill, and selecting **Discrete**.

18. From **Measures**, drag the calculated field **Rows** to the **Rows** shelf, to the left of **SUM(Population)**.

19. Right-click on the **Rows** pill in the **Rows** shelf, and select **Compute Using by Country Name**.

20. Change **Rows** pill to discrete by right-clicking on this pill, and selecting **Discrete**.

21. Click on **Label** in the **Marks** card, and use the following settings:

   ❑   Marks to Label: **Line Ends**

   ❑   Options: **Allow labels to overlap other marks**

   ❑   Options: **Label start of line**

   ❑   Alignment: **Custom**

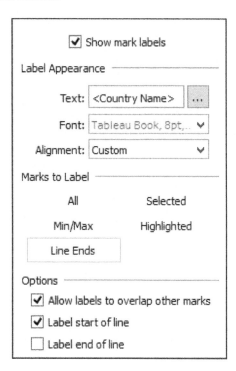

22. Right-click on the **Columns** heading and choose **Hide Field Labels for Columns**.

23. Right-click on the **Rows** pill in the **Rows** shelf and uncheck **Show Header**.

24. Right-click on the **Year** pill in the **Columns** shelf and uncheck **Show Header**.

25. Right-click on the **% Difference in Population** axis and:

  ❑ Change the **Title** to `$ Diff`

  ❑ Change **Range** to **Fixed**, starting at `-0.4`

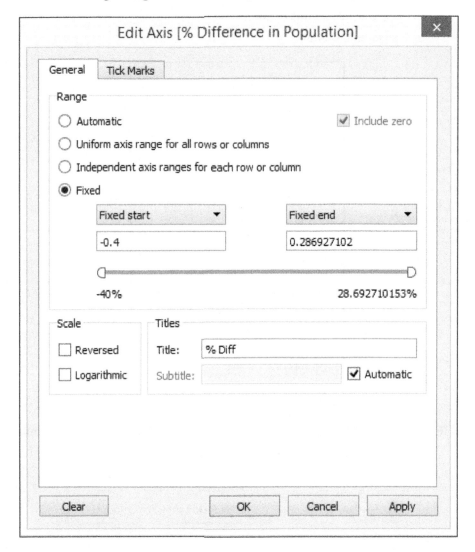

26. Go to the **Format** menu, and choose **Lines**. This will show a formatting sidebar.

27. Under the tabs **Sheet**, **Rows**, and **Columns**, set the **Grid Lines** to **None**. Close the formatting sidebar when done.

28. Test the parameter. Change the column size and confirm that the chart adjusts the number of columns shown.

How it works...

A **trellis chart** is a small multiple chart that is called by many other names such as panel chart or grid chart. A trellis chart is composed of multiple similar, small charts that allow for easier side-by-side comparison of the items being visualized.

 See Creating a small multiple chart recipe in *Chapter 2, Advanced chart*, for additional examples and explanation.

This recipe adds a parameter to a typical small multiple, which allows the consumer of the view to decide or experiment with how many columns side by side would be most effective for the data analysis.

It is important to note that by default, a chart becomes a small multiple when it is sliced into discrete dimensions. If we wanted a small multiple that has columns and rows, we need to add at least one discrete dimension in the Columns shelf, and another in the Rows shelf.

In our recipe, however, we are not slicing our chart based on any other dimensions. We simply want to display the small charts using a specific number of columns and rows. To do this, we need to introduce a discrete dimension in Columns based on what our end user enters in the # of Columns parameter, and then calculate how many rows will result based on the number of columns.

The calculated field called Columns has the following formula:

Columns   Population (WDI 1966-2016)

```
IIF([Index]%[# of Columns]==0,
    [# of Columns],
    [Index]%[# of Columns]
  )
```

To create a trellis chart with # of Columns parameter value, we need to technically assign each small graph a number. This is achieved by using the INDEX() function used in the Index calculated field, which assigns a sequential number to each value specified in the Compute Using. This formula then takes the index assigned to each country, and checks for the modulo based on the parameter value. The modulo operator is the %, and this operator finds the remainder after dividing the number by another number.

To visualize this, let's assume that the `# of Columns` parameter value is 4. The corresponding values are as follows:

Country	INDEX()	INDEX() % 4	Column	Row
Afghanistan	1	1	1	
Albania	2	2	2	
Algeria	3	3	3	
American Samoa	4	0	4	
Andorra	5	1	1	
Angola	6	2	2	

The number of columns indirectly defines the number of rows. The **Rows** calculated field determines in which row number a country would be placed, based on that country's **Index** value divided by the `# of Columns` parameter value.

Rows	🛢 Population (WDI 1966-2016)
`(INT(([Index]-1)/[# of Columns])) + 1`	

The resulting row values are as follows:

Country	INDEX()	(INDEX()-1) / 4	((INDEX()-1) / 4) + 1	Column	Row
Afghanistan	1	0	1	1	1
Albania	2	0	1	2	1
Algeria	3	0	1	3	1
American Samoa	4	0	1	4	1
Andorra	5	1	2	1	2
Angola	6	1	2	2	2

The dynamic column/row trellis chart is really just a play on modulo and integer division. To confirm, when we plug in 4 as our parameter, our chart looks like this, with the headers for **Rows** and **Columns** turned on:

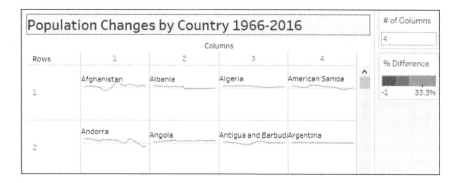

See also

▶ Please refer to the recipe in Creating a small multiple chart recipe in *Chapter 2, Advanced chart*

Creating a top/bottom N filter

In this recipe, we will create a bar chart that can display the top *N* or bottom *N* countries based on CO2 emission, a **world development indicator** (**WDI**) tracked by the World Bank.

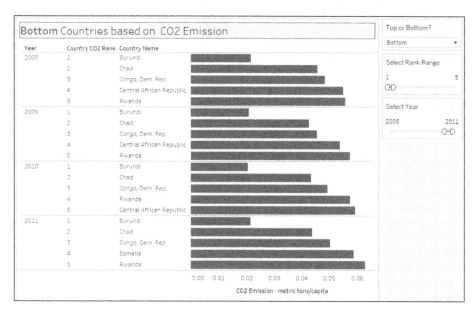

Getting ready

To follow this recipe, open B05527_03 - STARTER.twbx. Use the worksheet called Top N Bottom N, and connect to the CO2 (Worldbank) data source.

How to do it...

The following are the steps to create a bar chart with a top/bottom N filter:

1. From **Dimensions**, drag **Year** to the **Rows** shelf.

2. From **Dimensions**, drag **Country Name** to the **Rows** shelf, to the right of the **Year** pill.

3. From **Measures**, drag **CO2 Emission** to the **Columns** shelf.

4. Right-click the arrow beside the **Dimensions** section in the side bar, and select **Create Parameter**.

5. Create a string parameter called **Top or Bottom?** with the following settings:

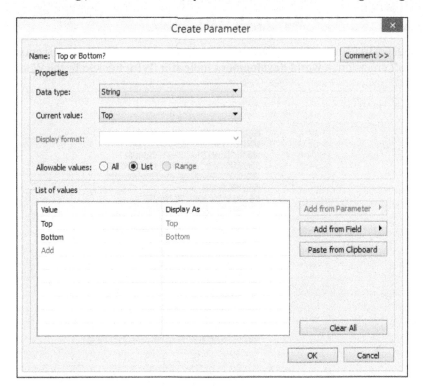

6. Show the parameter control for **Top or Bottom?**. You can do this by right-clicking on the parameter, and selecting **Show Parameter Control**.

7. Create a calculated field called `Country CO2 Rank`, with the following formula:

Country CO2 Rank	🗂 CO2 (Worldbank)

```
IF [Top or Bottom?] = "Top"
THEN RANK(SUM([CO2 Emission]), 'desc')
ELSEIF [Top or Bottom?] = "Bottom"
THEN RANK(SUM([CO2 Emission]),'asc')
END
```

8. Drag the new calculated field **Country CO2 Rank** to the **Rows** shelf. By default, since this is a continuous field, it can only be placed to the right of **Country Name** and will produce an axis.

9. Right-click on the **Country CO2 Rank** in the **Rows** shelf and select **Discrete**. This will change the pill color from green to blue.

10. Move the discrete **Country CO2 Rank** pill and place it between **Year** and **Country Name**. Your **Rows** and **Columns** shelves should now look like the following:

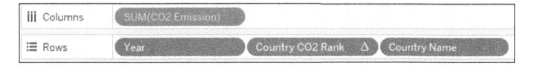

11. Right-click on the **Country CO2 Rank** pill, and change the **Compute Using** to **Pane (down)**.

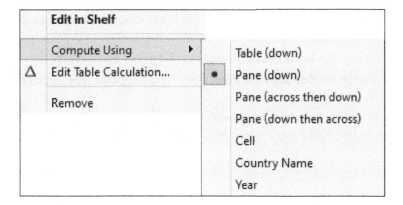

12. Control drag the blue **Country CO2 Rank** in the **Rows** shelf to the **Filters** shelf to copy this pill.

13. Click on **OK** to accept the defaults in the **Filters** window that appears. This leaves all the countries selected by default.

14. Right-click on the **Country CO2 Rank** pill in the **Filters** shelf and select **Continuous**.

15. Change the range in the window that appears to show 1 to 5.

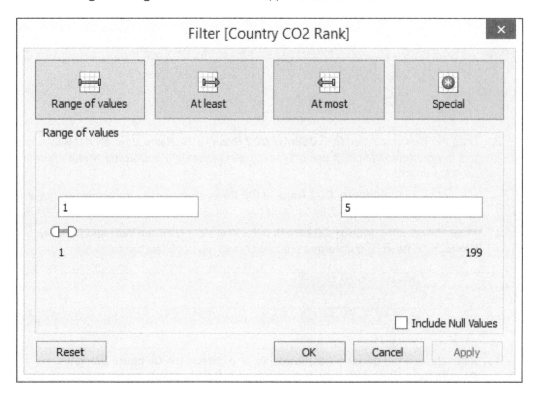

16. After you click **OK**, notice that the pill color of the **Country CO2 Rank** pill in the **Filters** card changes the pill from blue to green.

17. Right-click on the **Country CO2 Rank** filter and select **Show Filter**.

18. Right-click on the **Country CO2 Rank** filter, and select **Edit Title**. Change the title to **Rank**.

19. Control drag the **Year** from the **Rows** shelf to the **Filters** shelf to create a copy of it. Accept all the defaults in the filter window that comes up.

20. Right-click on the **Year** pill in the **Filters** shelf and select **Continuous**.

21. Change the range in the window that appears to show 2008 to 2011.

22. Right-click on the **Year** filter and select **Show Filter**.

23. Edit the **CO2 Emission** axis. Change the title to **CO2 Emission - metric tons/capita**.

24. Test the **Top or Bottom?** parameter. Check that when you select **Top**, the graph shows the highest emitting countries. When you select **Bottom**, the graph should show the least emitting countries.

How it works...

In this recipe, we allow the end users to select whether they want to display the top *N* countries (that is, countries with the most CO2 emissions) or bottom *N* countries (that is, countries with the least CO2 emissions). To do this, we need to use a parameter that determines if they went to the top or bottom.

To ascertain which countries belong to top or bottom, we can use the table calculation function **Rank**. In the **Country CO2 Rank** calculated field below, we determine whether the rank sorting is in ascending or descending fashion. If Top is selected, we want to sort descending (that is, the most first). If it is Bottom, SUM([CO2 Emission]) should be sorted in ascending fashion (that is, least first).

```
Country CO2 Rank                    ⬁ CO2 (Worldbank)

IF [Top or Bottom?] = "Top"
THEN RANK(SUM([CO2 Emission]), 'desc')
ELSEIF [Top or Bottom?] = "Bottom"
THEN RANK(SUM([CO2 Emission]),'asc')
END
```

A key step to making sure the ranking works is that this Country CO2 Rank calculated field with the rank calculation needs to be placed as a discrete field between Year and Country Name. This will allow us to limit the scope per year, therefore allowing us to reset the ranking for each year. The field also needs to be discrete, because we cannot place a green (or continuous) pill between two blue (discrete) pills.

We have also re-used the `Country CO2 Rank` pill in the `Rows` shelf. We copied it to our `Filter` shelf so we can easily change which years are to be shown on the chart. By default, when we copy it, the pill is discrete and therefore shows all the values as checkboxes.

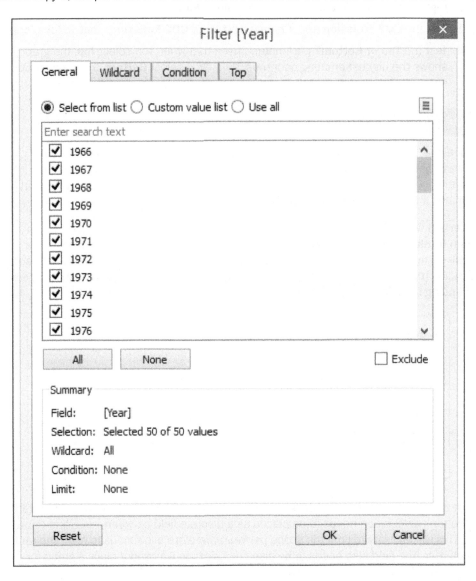

Leaving the **Year** filter as **Discrete** is not very user friendly. It will become quite tedious, and annoying, to have to check or uncheck each box every time the year range needs to change. For this reason, we change this copied field to **Continuous**.

You will most likely find yourself copying pills with table calculations around, and changing some of them to discrete and perhaps changing some of them back to continuous. Don't worry! This is a pretty common trick. We change the fields as we need them. Just remember that as soon as you copy, that pill becomes another pill that is no longer connected to the original pill. If you need to make changes, you need to remember you may need to change them in the other copies.

See also

Please refer to the recipe in *Appendix A, Calculated Fields Primer*.

Comparing one to everything else

In this recipe, we will create a bar chart that shows how much more or less other athletes earned compared to a selected athlete.

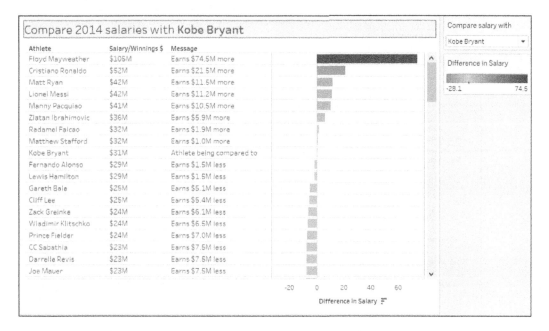

Getting ready

To follow this recipe, open `B05527_03 - STARTER.twbx`. Use the worksheet called `Compare one against everything else` and connect to the `Top Athlete Salaries (Global Sport Finances)` data source.

How to do it...

The following are the steps to create a chart that allows a selected item to be compared with all other items in the view:

1. Right-click the arrow beside the **Dimensions** section in the sidebar, and select **Create Parameter**.

2. Create a string parameter called `Compare salary with` the following settings:

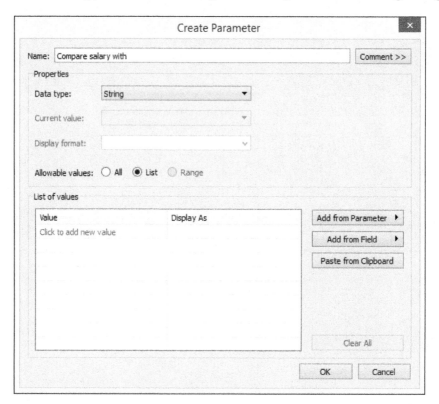

3. Click on the **Add from Field** button, choose the data source **Top Athlete Salaries (Global Sport Finances)**, and then select **Athlete**.

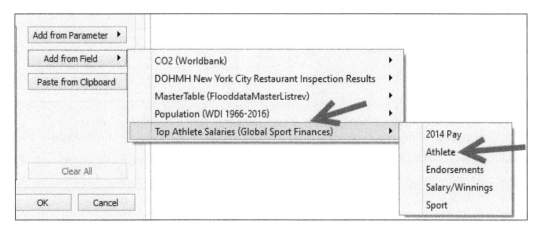

4. Click on **OK** when done.

5. Show the parameter control for **Compare salary with**. You can do this by right-clicking on the parameter, and selecting **Show Parameter Control**.

6. Create a calculated field called **Selected Athlete Salary**, which uses the following **LOD** (**Level of Detail**) expression:

```
Selected Athlete Salary                    ☐ Top Athlete Salaries (Global Sport Finances)

//this is a fixed LOD expression
{
    SUM (
        IF [Athlete] = [Compare salary with]
        THEN [Salary/Winnings $]
        ELSE 0
        END
    )
}
```

7. Create another calculated field called `Difference in Salary`, which uses the following formula:

Difference in Salary   ⬚ Top Athlete Salaries (Global Sport Finances)

```
SUM([Salary/Winnings $]) - SUM([Selected Athlete Salary])
```

---

8. Create one more calculated field called **Message**, which determines what string message to display depending on the calculated salary difference. The formula is as follows:

Message   ⬚ Top Athlete Salaries (Global Sport Finances)

```
IF [Difference in Salary] < 0
THEN "Earns $" +
     STR(ROUND(ABS([Difference in Salary]),1))  + "M less"
ELSEIF [Difference in Salary] > 0
THEN "Earns $" +
     STR(ROUND(ABS([Difference in Salary]),1)) + "M more"
ELSEIF [Difference in Salary] = 0
       AND ATTR([Athlete]) = [Compare salary with]
THEN "Athlete being compared to"
ELSEIF [Difference in Salary] = 0
       AND ATTR([Athlete]) = [Compare salary with]
THEN "Earns the same"
ELSEIF ISNULL([Difference in Salary])
THEN "N/A"
END
```

---

9. From **Dimensions**, drag **Athlete** to the **Rows** shelf.

10. From **Measures**, drag **Salary/Winnings $** to the **Rows** shelf, to the right of **Athlete**.

11. Right-click on the **SUM(Salary/Winnings $)** pill in the **Rows** shelf, and select **Discrete** to show this as a text column beside **Athlete**.

12. From **Measures**, drag **Message** to the **Rows** shelf, to the right of **SUM(Salary/ Winnings $)**.

13. From **Measures**, drag **Difference in Salary** to the **Columns** shelf. This should produce a bar chart.

14. This is what you should have now in your **Rows** and **Columns** shelves:

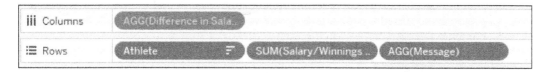

15. From **Measures**, drag **Difference in Salary** to **Color** in the **Marks** card.
16. Right-click on the **Athlete** pill in the **Rows** shelf, and select **Sort**.
17. Sort the **Athlete** field in **Descending** order, using the **Difference in Salary** field.

18. Click **OK** when done.

19. Test the parameter. Select different athletes and confirm that the bars and message are adjusted based on the difference between the selected athlete's salary is compared to everyone else in the list.

How it works...

It is not uncommon to want to compare one item against all other items in a chart or viz. This has become easier to achieve in Tableau, thanks to the addition of LOD expressions starting in V9.

In this recipe, we wanted to compare how much more or less athletes are making compared to one athlete we select. This may seem to be a simple calculation, but it quickly becomes tricky if we recall how Tableau works. The grain (or granularity) of measures in Tableau by default depends on the dimensions that are present in the view. For example, the granularity of the following measure **SUM(Salary/Winnings $)** in the **Columns** shelf is per **Sport**.

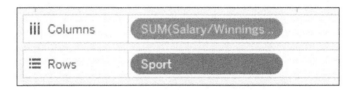

If another dimension is added, this means **SUM(Salary/Winnings $)** is further sliced. In the following example, it means that the measure is now by **Sport** and by **Athlete**.

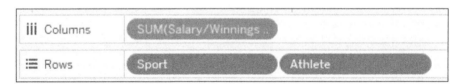

By default, the level of detail presented in a Tableau chart is affected by the data fields used in any of the cards and shelves. However, with LOD expressions, the level of detail can be different from what is in the canvas.

Let us start by attempting to display the salary differences between the selected athlete in the **Compare salary with** parameter and the rest of the athletes using a simple SUM formula:

Selected Athlete Salary Non LOD	☐ Top Athlete Salaries (Global Sport Finances)

```
SUM
(
    IF [Athlete] = [Compare salary with]
    THEN [Salary/Winnings $]
    ELSE 0
    END
)
```

When we select **Kobe Bryant**, we can see that we are not able to display his salary side by side with other athletes using the non-LOD calculated field. His salary appears to be zero for everyone else but him.

Compare 2014 salaries with **Kobe Bryant**

Athlete	Salary/Winnings $	Selected Athlete Salary Non LOD
Floyd Mayweather	$105M	0
Cristiano Ronaldo	$52M	0
Matt Ryan	$42M	0
Lionel Messi	$42M	0
Manny Pacquiao	$41M	0
Zlatan Ibrahimovic	$36M	0
Radamel Falcao	$32M	0
Matthew Stafford	$32M	0
Kobe Bryant	$31M	30.5
Fernando Alonso	$29M	0
Lewis Hamilton	$29M	0

This is problematic because this will give us incorrect salary differences.

However, using a `FIXED` LOD expressed, we can keep this number static. We can use the previous formula and just enclose it in curly braces.

The syntax of LOD expressions is:

```
{[FIXED | INCLUDE | EXCLUDE] <dimension declaration > : <aggregate expression>}
```

The `FIXED` keyword can be omitted if the LOD expression is not being fixed to any specific dimensions. When we display this in our view, we can see that Kobe Bryant's salary is persisted for each row.

Compare 2014 salaries with **Kobe Bryant**

Athlete	Salary/Winnings $	Selected Athlete Salary Non LOD	Selected Athlete Salary LOD
Floyd Mayweather	$105M	0	30.5
Cristiano Ronaldo	$52M	0	30.5
Matt Ryan	$42M	0	30.5
Lionel Messi	$42M	0	30.5
Manny Pacquiao	$41M	0	30.5
Zlatan Ibrahimovic	$36M	0	30.5
Radamel Falcao	$32M	0	30.5
Matthew Stafford	$32M	0	30.5
Kobe Bryant	$31M	30.5	30.5
Fernando Alonso	$29M	0	30.5
Lewis Hamilton	$29M	0	30.5

Calculating the difference is now easier, because the calculated field with LOD expression maintains the chosen athlete's salary.

Difference in Salary	🗋 Top Athlete Salaries (Global Sport Finances)

```
SUM([Salary/Winnings $]) - SUM([Selected Athlete Salary])
```

You are probably wondering why we are enclosing the `Selected Athlete Salary` calculated field in `SUM` when it is already a `SUM`. The reason is because as far as Tableau is concerned, an LOD expression is still a non-aggregated field. If we tried to use this without an aggregation and subtract this from an aggregated expression, we would get the classic error on mixing aggregate and non-aggregate fields:

Difference in Salary	🗋 Top Athlete Salaries (Global Sport Finances)

```
SUM([Salary/Winnings $]) - [Selected Athlete Salary]
```

The calculation contains errors ▼

Cannot mix aggregate and non-aggregate arguments with this function.

The good thing is we simply need to enclose the field with the LOD expression in an aggregated function, like a `SUM`, `MIN`, or `MAX`. The `SUM`, `MIN`, or `MAX` of one value is still that value, so it will not affect the calculation and it will allow us get around the mixed aggregation error.

One more thing we did in this recipe is create another calculated field for a text message we are displaying as a column. This calculated field, called Message, uses several IF... ELSEIF statements to see if the salary difference is more, less, or equal, and composes the appropriate string message to be displayed:

Message   🗍 Top Athlete Salaries (Global Sport Finances)

```
IF [Difference in Salary] < 0
THEN "Earns $" +
     STR(ROUND(ABS([Difference in Salary]),1))  + "M less"
ELSEIF [Difference in Salary] > 0
THEN "Earns $" +
     STR(ROUND(ABS([Difference in Salary]),1)) + "M more"
ELSEIF [Difference in Salary] = 0
        AND ATTR([Athlete]) = [Compare salary with]
THEN "Athlete being compared to"
ELSEIF [Difference in Salary] = 0
        AND ATTR([Athlete]) = [Compare salary with]
THEN "Earns the same"
ELSEIF ISNULL([Difference in Salary])
THEN "N/A"
END
```

There's more...

LOD expressions were introduced in Tableau V9—one of most anticipated, if not the most anticipated, features of this release.

LOD expressions are very powerful, and allow us to simplify what used to be complicated calculations from before their introduction. The problem we solved in this recipe might have required a blend, or a subquery at the data source, had we not had access to LODs.

The syntax for LOD expressions is as follows:

```
{[FIXED | INCLUDE | EXCLUDE] <dimension declaration > : <aggregate
expression>}
```

While powerful, one of the limitations is that the dimension declaration must be a persistent field. We can definitely get around this, but this requires creating additional fields that may be used only within the LOD expression.

Tableau V10 now allows expressions to be used instead of dimension field names. For example, if you wanted to fix sales per year, you can simply use the YEAR function in your LOD expression:

```
{ FIXED YEAR([Order Date]):SUM([Sales]) }
```

There are many scenarios where LOD expressions can prove to be useful and efficient. If you're new to LOD expressions, or looking to understand them better, I encourage you to check out the following resources:

- Top 15 LOD Expressions (`http://bit.ly/top15LOD`)

- Understanding Level of Detail Expressions (`http://bit.ly/UnderstandingLOD`)

See also

- Please refer to the recipe in *Appendix A, Calculated Fields Primer*

Dynamically displaying dimensions

In this recipe, we will explore how to display different dimensions in the same graph using a parameter and calculated field.

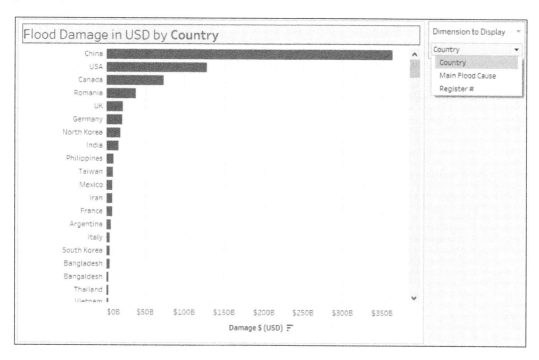

Getting ready

To follow this recipe, open B05527_03 - STARTER.twbx. Use the worksheet called Dynamic Dimension, and connect to the MasterTable (FlooddataMasterListrev) data source.

Data	Analytics	⬍
🗄 MasterTable (FlooddataMasterListrev)		▼

How to do it...

The following are the steps to create a chart with dynamic dimensions:

1. Right-click the arrow beside the **Dimensions** section in the sidebar, and select **Create Parameter**.

2. Create a string parameter called Dimension to Display with the following settings:

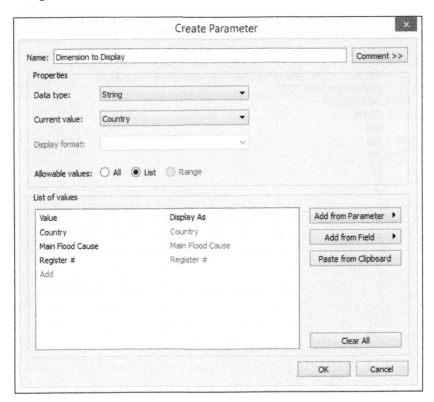

3. Show the parameter control for **Dimension to Display**. You can do this by right-clicking on the parameter, and selecting **Show Parameter Control**.

4. Create a calculated field called `Selected Dimension`, with the following formula:

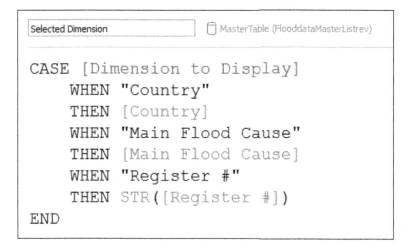

5. From **Dimensions**, drag the calculated field **Selected Dimension** to the **Rows** shelf.

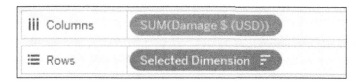

6. From **Measures**, drag **Damage $ (USD)** to the **Columns** shelf.

7. Right-click on the **SUM(Damage $ (USD))** pill in the **Columns** shelf, and select **Format**.

8. In the side bar, change the **Numbers** in the **Scale** section, and select **Currency (Custom)** with the following additional settings:

   ❑ Zero (0) decimal places

   ❑ Units in **Billions (B)**

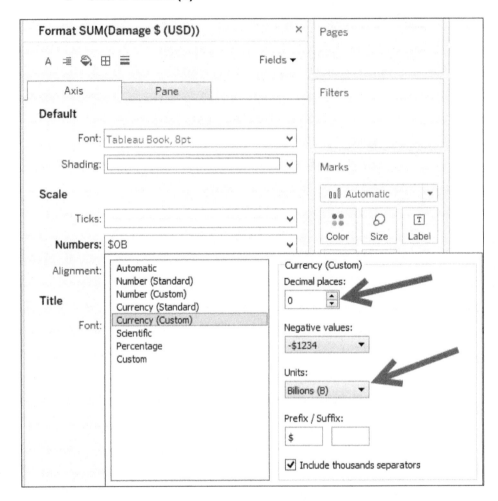

9. Hover your mouse pointer over the **Damage $ (USD)** axis and click the sort icon once to sort the bars in descending fashion.

10. Test the parameter. Ensure that as you change the parameter selection, the labels for the bars also change.

How it works...

Normally when we create our charts, we choose the dimensions and measures to display and place them on the appropriate shelves or cards.

For example, if we wanted to show flood damage by **Country**, our **Rows** and **Columns** shelves would look like this:

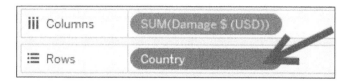

If we wanted to show it by **Main Flood Cause**, we would replace the **Country** pill in the **Rows** shelf with **Main Flood Cause**:

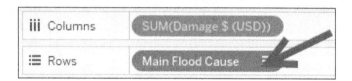

What we have done in this recipe is introduce a parameter so that our end users can decide which dimension they want used in the **Rows** shelf. The parameter called **Dimension to Display** elicits the choice from our end users. Once the choice is made, a calculated field identifies which dimension should be used:

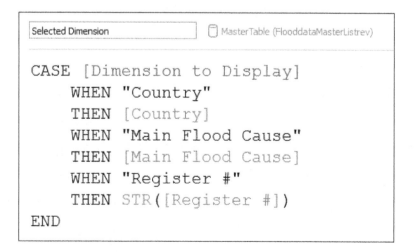

This calculated field needs to replace the dimension pill we have in the **Rows** shelf.

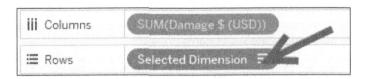

With the calculated field **Selected Dimension** in place, what is being displayed can now be dynamic, as the dimension changes when the parameter choice changes.

See also

▸   Please refer to the recipe in this chapter *Dynamically displaying and sorting measures*

Dynamically displaying and sorting measures

In this recipe, we will walk through the strategy to display and sort measures based on user selection.

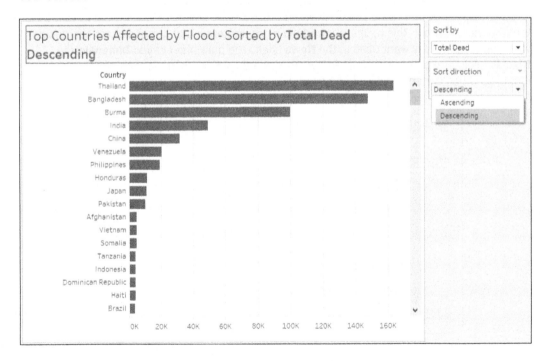

Getting ready

To follow this recipe, open `B05527_03 - STARTER.twbx`. Use the worksheet called `Dynamic Measure Display and Sort`, and connect to the `MasterTable (FlooddataMastListrev)` data source.

How to do it...

The following are the steps to create a chart that enables displaying and sorting measures through a parameter:

1. Right-click the arrow beside the **Dimensions** section in the side bar, and select **Create Parameter**.

2. Create a string parameter called **Sort by** with the following settings:

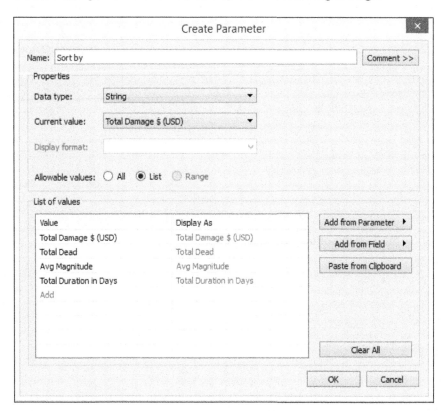

3. Show the parameter control for **Sort by**. You can do this by right-clicking on the parameter, and selecting **Show Parameter Control**.

4. Create another parameter called Sort direction with the following settings:

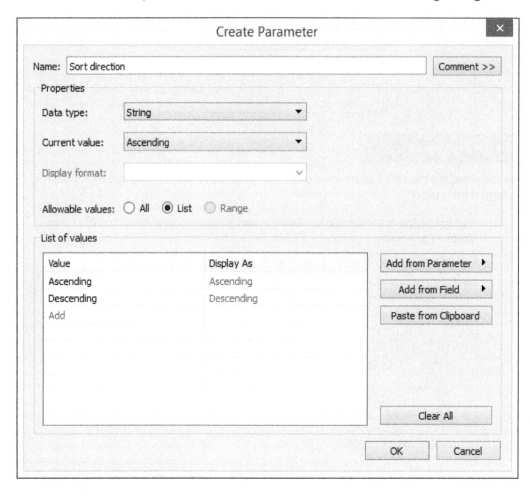

5. Show the **Sort direction** parameter control.

6. Create a calculated field called `Chosen Sort by` with the following formula:

┌──┐
│ Chosen Sort by   ⬚ MasterTable (FlooddataMasterListrev) │
├──┤

```
CASE [Sort by]
    WHEN "Total Damage $ (USD)"
    THEN SUM([Damage $ (USD)])
    WHEN "Total Dead"
    THEN SUM([Dead])
    WHEN "Avg Magnitude"
    THEN AVG([Magnitude (M)**])
    WHEN "Total Duration in Days"
    THEN SUM([Duration in Days])
END
```

7. Create another calculated field called `Chosen Sort by with direction`, which takes into account the selected direction.

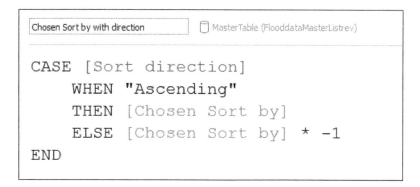

┌──┐
│ Chosen Sort by with direction   ⬚ MasterTable (FlooddataMasterListrev) │
├──┤

```
CASE [Sort direction]
    WHEN "Ascending"
    THEN [Chosen Sort by]
    ELSE [Chosen Sort by] * -1
END
```

8. From **Measures**, drag the calculated field **Chosen sort by** to the **Columns** shelf.

9. From **Dimensions**, drag **Country** to the **Rows** shelf.

10. Right-click on the **Country** pill in the **Rows** shelf, and select **Sort**.

11. Sort the **Country** based on the calculated field **Chosen sort by with direction** in **Ascending** order.

12. Click **OK** when done.
13. From **Measures**, drag **Chosen sort by** to the **Filters** shelf.

14. Choose **Special**, and select **Non-null values**.

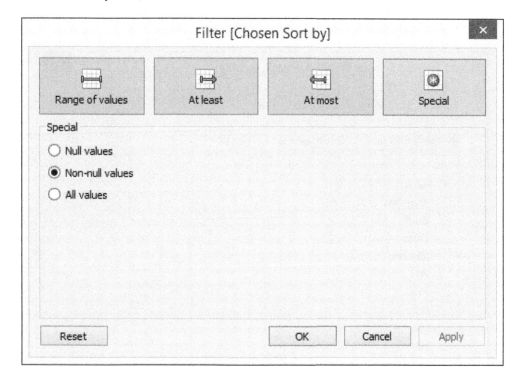

15. From **Dimensions**, drag **Country** to the **Filters** card.

16. Under the **General** tab, check the **Exclude** option, and select **Null**. Notice that selecting something when the **Exclude** option is checked adds a strikethrough to the selected item, meaning that item will be excluded.

17. Click **OK** when done.
18. Test the parameters. Ensure that as you change the parameter selection, the measures and the sorting change accordingly.

How it works...

In this recipe, we put the end users in the driver's seat and let them change the measures being displayed as they require, as well as how the measures are sorted.

Normally we place the measures we want to display in the shelves or cards. However, to allow end users to change this on demand, we must first enable them to specify their choice through a parameter. In our recipe, we called this parameter Sort by. This parameter is used in a calculated field that determines the actual measure to be used in the visualization, as well as the appropriate aggregation function:

```
Chosen Sort by                          ▯ MasterTable (FlooddataMasterListrev)

CASE [Sort by]
     WHEN "Total Damage $ (USD)"
     THEN SUM([Damage $ (USD)])
     WHEN "Total Dead"
     THEN SUM([Dead])
     WHEN "Avg Magnitude"
     THEN AVG([Magnitude (M)**])
     WHEN "Total Duration in Days"
     THEN SUM([Duration in Days])
END
```

In addition to this, we also created another parameter called Sort direction. The Sort direction parameter is used in a calculated field called Chosen Sort by with direction that either keeps the value of the calculated field Chosen Sort by as is if ascending, or reverses it by multiplying it by -1 if descending.

```
Chosen Sort by with direction           ▯ MasterTable (FlooddataMasterListrev)

CASE [Sort direction]
     WHEN "Ascending"
     THEN [Chosen Sort by]
     ELSE [Chosen Sort by] * -1
END
```

This calculated field is to be used with the sort direction for the **Country** dimension.

When the parameter choices change, the respective calculated fields will trigger the change in the chart, and show the appropriate measure and sort direction.

There's more...

One trick when working with dynamic measures is adding the parameter in the same shelf as the dynamic measure.

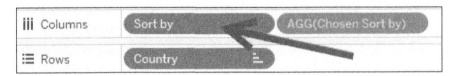

This allows for the actual measure name to be displayed as a header in the view.

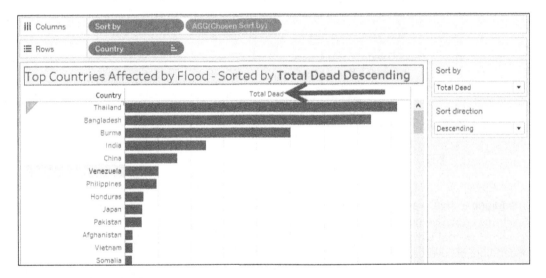

See also

▸ Please refer to the recipe in this chapter *Dynamically displaying dimensions*

Creating a custom date period filter

In this recipe, we will create a custom date period that will drive the labels and detail shown in our time series graph.

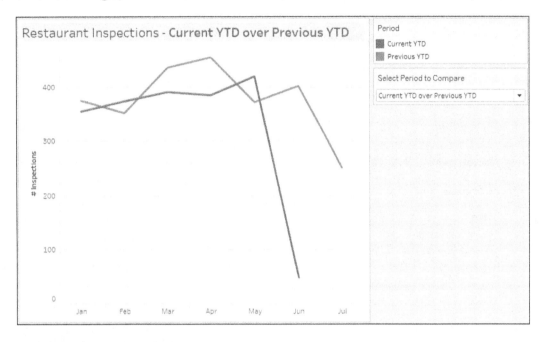

Getting ready

To follow this recipe, open `B05527_03 - STARTER.twbx`. Use the worksheet called `Custom Date Period`, and connect to the `DOHMH New York City Restaurant Inspection Results` data source.

How to do it...

The following are the steps to create a chart with a custom date period parameter:

1. Right-click the arrow beside the **Dimensions** section in the sidebar, and select **Create Parameter**.

2. Create a string parameter called `Select Period to Compare` with the following settings:

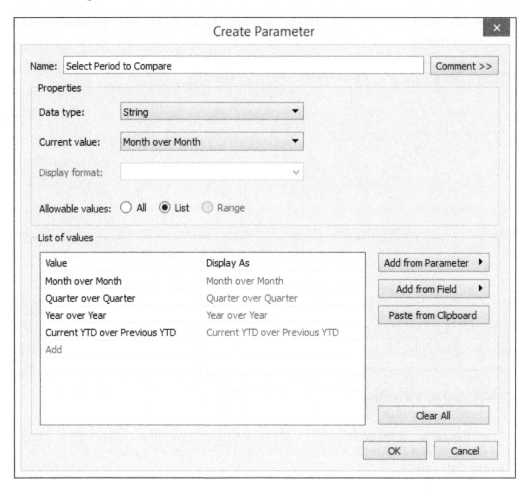

3. Show the parameter control for `Select Period to Compare`. You can do this by right-clicking on the parameter, and selecting `Show Parameter Control`.

4. Create a calculated field called `Period` with the following formula. Don't worry if this is a little bit long, we will explain what each block does in the following *How it works* section.

```
Period                              📄 DOHMH New York City Restaurant Inspection Results

IF [Select Period to Compare] = "Year over Year"
THEN IF YEAR([Inspection Date]) = [Current Year]
     THEN "Current Year"
     ELSEIF  YEAR([Inspection Date]) = [Current Year]-1
     THEN "Previous Year"
     END
ELSEIF [Select Period to Compare] = "Current YTD over Previous YTD"
THEN IF YEAR([Inspection Date]) = [Current Year]
     AND [Inspection Date] <= TODAY()
     THEN "Current YTD"
     ELSEIF (YEAR([Inspection Date]) = [Current Year] - 1 )
     AND ([Inspection Date] <= DATEADD('year', -1, TODAY()))
     THEN "Previous YTD"
     END
ELSEIF [Select Period to Compare] = "Quarter over Quarter"
THEN IF DATEPART('quarter',[Inspection Date]) = [Current Quarter]
     THEN "Current Quarter"
     ELSEIF ([Current Quarter] > 1
          AND DATEPART('quarter',[Inspection Date])  = [Current Quarter] -1 )
     OR ([Current Quarter] = 1 AND DATEPART('quarter',[Inspection Date]) = 4
        AND YEAR([Inspection Date]) = [Current Year] -1 )
     THEN "Previous Quarter"
     END

ELSEIF [Select Period to Compare] = "Month over Month"
THEN IF MONTH([Inspection Date]) = [Current Month]
     THEN "Current Month"
     ELSEIF ([Current Month] > 1
          AND MONTH([Inspection Date]) = [Current Month] -1 )
     OR ([Current Month] = 1 AND MONTH([Inspection Date]) = 12
        AND YEAR([Inspection Date]) = [Current Year] -1 )
     THEN "Previous Month"
     END
END
```

5. Create another calculated field called `Custom Period Label` for the axis labels. The formula is as follows:

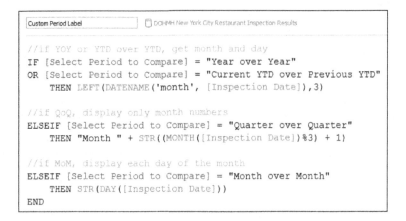

```
Custom Period Label                     ▢ DOHMH New York City Restaurant Inspection Results

//if YOY or YTD over YTD, get month and day
IF [Select Period to Compare] = "Year over Year"
OR [Select Period to Compare] = "Current YTD over Previous YTD"
    THEN LEFT(DATENAME('month', [Inspection Date]),3)

//if QoQ, display only month numbers
ELSEIF [Select Period to Compare] = "Quarter over Quarter"
    THEN "Month " + STR((MONTH([Inspection Date])%3) + 1)

//if MoM, display each day of the month
ELSEIF [Select Period to Compare] = "Month over Month"
    THEN STR(DAY([Inspection Date]))
END
```

6. From **Dimensions**, drag the calculated field **Period** to the **Filter** shelf, and exclude **Null**. You can do this by checking the **Exclude** option, and then checking **Null**. Notice that the selected **Null** gets a strikethrough, meaning it is being excluded.

7. From **Dimensions**, drag **Inspection Date** to the **Filters** card and choose **Years**.

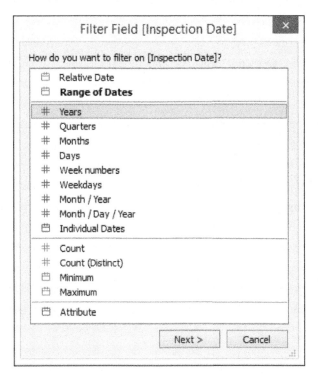

8. Exclude **1900** from the list of the years, and click **OK** when done.

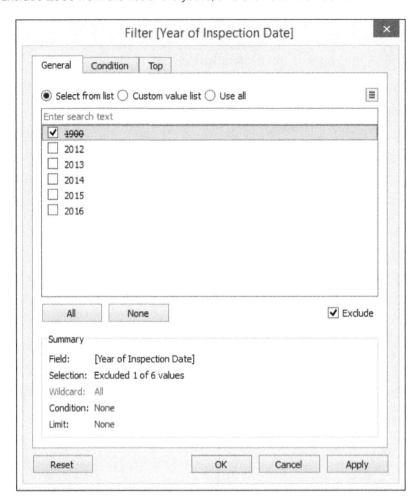

9. From **Dimensions**, drag the calculated **field Custom Period Label** to the **Columns** shelf.

10. From **Measures**, drag the **Number of Records** field to Rows.

11. From **Dimensions**, drag the calculated field **Period** to **Color** in the **Marks** card.

12. Right-click on the **Custom Period Label** header, and choose to **Hide Field Labels for Columns**.

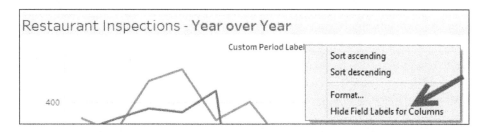

13. Right-click on the **Number of Records** axis, and select **Edit Axis**.

14. Change the axis title to **# Inspections**.

15. For each of the parameter selection, edit the colors in the color legend so that all "Current" periods are assigned one color, and all "Previous" periods are assigned a different color.

16. Test the parameter. Confirm that when the parameter choice changes, the detail of the time series graph and the corresponding labels change.

How it works...

Tableau allows for relative date filters out of the box. When you drag a date field onto the **Filters** shelf, you can choose **Relative Dates**. The following window allows you to choose the configuration of relative dates.

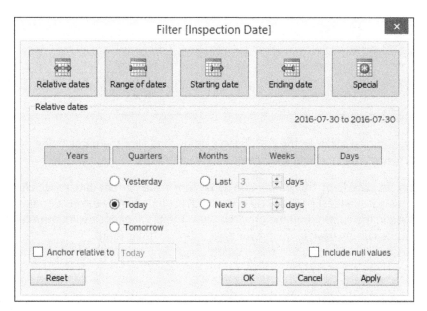

Tableau, however, does not have the built in capability to allow you to compare periods, like this month vs last month, or current year-to-date (YTD) vs previous year's YTD.

In this recipe, we worked around this limitation by using parameters and calculated fields. First, we created a parameter that allows us to specify which periods we want to make available.

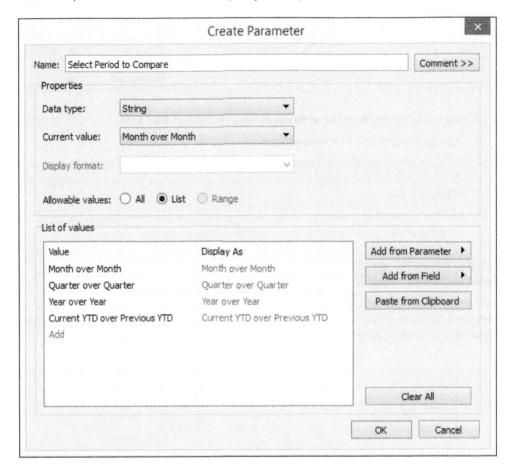

The parameter choice will drive the calculated field used to filter the dates being displayed in the view, as well as the labels for the dates.

In this recipe, we have kept the comparison consistent – the current date range compared to the previous date range. For a Year over Year (YOY) comparison, we consider anything that happened in the current and the previous year. The block of code will separate what happened in the current year, in the previous year, and in other years.

```
IF [Select Period to Compare] = "Year over Year"
THEN IF YEAR([Inspection Date]) = [Current Year]
     THEN "Current Year"
     ELSEIF  YEAR([Inspection Date]) = [Current Year]-1
     THEN "Previous Year"
     END
```

If the inspection happened earlier than the previous year, those records will be assigned a **Null** label, which we will exclude in the view.

If we are looking for Current Year-to-Date (YTD) over Previous YTD, meaning we only want inspections that happened until the current month and day for both years, the following block restricts the comparison to the current month and day.

```
ELSEIF [Select Period to Compare] = "Current YTD over Previous YTD"
THEN IF YEAR([Inspection Date]) = [Current Year]
     AND [Inspection Date] <= TODAY()
     THEN "Current YTD"
     ELSEIF (YEAR([Inspection Date]) = [Current Year] - 1 )
     AND ([Inspection Date] <= DATEADD('year', -1, TODAY()))
     THEN "Previous YTD"
     END
```

The DATEADD function allows us to add or subtract time intervals to a given date. If we provide a positive value for the second argument, then we are adding the time interval. If we provide a negative value, we are technically subtracting the time interval.

If we are comparing quarters, that is, current quarter over previous quarter, the formula becomes a little bit tricky. We cannot simply check for current quarter number compared to current quarter number minus 1. We need to consider that, if the current quarter is the first quarter, if we simply subtracted 1, we are going to be looking for quarter 0, which will be incorrect. If the current quarter is 1, we need to compare the current quarter with the previous year's fourth quarter. This logic is handled in the following block of code.

```
ELSEIF [Select Period to Compare] = "Quarter over Quarter"
THEN IF DATEPART('quarter',[Inspection Date]) = [Current Quarter]
     THEN "Current Quarter"
     ELSEIF ([Current Quarter] > 1
          AND DATEPART('quarter',[Inspection Date])  = [Current Quarter] -1 )
     OR ([Current Quarter] = 1 AND DATEPART('quarter',[Inspection Date]) = 4
          AND YEAR([Inspection Date]) = [Current Year] -1 )
     THEN "Previous Quarter"
     END
```

The Month over Month comparison, that is, comparing the current month with the previous month, shares the same challenge as Quarter over Quarter. We cannot simply compare current month number to current month number minus one. If we are currently on month number one, or January, we should compare it to last year's month twelve, or December. The following block of code handles this logic.

```
ELSEIF [Select Period to Compare] = "Month over Month"
THEN IF MONTH([Inspection Date]) = [Current Month]
     THEN "Current Month"
     ELSEIF ([Current Month] > 1
            AND MONTH([Inspection Date]) = [Current Month] -1 )
     OR ([Current Month] = 1 AND MONTH([Inspection Date]) = 12
        AND YEAR([Inspection Date]) = [Current Year] -1 )
     THEN "Previous Month"
     END
```

The other tricky part in this recipe is the labels for the period. We wanted to make sure that the previous period and current period line up. This is not an issue when we want to compare Year over Year, or current YTD over previous YTD, because we can simply display the months.

```
Custom Period Label              ☐ DOHMH New York City Restaurant Inspection Results

//if YOY or YTD over YTD, get month and day
IF [Select Period to Compare] = "Year over Year"
OR [Select Period to Compare] = "Current YTD over Previous YTD"
    THEN LEFT(DATENAME('month', [Inspection Date]),3)
```

The labels become more of an issue when we are looking at Quarter over Quarter (QoQ) or Month over Month (MoM). We cannot use months when we are dealing with QoQ, because the months in the current quarter will not line up with the months from the previous quarter in a time series graph. For quarters, we can simply display the month number in that quarter.

```
//if QoQ, display only month numbers
ELSEIF [Select Period to Compare] = "Quarter over Quarter"
    THEN "Month " + STR((MONTH([Inspection Date])%3) + 1)
```

This is what the graph will look like when Quarter over Quarter is chosen:

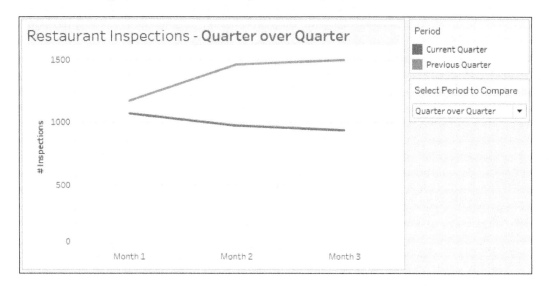

When we are looking at Month over Month (MoM), we also cannot just look at months, as this will produce just two dots – one for each month – that don't line up. We have to display the graph based on the days in the month, so that the points still line up. This is what the graph will look like when Month over Month is chosen:

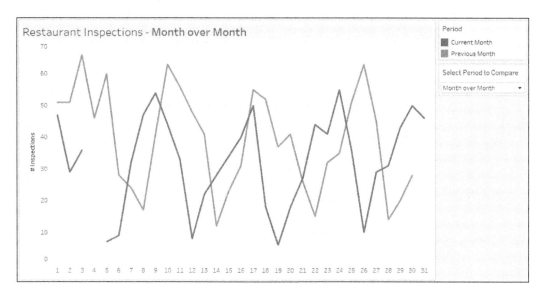

If you need to display custom date periods in your Tableau dashboards, you can use the techniques presented in this recipe as a reference or starting point. You can expand the selection, or integrate additional logic into your graphs using parameters and calculated fields.

See also

Please refer to the recipe in *Appendix A, Calculated Fields Primer*.

4
Dashboards and Story Points

In this chapter, we will cover:

- ▸ Creating a filter action
- ▸ Creating a highlight action
- ▸ Creating a URL action
- ▸ Creating an Infographic-like dashboard
- ▸ Creating story points

Introduction

In this chapter, we tackle how we can put worksheets together to create dashboards and story points. Dashboards are containers for worksheets to relay information and insights in a more holistic manner. Story points, on the other hand, allow you to organize your topics and ideas for a presentation.

If you have not worked with dashboards and story points before, I highly recommend reading *Appendix C, Working with Tableau 10* first. This chapter has a section on dashboards and story points, and goes through the concepts and terminologies used in this area.

Creating a filter action

One of the ways to add interactivity to Tableau dashboards is by adding actions. Tableau supports three actions, and one of them is a filter action. A filter action enables one view to narrow down the information shown in other views, either in the same dashboard or different dashboards.

In this recipe, we will use one of the sheets in our dashboard to filter all other sheets in the dashboard.

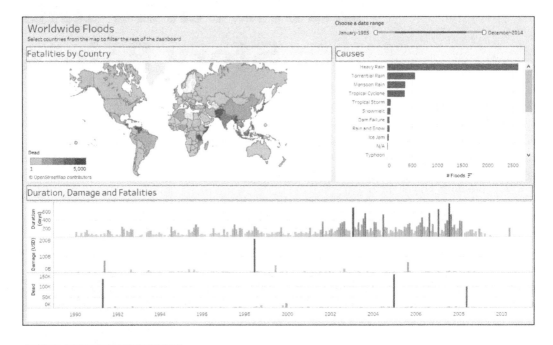

Getting ready

To follow this recipe, open B05527_04 – STARTER.twbx. We will use the following worksheets:

- ▸ Floods by Country
- ▸ Floods by Cause
- ▸ Flood Damage

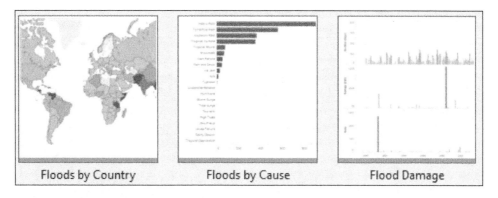

| Floods by Country | Floods by Cause | Flood Damage |

How to do it...

The following are the steps to create the dashboard in this recipe:

1. At the bottom of your Tableau design area are sheet tabs. There are three tabs with plus signs, which allow you to create a new sheet, dashboard and story point respectively. Click on the middle icon with the grid to create a new dashboard.

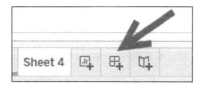

2. When in the dashboard design area, the sidebar becomes a Dashboard bar, showing the available worksheets and other dashboard components.

3. Check the **Show dashboard title** checkbox, located at the bottom of the **Objects** section. This will show the dashboard title text box in the dashboard.

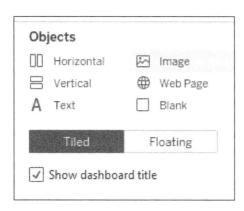

4. Change the dashboard title to show the following:

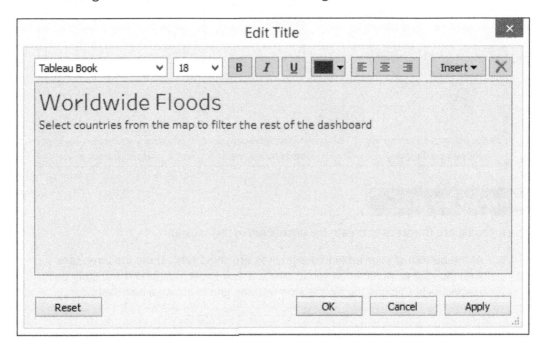

5. Right-click on the dashboard title, and select **Format Title**. Choose a light gray background to the title.

6. If needed, adjust the height of dashboard title so the whole text is visible.

7. Under the **Objects** section, ensure that **Tiled** is selected and not **Floating**.

8. Under the **Sheets** section in the **Dashboard** tab, drag the related worksheets onto the dashboard:

   ❏ Drag **Floods by Country**. By default, when **Tiled** is selected, this will occupy the whole dashboard space.

   ❏ Drag the **Flood Damage** worksheet and place it below **Floods by Country**. When you drag it, you will notice certain areas will get shaded. Release your mouse only when the shaded area is underneath the **Floods by Country** worksheet.

   ❏   Drag **Floods by Cause** to the right of **Floods by Country** and above **Flood Damage**.

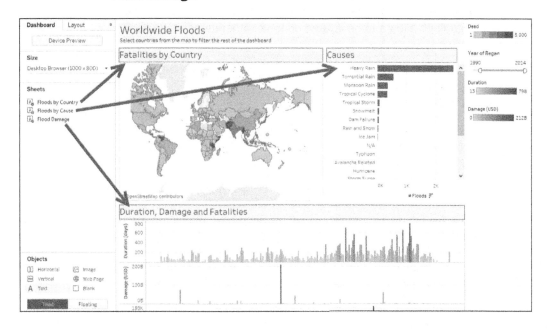

9. Increase the width of **Fatalities by Country** so it is wider than the **Floods by Cause** worksheet.

10. Remove the **Duration** and **Damage (USD)** color legends by clicking on the **X** mark.

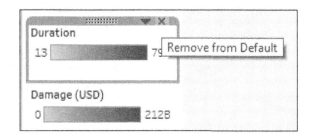

11. Set the **Dead** color legend to **Floating**. You can do this by selecting the color legend, which will show the legend's gray border. Click on the drop-down arrow in the top-right corner, and select **Floating**. Selecting the **Floating** option will take the legend out of the grid and allow it to be layered on top of other items in the dashboard.

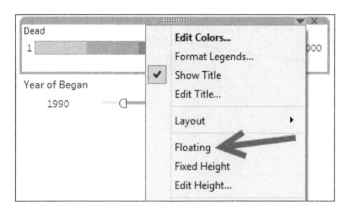

12. Place the **Dead** color legend closer to the **Fatalities by Country** map worksheet, closer to the bottom-left area so it does not cover any countries in the map.

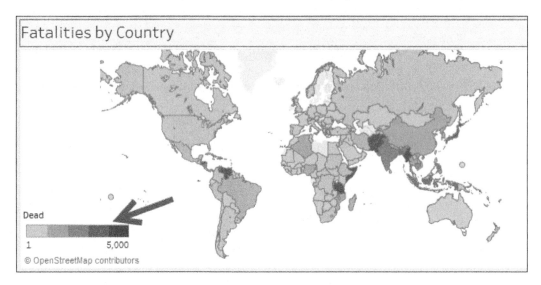

13. Change the title of the **Year of Began** filter to Choose a date range. To do this:

   ❑ Click on the **Year of Began** filter to show the gray border

   ❑ Click on the drop-down menu in the top-right corner

   ❑ Select **Edit Title** and make the changes

14. Change the scope of the date filter to all worksheets in the dashboard.

❑ Click on the dropdown of the filter, and choose **Apply to Worksheets**, and then **Selected Worksheets**.

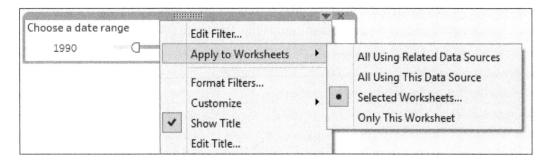

❑ Click the **All on dashboard** button in the **Apply Filter to Worksheets** window that appears. Click on **OK** when done.

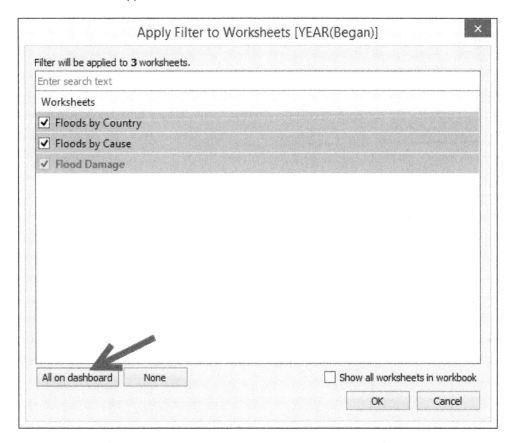

15. Format the filter to have light gray shading using the same color as the dashboard title. You can do this by selecting the filter, and clicking on the drop-down arrow in the top-right corner. From here, you can choose **Format Filters**. You can change the shading from the formatting sidebar that appears.

16. Click on the dropdown of the date filter, and choose **Float**. Place the filter in the top-right corner of the dashboard, beside the dashboard title.

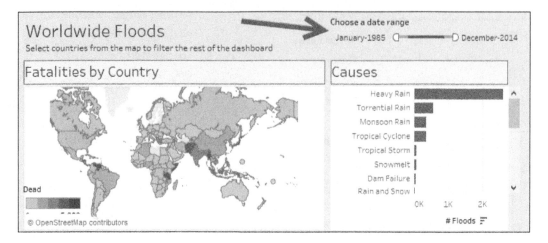

17. Click on the **Floods by Country** worksheet, and click on the funnel icon that appears in the top-right corner. This enables the map to filter all the worksheets in the dashboard.

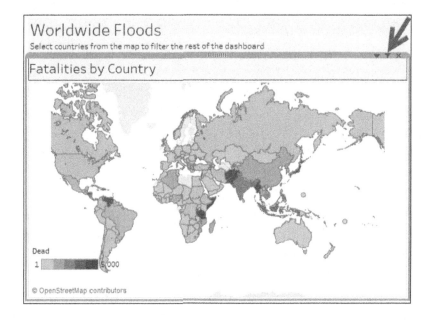

18. Change the dashboard name to `Flood Dashboard`. You can double-click on the dashboard tab, and rename from there.

19. Test the dashboard. Use the presentation mode (or press *F7*) to see what the end users will see. Click on countries in the map and/or change the date range in the filter. Confirm that the rest of the worksheets are filtered by that country.

How it works...

Dashboards in Tableau allow multiple worksheets to be put together, so provide a more comprehensive view of the insights you are trying to provide. Dashboards also allow additional interactivity between the worksheets, and even other dashboards, using what are called actions. There are three types of action—**Filter**, **Highlight**, and **URL**.

In this recipe, we simply used the **Filter** action, using the quick icon that is made available within the worksheet's options. This icon was introduced in Tableau V9.2.

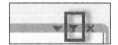

We can also enable this option by using the drop-down arrow and selecting **Use as Filter**.

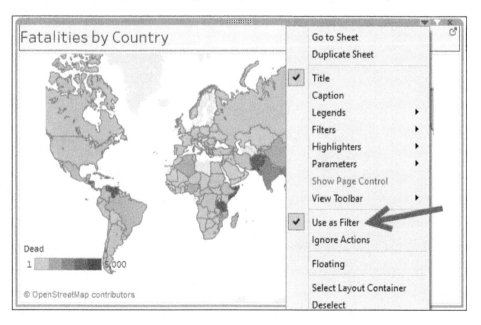

When a sheet is enabled as a filter, Tableau auto-generates a filter action which filters all other worksheets in the dashboard using the values that were selected in the sheet.

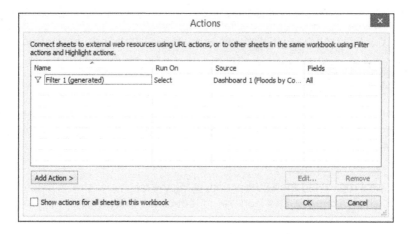

Under the covers, the following are the settings for the auto-generated filter action:

Notice that the source and target are the current dashboard. The filter happens on **Select**, which triggers the action when the consumer of the dashboard clicks on a label or mark from the source sheet. The fields that are used for filtering are all fields that are common among the worksheets.

There are two other options under **Run action on:**, which are **Hover** and **Menu**. **Hover** triggers the action when the mouse pointer is moved over a label or mark, while the **Menu** shows a hyperlink after a label or mark is clicked. We will see these other options in action in later recipes.

Adding filter actions is a great way to make Tableau dashboards more interactive. It allows the user of the dashboard to focus on specific items by narrowing down other views and only retaining values based on what they selected. It also encourages the end users to explore the data sets more, and see how each of the graphs vary based on how they filter them.

We can create the filter actions manually by going to the **Dashboard** menu, and selecting **Actions**.

When setting up the action, the target can be a different dashboard altogether.

When setting up actions that allow your end users to jump from one dashboard to another, ensure you provide a way to go back to the previous dashboard. This can be done by creating another filter action, and reversing the source and destination dashboards.

Pay attention to the source and target item icons.

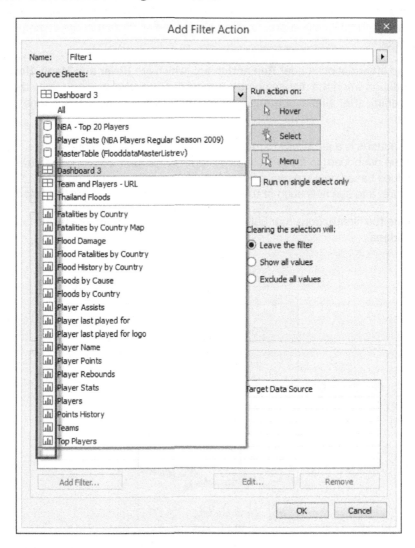

Typically, we target dashboards instead of individual sheets. In addition, when we target an individual sheet that is not in the dashboard, the action would take them to that specific worksheet. This may create a confusing effect especially if the look and feel of the dashboard is different from that individual sheet's.

There's more...

We have used a mix of **Tiled** and **Floating** components in this exercise. Tiled makes all the components (worksheets, containers, legends, filters, and so on) occupy a single layer in a grid. All of these components together occupy 100% of the dashboard space. When components are tiled, there is no control over the position or size of the items.

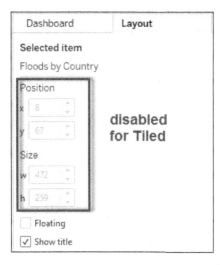

Floating allows these layers to overlap each other, and either be placed on the front or at the back of any sheet. **Floating** is great if you want to have more control over the design of your dashboards, especially if you are following more stringent constraints on sizing, such as needing to print the dashboard on letter or legal paper, or targeting specific devices.

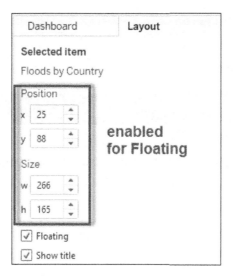

Floating is also great for placing legends, parameters, and filters nearer the views they refer to. By default, these components are placed on the right-hand section of the dashboard. However, this placement may be disruptive if the view they relate to is not within the proximity of the control.

In this recipe, we also made use of filters (not filter action, but filter control). When you add a filter to the dashboard, it is possible to change the scope of that filter to affect not only the worksheet it belongs to, but other worksheets as well.

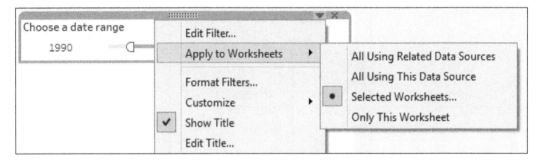

As can be seen in the screenshot, the **Apply to Worksheets** menu shows four options:

- **Only This Worksheet**
- **Selected Worksheets**
- **All Using This Data Source**
- **All Using Related Data Sources**

These options illustrate how flexible filters can be. It is possible for one filter to affect multiple selected sheets, or even all sheets that share the same data source. In Tableau V10, the option **All Using Related Data Sources** was introduced, which allows the filter to work across different data sources. This is a very welcome addition, as this simplifies filtering in dashboards. In previous versions, the only ways to filter across different data sources were either using filter actions or creating parameters and calculated fields in all related sheets.

Creating a highlight action

The highlight action in Tableau dashboards allows related marks in other views to be emphasized by retaining their colors and dimming the colors of all other unrelated marks.

In this recipe, we will use a highlight action on mouse hover to highlight the points history and players for a specific NBA team.

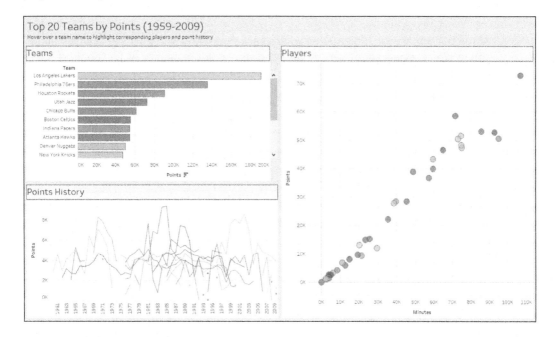

Getting ready

To follow this recipe, open B05527_04 - STARTER.twbx. We will use the following worksheets:

- ▸ Teams
- ▸ Players
- ▸ Points History

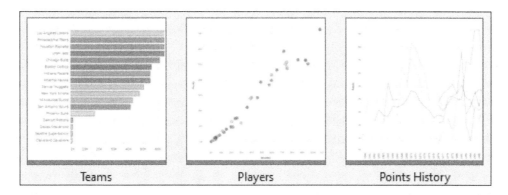

How to do it...

The following are the steps to create the dashboard in this recipe:

1. At the bottom of your Tableau design area are three tabs with plus signs, which allow you to create a new sheet, dashboard, and story point respectively. Click on the middle icon with a grid to create a new dashboard.

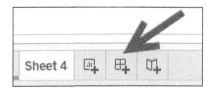

2. When in the dashboard design area, the sidebar becomes a Dashboard bar, showing the available worksheets and other dashboard components.

3. Change the dashboard name to `Team and Players - Highlight`.

4. Check the **Show dashboard title** checkbox located at the bottom of the sidebar. This will show the dashboard title text box in the dashboard.

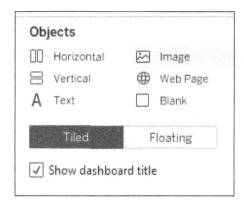

5. Change the dashboard title to show the following:

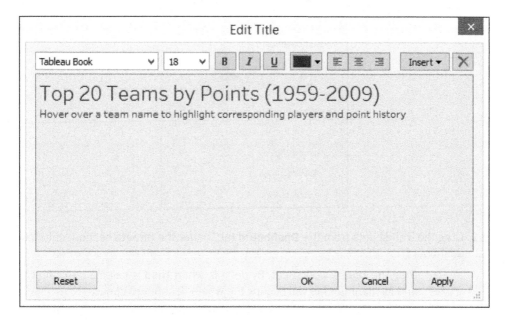

6. Right-click on the dashboard title, and select **Format Title**. Choose a light gray background to the title.

7. If needed, adjust the height of the dashboard title so the whole text is visible.

8. Under the **Objects** section, ensure that **Tiled** is selected and not **Floating**.

9. Click on the **Dashboard** menu, and choose **Format**.

10. Under **Dashboard Shading**, change the color beside **Default** to a light color. This will set the dashboard background color.

11. Drag the worksheets from the **Dashboard** tab, under the **Sheets** section, onto the dashboard.

   ❑ Drag the **Teams** worksheet. By default, when **Tiled** is selected, this first sheet and its components will occupy the whole dashboard space.

   ❑ Drag the **Players** worksheet to the right of **Teams**. When you drag it, you will notice certain areas will get shaded. Release your mouse only when the shaded area is to the right of the **Teams** worksheet.

   ❑ Drag the **Points History** worksheet and place it below **Teams**, and to the left of **Players**.

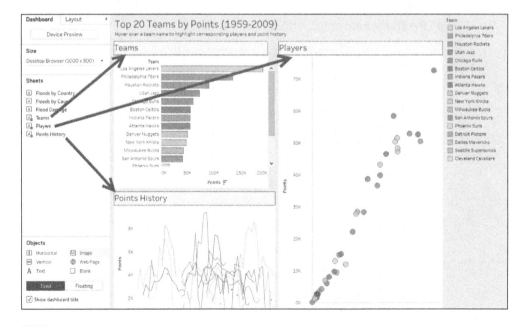

12. Click the drop-down arrow on the color legend, and choose **Select Layout Container**. This selects the container that the legend belongs to, and is identified by a dark blue border.

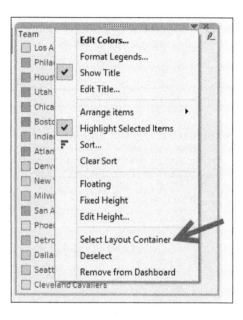

13. Click on the **X** on the top-right corner of the container border to remove the layout container.

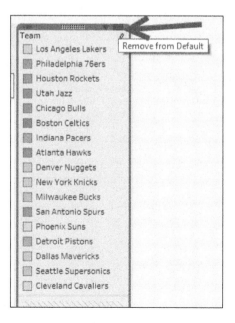

14. Click on **Delete** when you receive a warning about removing the layout container.

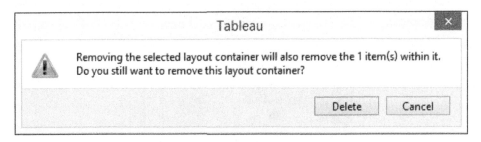

15. Click on the **Dashboard** menu and select **Actions**.

16. In the **Actions** window, click on **Add Action**, and choose **Highlight**.

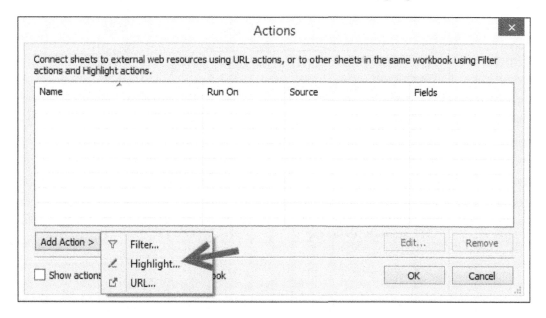

17. In the **Add Highlight Action** window:
- ❑ Change the **Name** to Highlight Team
- ❑ Change the **Run action on:** to **Hover**

    ❑   Leave everything else as the default, and select **OK** to close the window

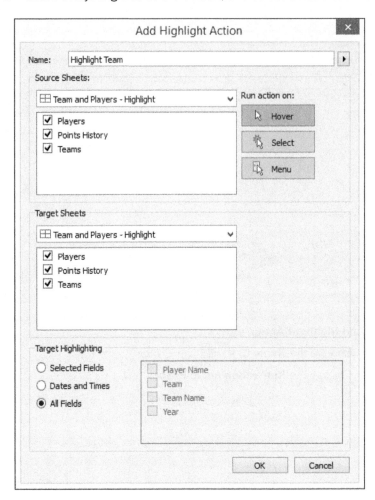

18. Test the dashboard. Use the presentation mode (or press *F7*) to see what the end users will see. Confirm that when you hover over any of the teams in the bar chart, you see the corresponding points history for that team highlighted in the time series graph, as well as the players on that team highlighted in the scatter plot.

How it works...

The **Highlight** action emphasizes the selected values, and blurs everything else to the background.

Before I continue, I would like to apologize for the many colors in the sheets! Yes, yes I can hear you say *Skittles* in the background. As a rule of thumb in visual analytics, we do not want to use color as a way to differentiate different dimensions where there are more than a handful of values. However, in this recipe, I wanted to make it clear what the highlight action does. Once set up, when you hover over a team, all other team marks in other worksheets are highlighted. This is more obvious with the consistency of colors in the three worksheets.

In this recipe, we used a highlight action on mouse hover for our three worksheets. The three worksheets all use **Team** field. When we created the **Highlight** action using **All Fields**, all fields that are common to the three worksheets are matched up. Therefore, when a team is highlighted on any of the sheets, the other two sheets' corresponding team marks are highlighted. All other teams' marks are dimmed.

The highlight action can be triggered on **Select**, **Hover**, or **Menu**. **Select** requires that the mark or label be clicked. The **Hover** action activates when the mouse pointer is over a mark or label—these don't have to be clicked. **Menu** creates a hyperlink for each action that uses **Menu**, and these will show when a mark or label is clicked.

There's more...

We have to be careful to use highlighting on sheets that have common fields. If we target a sheet that does not use the field used in the highlight, then we will see that graph grayed out altogether, as seen in the following screenshot:

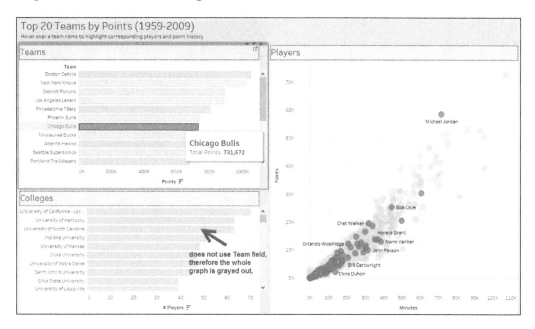

Since the whole chart gets grayed out, almost looking like the whole view is disabled, a mismatch in the highlighted fields may create the impression that the dashboard is broken. It is best to not target worksheets that do not have common columns to avoid this effect.

Creating a URL action

The URL action allows the dashboard to invoke a webpage, either using the user's default web browser or using a web page placeholder that exists in the dashboard. Adding a URL action can add a lot of value to a dashboard because it can allow additional information to be searched or fetched in addition to information the dashboard already offers. This can definitely engage the end users.

In this recipe, we will create a dashboard that uses a URL action to look up information about an NBA team from Wikipedia.

Getting ready

To follow this recipe, open B05527_04 - STARTER.twbx. We will use the following worksheets:

- ▶ Teams
- ▶ Points History

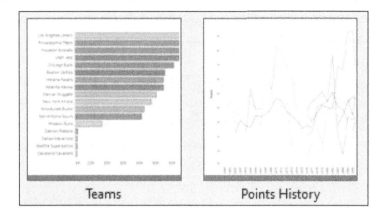

| Teams | Points History |

How to do it...

The following are the steps to create the dashboard in this recipe:

1. At the bottom of your Tableau design area are three tabs with plus signs, which allow you to create a new sheet, dashboard, and story point respectively. Click on the middle icon with the grid to create a new dashboard.

2. When in the dashboard design area, the sidebar becomes a **Dashboard** bar, showing the available worksheets and other dashboard components.

3. Change the dashboard name to `Team and Players – Embed URL`.

4. Check the **Show dashboard title** checkbox. This will show the dashboard title text box in the dashboard.

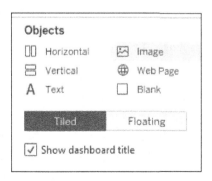

5. Change dashboard title to show the following:

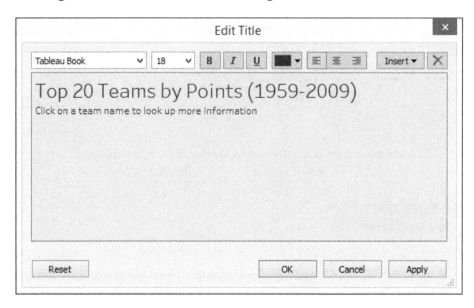

6. Right-click on the dashboard title, and select **Format Title**. Choose a light gray background to the title.

7. If needed, adjust the height of dashboard title so the whole text is visible.

8. Under the **Objects** section, ensure that **Tiled** is selected and not **Floating**.

9. Click on the **Dashboard** menu, and choose **Format**.

10. Under **Dashboard Shading**, change the color beside **Default** to a light color. This will set the dashboard background color.

11. Drag the worksheets from the **Dashboard** tab, under the **Sheets** section, onto the dashboard.

> ❑ Drag the **Teams** worksheet. By default, when **Tiled** is selected, this worksheet will occupy the whole dashboard space.
>
> ❑ Drag **Web Page** from the **Objects** section to the right of **Teams**.
>
> ❑ Drag **Points History** below **Teams**, but to the left of the web page component.

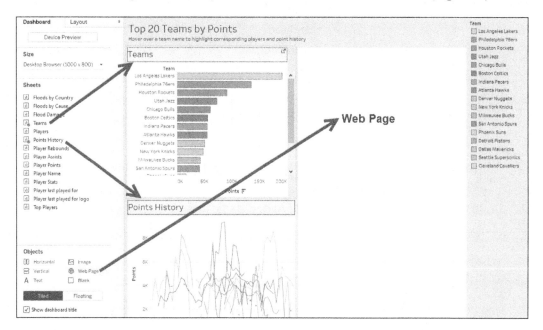

12. Click the color legend to activate it, and select the **X** in the top-right corner to remove it from the dashboard.

13. Click on the **Dashboard** menu and select **Actions**.

14. In the **Actions** window, click on **Add Action**, and choose **URL**.

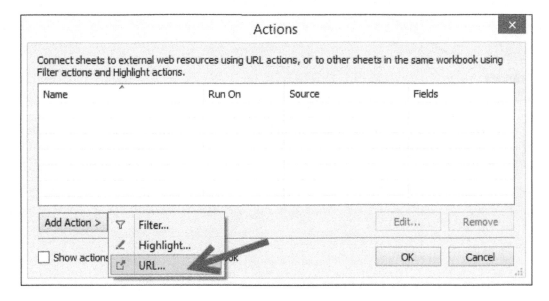

15. In the **Add URL Action** window:

- ❑ Change the **Name** to `Check out the <Team> NBA.com home page`
- ❑ Change the **Run action on:** to **Menu**

❑ Add the URL `http://www.nba.com/<Team>/`

❑ Click **OK** to close the window

16. Add another URL action with the following settings:

❑ Change the **Name** to `Look for <Team> information on Wikipedia`

❑ Change the **Run action on:** to **Menu**

❑ Add the URL `http://www.nba.com/<Team>/`

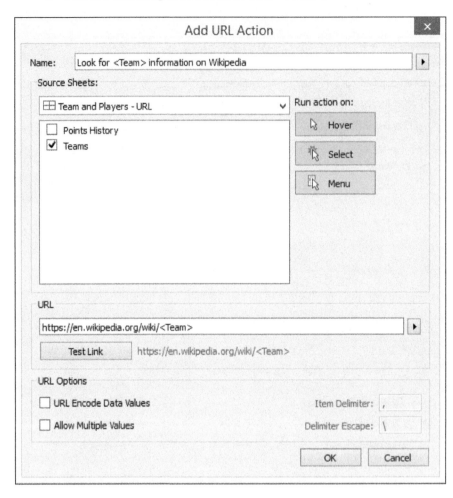

❑ Add a filter action with the following settings:

❑ Change the **Name** to `Filter dashboard for <Team>`

❑ Change the **Run action on:** to **Select**

❑ Under **Source Sheets**, ensure **the Team and Players – URL** dashboard is selected (icon should be the grid), and the **Teams** worksheet is checked

❑ Under **Target Sheets**, ensure the **Team and Players – URL** dashboard is selected (icon should be the grid), and the **Points History** worksheet is checked

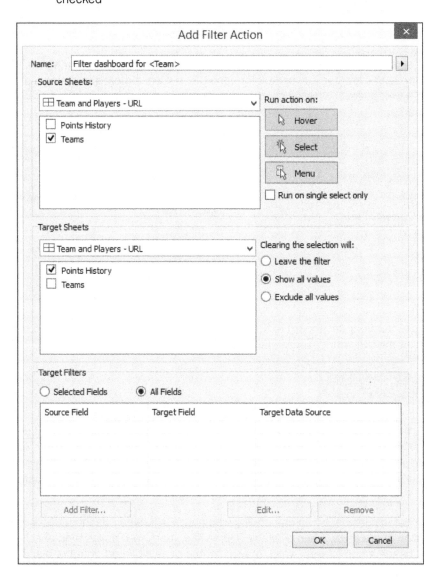

17. Test the dashboard. Use the presentation mode (or press *F7*) to see what the end users will see. Confirm that when you hover over any of the teams in the bar chart, you see the corresponding points history for that team highlighted in the time series graph, as well as the players on that team highlighted in the scatter plot.

How it works...

The URL action allows us to specify a URL that our dashboard can navigate to. If there is a web page object in the dashboard, the URL action displays the web page in that object. If there is no web page object, the URL is opened in the default web browser.

As with the other actions, the URL action can be used with **Select**, **Hover**, or **Menu**. **Menu** is quite popular as this creates a hyperlink for each URL action, almost simulating a drop-down menu from a web page. The hyperlink can be customized, and can include values we have in the dashboard.

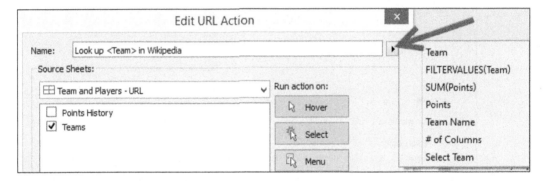

To feed values from our dashboard to the target URL, the target URL must be able to accept parameters at the URL string. These are called GET parameters.

There's more...

The URL action opens up a world of possibilities. However, be wary that when websites are embedded, the behavior may change as the providers change their agreement, code, and so on. For example, a while back, it was pretty easy to embed YouTube videos into Tableau dashboards and play them on Tableau Desktop. However, this behavior has changed and the dashboard is now required to be published to Tableau Server/Online/Public before the video plays.

Another aspect to consider when embedding web pages in Tableau dashboards is using the mobile version of the page, when available. Otherwise, many web pages tend to show all the extraneous headers and footers, which may make the page look odd or out of place.

One current limitation is if you have multiple URLs and want to direct them to different web page objects in your dashboard, you cannot. You also cannot choose to open the web page in a new window if you have a web page object in your dashboard.

See also

Please refer to the *Creating a filter action* recipe in this chapter

Creating an Infographic-like dashboard

Infographics is a shortened term for information graphics, which is a way to visualize data using a lot of graphics and is designed to make the make the visual more graphic and eye-catching. Tableau has the components to add more visual elements to a dashboard and making it look more like the typical infographic.

In this recipe, we will create an infographic-like dashboard that incorporates free form images and text.

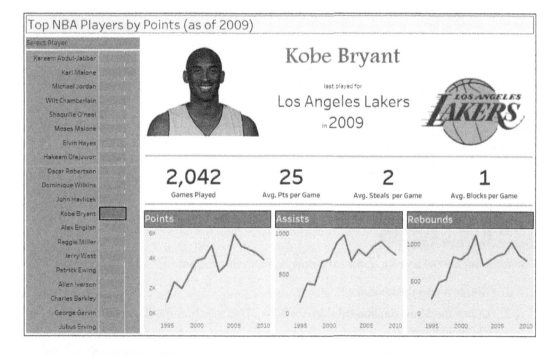

Getting ready

To follow this recipe, open B05527_04 - STARTER.twbx. We will use the following worksheets:

▸ Top Players

▸ Player Points

▶ Player Assists

▶ Player Rebounds

▶ Player Name

▶ Player Stats

▶ Player last played for

▶ Player last played for logo

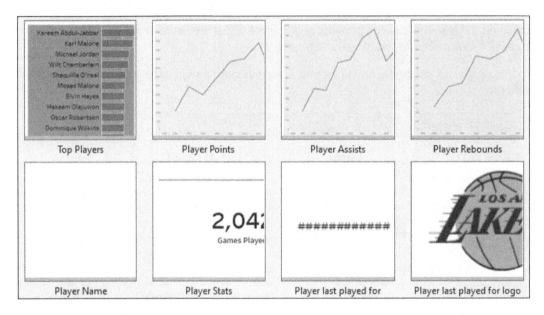

| Top Players | Player Points | Player Assists | Player Rebounds |
| Player Name | Player Stats | Player last played for | Player last played for logo |

How to do it...

The following are the steps to create the dashboard in this recipe:

1. Create a new dashboard.

2. Check the **Show dashboard title** checkbox. This will show the dashboard title text box in the dashboard.

3. Change the dashboard title to `Top NBA Players by Points (as of 2009)`.

4. Ensure that **Tiled** is selected under the **Objects** section.

5. Drag the **Top Players** worksheet to your dashboard. By default, this will occupy the whole space of the dashboard.

6. From the **Objects** section, drag a **Blank** object to the right of the **Top Players** worksheet. Adjust the width of the **Blank** object so that it occupies about 75% of the space.

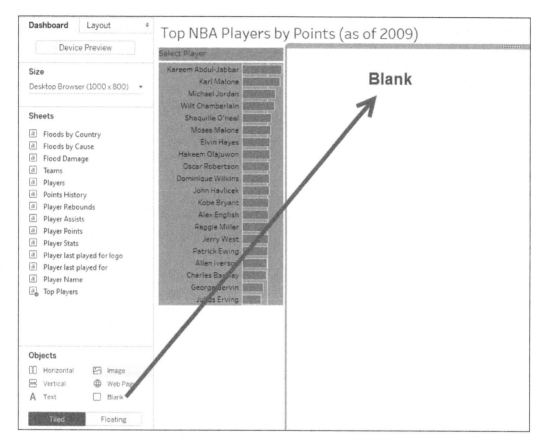

7. Drag the **Player Stats** worksheet and place it below the **Blank** space, to the right of the **Top Players** worksheet.

8. Click on the dropdown of the **Player Stats** worksheet. Under **Fit**, choose **Entire View**.

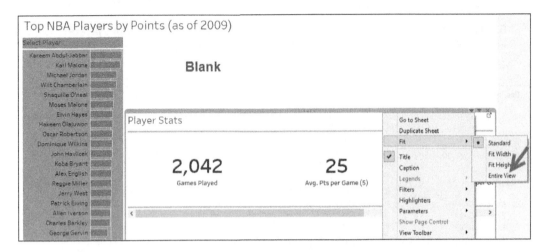

9. Under **Objects**, drag **Horizontal** (which is a layout container) and place it underneath the **Player Stats** worksheet, to the right of the **Top Players** worksheet.

10. Under **Objects**, drag another **Blank**. Place it underneath the **Horizontal Layout Container**.

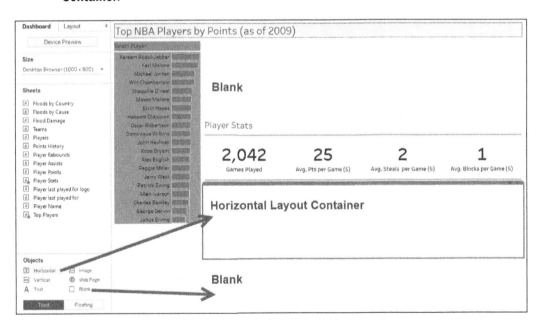

11. Hide the title for **Player Stats**. To do this, you can right-click on the **Player Stats** title, and choose **Hide Title**.

12. Drag the following player worksheets:

 ❏ Drag the **Player Points** worksheet and place it on the **Horizontal** layout container. By default, it will occupy all the space in that layout container.

 ❏ Drag the **Player Rebounds** worksheet and place it to the right of the **Player Points** worksheet.

 ❏ Drag the **Player Assists** worksheet and place it in the middle of the **Player Points and Player Rebounds** worksheets.

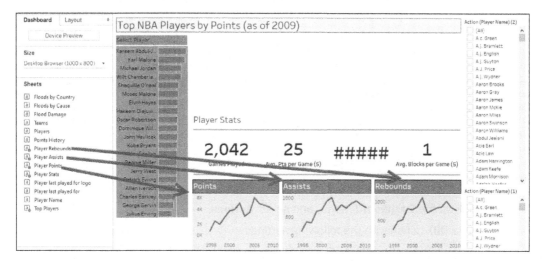

13. Remove all the filters that were added to the right hand side of the dashboard. You can do this by selecting the respective filters, and clicking on the X mark.

14. Under **Objects**, select **Floating**.

15. Add the following as floating objects. A screenshot of the expected layout is provided as well:

 ❏ Add a web page to top. Leave URL as blank for now. We will add the URL action later.

 ❏ Drag **Player Name** to the right of the **Blank** web page.

 ❏ Drag **Player last played for**, and place it below the **Player Name** worksheet.

❑ Drag **Player** last played for to the right of **Player Name** and **Player last played for**.

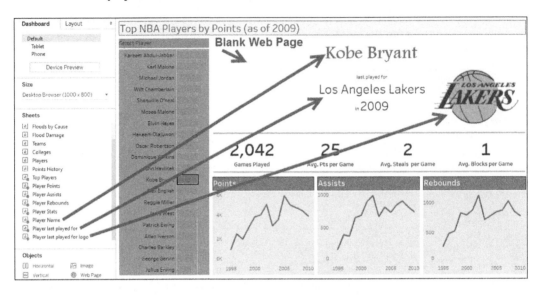

16. Click on the **Dashboard** menu, and select **Actions**.

17. Add a URL action with the following settings:

❑ Change the **Name** to Player Image

❑ Change the **Run action on:** to **Select**

❑ Set the **URL** to **<Image>**

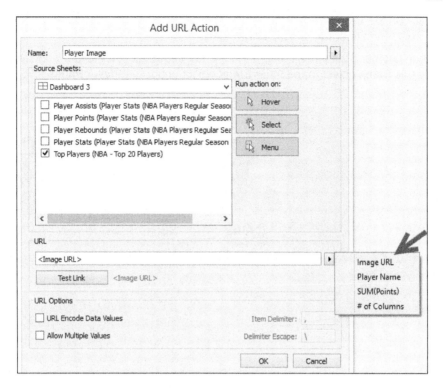

18. Test to ensure that the image is showing properly. Click on any player name, and the image of that player should show up.

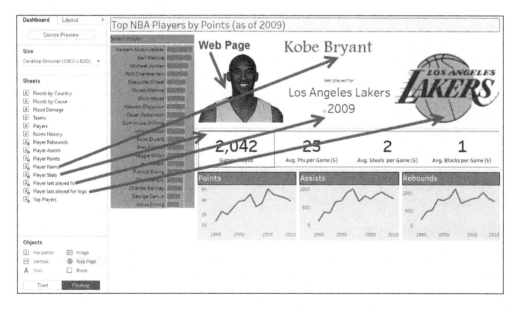

19. Click on the **Top Players** worksheet to select it. Click on the dropdown on the top-right corner, and under **Fit**, choose **Entire View**.

20. Drag another **Blank** object and place it underneath the **Top Players** worksheet. Line up this **Blank** object to the other **Blank** object under the **Player Points** row.

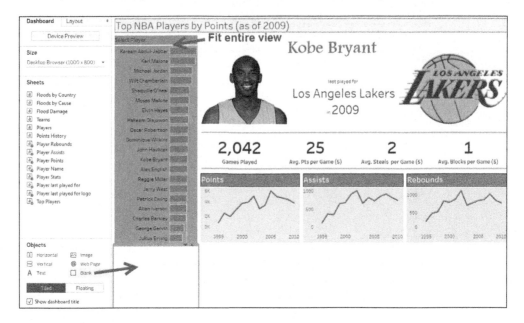

21. Change dashboard name to Top NBA Players by Points.

How it works...

Creating an infographic-like dashboard in Tableau can be quite involved. Often times, this task will encompass creating multiple worksheets with individual components or pieces of information, and putting these all together creatively so that the design elements flow according to the infographic design.

What we have done in this recipe is a fairly simplistic take on the infographic possibility with Tableau, but it should give you a clearer idea of how to do it. If you check the individual worksheets we used, many of them have single pieces of information. For example, one worksheet contained only the name of the player. Another worksheet contained only the logo of the team that player last played with.

There's more...

Just a word of caution. The URL cannot come from a secondary data source, in the case of blended data sources. The URL information has to be from the primary data source.

See also

Please refer to the *Creating a filter action* recipe in this chapter

Please refer to the *Creating a URL action* recipe in this chapter

Creating story points

Story Points allow us to organize our topics and views into a sequence of points that aid in presenting data. Story Points can leverage any views or dashboards in the workbook and use any of those in each point.

In this recipe, we will explore where fatal floods have happened over time using Tableau's story points.

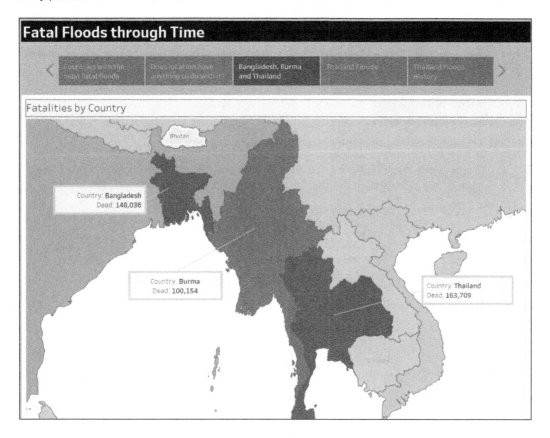

Getting ready

To follow this recipe, open *B05527_04 – STARTER.twbx*. We will use the following worksheets:

- ▸ Fatalities by Country
- ▸ Fatalities by Country Map
- ▸ Flood History by Country

    We are also going to use the following dashboard which shows **Thailand Floods** data:

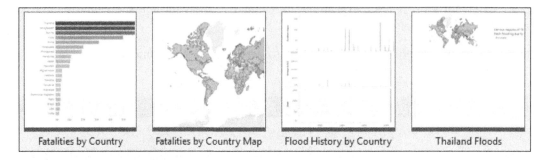

| Fatalities by Country | Fatalities by Country Map | Flood History by Country | Thailand Floods |

How to do it...

The following are the steps to create the story points in this recipe:

1. Create a new story point. You can click on the new Story Point tab, which looks like a book with a plus sign, at the bottom of the canvas.

2. Double-click on the title, and change story title to `Fatal Floods over Time`.

3. Click on the **Story** menu at the top, and select **Format**.

4. Format the story using the following settings:
   - ❑ **Story Shading** to gray
   - ❑ **Story Title Font** to 22 pt bold, **Tableau Bold** font family, white color
   - ❑ **Story Title Shading** to black
   - ❑ **Navigator Font** to 10 pt, **Tableau Book** font family
   - ❑ **Navigator Shading** to dark red

5. Change the **Story size** to **Automatic**.

6. Click on **New Blank Point** to create a new story point.

❑ Change the text of the navigator to `Countries with the most fatal floods`

❑ Drag the **Fatalities by Country** worksheet to the Story Point canvas

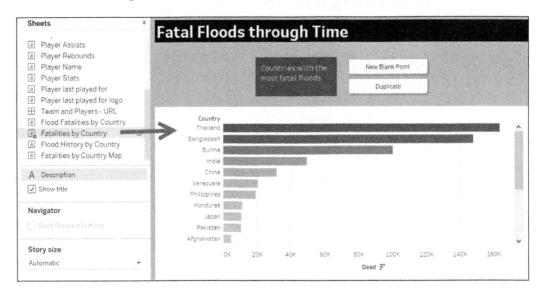

7. Click on **New Blank Point** to create another point.

- Set the new title to Does location have anything to do with it?

- Drag the **Fatalities by Country** worksheet, which is a filled map, to the current Story Point canvas

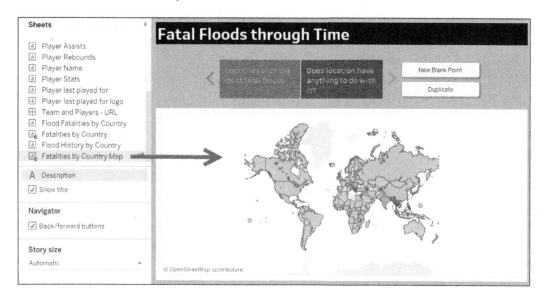

8. Zoom to where the reddest areas are. You can do this by clicking on the map's view toolbar, and using the magnifying lens to zoom to the area.

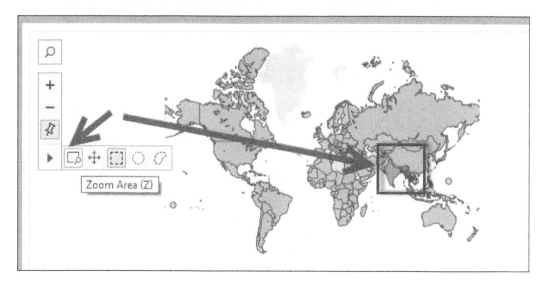

9. Add mark annotations onto the three countries with the reddest colors—Bangladesh, Burma, and Thailand. Leave the default text on the mark annotations, which should include the country name and the total fatalities for those countries.

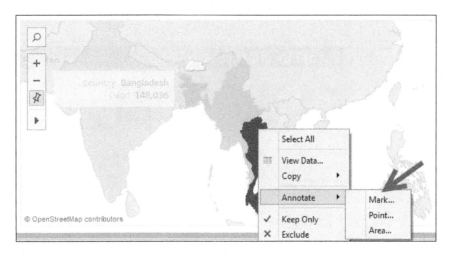

10. Right-click on each of the annotation boxes and select **Format**. Add a thick gray border to each of the annotations.

11. Click on **Save as a New Point** to save this view as a new point.

12. Change the text on this new point to Bangladesh, Burma, and Thailand.

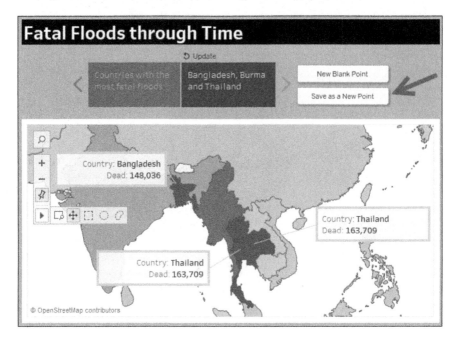

13. Click on **New Blank Point**, and change the text to `Thailand Floods`.

14. Drag the **Thailand Floods** dashboard from the **Sheets** onto this new story point.

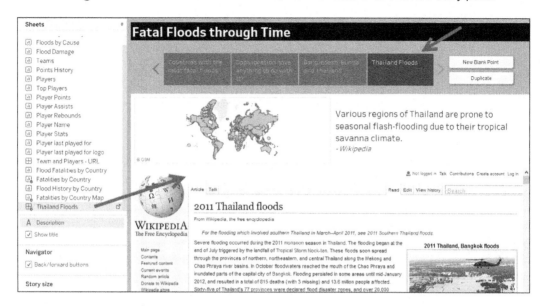

15. Click on **New Blank Point**, and change the text to `Thailand Floods History`.

16. Drag the **Flood History by Country** worksheet onto the story point.

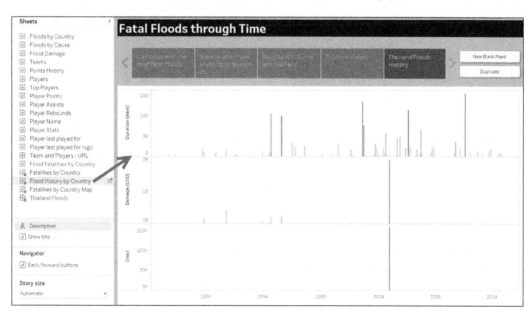

17. Click on the presentation mode, or press *F7*, and test the story points. You click on the navigator, or simply use the left and right arrows in your keyboard to move through the points.

How it works...

Story points help you organize your points and thoughts for a presentation. You may have done this in the past using different software applications. This, however, would have required you to export the worksheets and dashboards as images so they can be embedded into the presentation application. This does limit the interactivity, and you really lose the advantages that Tableau brings to the table.

Tableau is largely an interactive tool, and allows for the exploration of information. As you select, you may see other views get filtered. As you hover, you may get highlights. Story points allow you to present, as well as retain, the interactive components of Tableau. It provides a seamless flow of discussion and analysis.

There's more...

If you need to incorporate images and custom text, you will need to create a dashboard first with those objects and then use them in the story points.

What is presented in this recipe is just a starting point. Story points are completely dependent on your data story, your goal, and your audience. Although the formatting options for story points are fairly limited, you can still create very organized, interactive, and compelling presentations using Tableau's story points.

5

Maps and Geospatial
Visualization

In this chapter, we will cover the following topics:

- ▸ Adding data layers to the default map
- ▸ Creating custom territories
- ▸ Working with Web Map Service (WMS)
- ▸ Using Path to display movement on a map
- ▸ Mapping custom polygons
- ▸ Importing custom geocoding
- ▸ Using a custom background

Introduction

Back in the day, if I wanted to put any maps in my reports and dashboards, I remember I had to go through hoops to geocode my location data. I had to either learn an API (Application Programming Interface) to use some web services, or pay a third party for a database of locations with latitude and longitude information. I remember wishing the software tools I used just knew about the location information and mapped them. (Why does it have to be so hard, anyway?) A genie somewhere seems to have granted my wish—because Tableau knows about location data, and can map it!

When you install Tableau on your desktop, a database of locations and their corresponding latitude and longitude values are installed with it. This is why, whenever you have location data in your data source with standard field names, you will find a **Latitude (generated)** and a **Longitude (generated)** field under **Measures**.

Tableau supports postcode-level information for many countries, and in 2016 they have added a quarter of a million postcode-level records in their geocoding database.

The easiest way to map in Tableau is to double-click a geocoded field and let the magic happen. If Tableau can identify the location, there will be a small globe icon beside this field. When you double-click, Tableau will plot the corresponding latitude and longitude fields in the **Rows** and **Columns** shelves.

If the location information you have cannot be located by Tableau, you also have the option of either specifying an alternate place, or alternate latitude/longitude, or even importing your own geocoding information.

In a future release, it has been promised that shapefile file types will be supported. You will be able to connect to shapefiles directly from Tableau, instead of going through a series of steps to convert shapefile information to something that Tableau can read. Right now, the process to convert is quite involved, as documented here: `http://bit.ly/tableau-shapefiles`. Needless to say, I can't wait for the shapefile support!

In any case, let's dive into the wonderful world of mapping!

Adding data layers to map

Map layers can change the way maps look in Tableau. There are map layers that change the style of the map to use either a light, normal, or dark background. There are also data layers that overlay additional information, such as place names or population, on top of the existing map.

In this recipe, we will add coastline, state/province borders, and household growth layers to the default map that comes with Tableau:

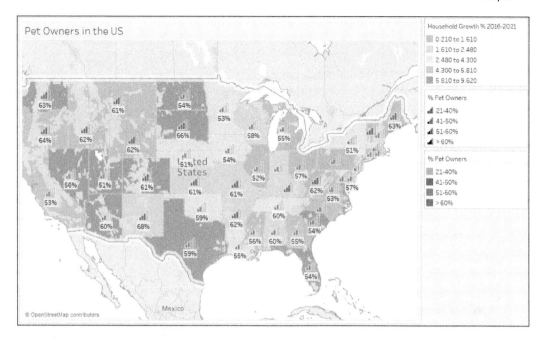

Getting ready

To follow this recipe, open B05527_05 - STARTER.twbx. Use the worksheet called **Map Data Layers**, and connect to the **States (catsvsdogs)** data source:

How to do it...

Here are the steps to add more layers to the default Tableau map:

1. Right-click on the **Location** field under **Dimensions**.

2. Go to **Geographic Role** and select **State/Province**:

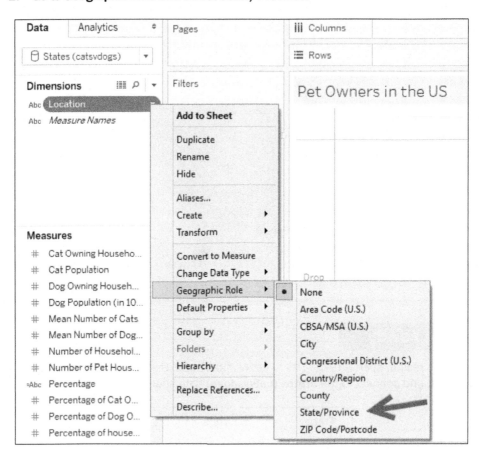

3. Double-click **Location**. **Latitude (generated)** is automatically placed in **Rows** and **Longitude (generated)** is automatically placed in **Columns**. The **Location** pill is also automatically placed in the **Details** property.

4. Under the **Marks** card, click on the dropdown and change the mark to **Shape:**

5. From **Measures**, drag the calculated field **Percentage** to **Shape** in the **Marks** card.

6. Click on the top-right drop-down arrow of the **Shape** legend and assign the following shapes from the **Bars** palette. To assign, click on a value on the left **Select Data Item** column, and then click on the appropriate icon you want to assign from the right column.

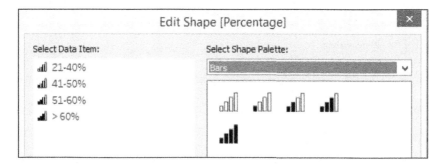

7. In this recipe, no shaded bars are assigned to **21-40%**, and four shaded bars is assigned to **> 60%**.

8. Click **OK** when done.

9. Click on **Size** in the **Marks** card and move the slider to the right to make the icons on the map a little bit bigger.

10. From **Measures**, drag the calculated field **Percentage** to **Color** in the **Marks** card.

11. From **Measures**, drag the field **Percentage** of households with pets to **Label** in the **Marks** card.

12. Go to the **Map** menu and select **Map Layers:**

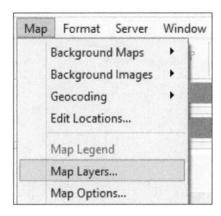

13. In the **Map Layers** sidebar that appears, do the following:

   ❑ Under **Map Layers**, check **Coastline** and **State/Province Borders**
   ❑ Under **Data Layer**, select **Housing Units Growth % 2016-2021**
   ❑ Under **Data Layer**, use the color palette **Orange-Blue Diverging**

14. Close the **Map Layers** sidebar when done.

How it works...

The default Tableau map comes with additional map and data layers. The data layers, however, are only available for US-related data.

To add the map and data layers, you simply need to go render the map in your view first, and then go to the **Map** menu and select **Map Layers**. The **Map Layers** pane will temporarily replace the data side bar.

The **Map Layer** allows additional information to be visualized onto the map, such as country/region names and borders:

Like the map layers, the data layers add more encoding onto the map, such as population or income information for US locations:

If you need data layers specific to your location or map, you may need to access your own GIS server that serves these extra map and data layers.

There's more...

The appearance of the maps can change subtly or dramatically depending on which layers you add. I encourage you to try out different combinations, and see which one can help deliver more impact to your dashboards.

Creating custom territories

Tableau 10 allows geographic regions to be selected and grouped, hence creating custom territories.

In this recipe, we will explore this option:

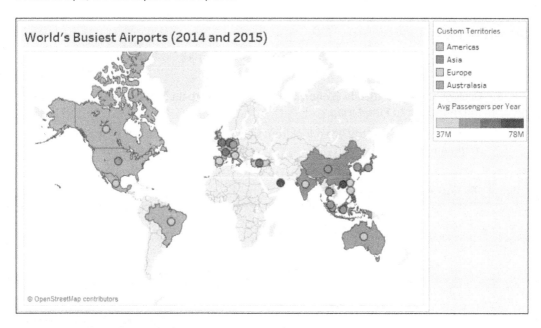

Getting ready

To follow this recipe, open `B05527_05 - STARTER.twbx`. Use the worksheet called **Custom Territories**, and connect to the **Worlds Busiest Airports** data source:

How to do it...

The following are the steps to create the custom territories in this recipe:

1. Double-click on the **Country** field under **Dimensions** in the side bar. The double-click action places this field in the **Details** property and creates a map with dots that represent the country of the respective airports, as well as the built-in **Latitude** and **Longitude** fields to **Rows** and **Columns** respectively.

2. Press *Ctrl* + drag the **Latitude (generated)** pill in the **Rows** shelf to the **Rows** shelf, to the right of the existing pill, to make a second copy. This will generate a second map in the view:

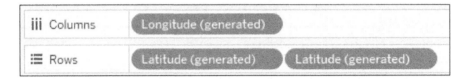

3. Click on the first **Latitude (generated)** field to activate its **Marks** card, and change the mark type to **Filled Map**.

4. For the top map, use the lasso tool from the view toolbar to select all the filled areas in the Americas:

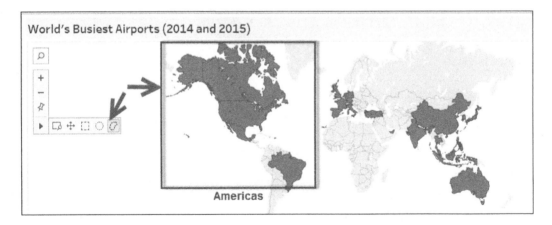

5. While these countries are selected, the command buttons will appear. Click on the paperclip to group these countries as a single territory:

6. Using the previous step as reference, create territories for three more groups of countries, as shown in the following screenshot:

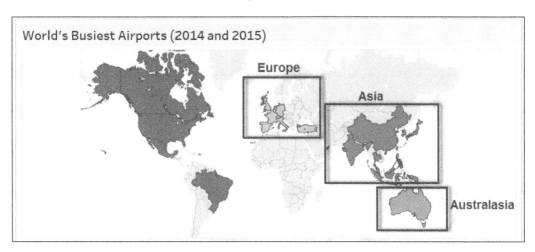

7. In the **Dimensions** section in the side bar, rename the **Country (group)** field to **Custom Territories**. You can do this by right-clicking on the field, and selecting **Rename**:

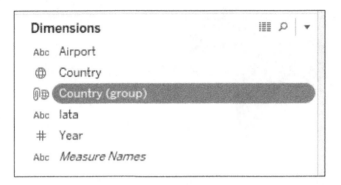

8. Right-click on the values that appear in the color legend, and select **Edit Alias**. Change the aliases to the corresponding territories:

9. Change the title of the color legend to **Custom Territories**. You can do this by clicking on the drop-down arrow in the top right corner of the color legend and selecting **Edit Title**.

10. Activate the second **Marks** card by clicking the second **Latitude (generated)** pill in the **Rows** shelf.

11. While the second **Latitude (generated) Marks** card is active, change the mark to **Circle.**

12. From **Measures**, drag **Passengers** to **Color** in the second **Marks** card.

13. Right-click on the **SUM(Passengers)** pill, and in the **Measure** option, select **Average** instead of **Sum**.

14. Edit the color of the passenger color legend. Change it to **Stepped Color**, with four steps:

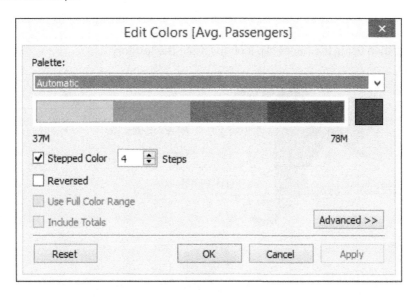

15. Click on the drop-down arrow on the second **Latitude (generated)** pill in the **Rows** shelf and check **Dual Axis**:

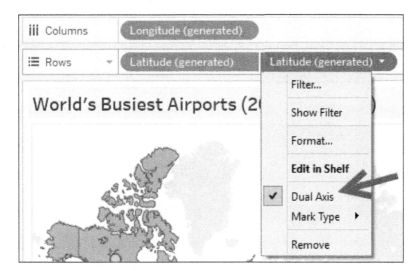

How it works...

Tableau 10 has a new feature that allows us to create custom territories. To create custom territories, we simply need to select all the marks in the map we want to include in the territory, and then using the paper clip icon to create the territory:

You may recall that the paperclip icon normally groups items together. The custom territory tool uses the same concept.

Instead of using the paperclip icon, you can also choose to right-click on the geolocation field on the side bar and use the menu items to group the locations:

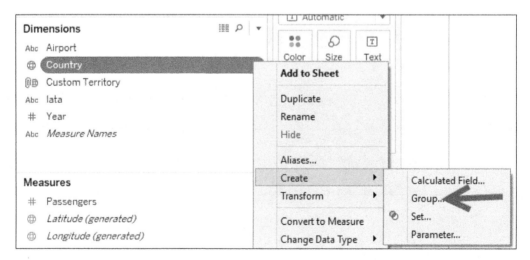

Once you create the group, you will notice a new field in the side bar represented by a globe with paperclip icon:

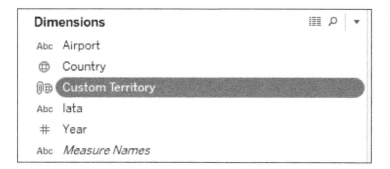

To make modifications, you can right-click on this new field and select **Edit**. In the **Edit** window, you can rename the groups or rearrange the members of the group as needed:

There's more...

We can add a lot of insights to maps by creating dual axis graphs – two marks on top of a map. To do this, we can simply duplicate either (or both) the latitude or longitude pill on either the **Rows** or **Columns** shelf and change the mark of one of the pills.

In the following example, we have a filled map with circle marks. To achieve this, we duplicated the latitude pill by using the *Ctrl* + drag shortcut from the pill to the **Rows** shelf. This produces two pills on **Rows** and two maps on the view, one on top of the other. This also introduces three **Marks** cards—one for the first pill, one for the second pill, and another one called **All**, which will affect both maps:

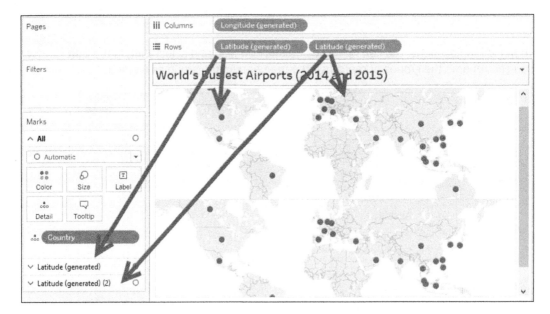

Because we have multiple **Marks** cards, we can now vary the marks we want to show. To overlay one map on top of the other, we can simply right-click on the second **Latitude (generated)** pill and select **Dual Axis**:

Pies on map? Shapes on map? Circles on map? All of these can be done using this technique!

See Also

▶ Please refer to the *Creating a combo chart (dual axis chart)* recipe in *Chapter 2, Advanced Charts*

▶ Please refer to the *Using path to display movement in map* recipe in this chapter

Working with Web Map Service (WMS)

Another way to change the appearance of maps is to connect to a service called Web Map Service, which serves map tiles, and use those instead of the default maps the come with Tableau.

In this recipe, we are going to plot some areas based on zip code and provide a map background based on a web map service:

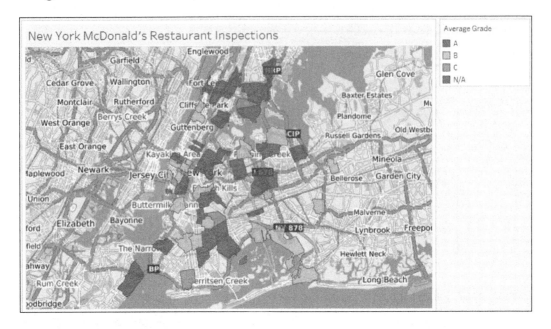

Getting ready

To follow this recipe, open B05527_05 - STARTER.twbx. Use the worksheet called WMS, and connect to the DOHMH New York City Restaurant data source:

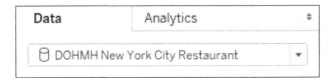

How to do it...

Here are the steps to create a map with a WMS background:

1. From **Dimensions** in the side bar, drag **DBA** to the **Filters** shelf and filter the values to only show **MCDONALD'S.**

2. In the **Dimensions** section, double-click on **Zipcode**. This will show the Tableau default map in the view.

3. From **Dimensions**, drag **DBA** to **Details** in the **Marks** card. This will update the map with circles representing locations of the McDonald's restaurants.

4. Click on the **Map** menu, and select **Map Services...**:

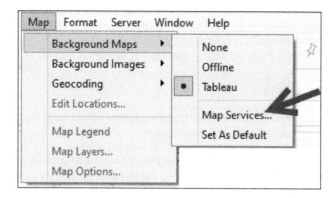

5. In the **Map Services** window that appears, select **Add** and then **WMS Servers...**:

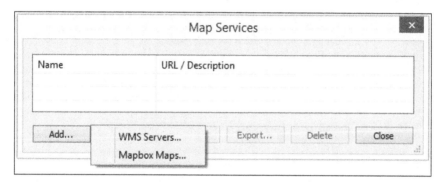

6. In the **Add WMS Server Connection** window, type the following in the URL field: `http://ows.terrestris.de/osm-gray/service?`:

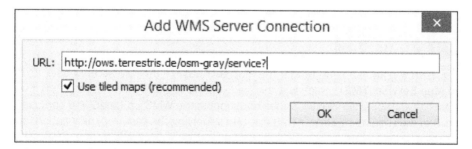

7. Close the **Map Services** window when done.

8. From **Measures**, drag **Cuisine Average Grade** to **Color**.

How it works...

Instead of the built-in Tableau map, we may want (or need) to use a map with a different feature, or different look and feel, with our geolocation data. One way to do this is by connecting to a Web Map Service (WMS) in Tableau. A web map service is defined in Open Geospatial Consortium (`http://www.opengeospatial.org/standards/wms`) as a service that does the following:

> *"Provides a simple HTTP interface for requesting geo-registered map images from one or more distributed geospatial databases"*

Some WMS servers can be publicly accessed, while others are private and/or commercial. To use a WMS server, we can simply add the URL to Tableau. This option can be found under the **Map Menu**, and **Map Services...**:

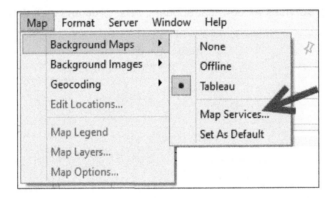

Once the URL is registered and Tableau verifies it can connect, the map tiles can be used. What we used in this recipe is a publicly available web mapping service from `http://ows.terrestris.de/dienste.html#openstreetmap-wms`.

There's more...

Ever wondered why Tableau can render the map very easily? Tableau actually uses its own **Tableau Map Service** (**TMS**), which is available from the Tableau Map Server. What if you want to connect to a mapping service that does not support the WMS protocol? You can use TMS to connect. This will require creating a TMS file, and supplying the required information, such as server, format, and request string. The full documentation is available from the following link:

`http://bit.ly/tableau-map-service`

Using path to display movement in map

We can visualize movements in Tableau by drawing lines between points. This takes advantage of the Line mark and the Path property.

In this recipe, we are going to visualize who Shaquille O'Neal played for from 1992 to 2011:

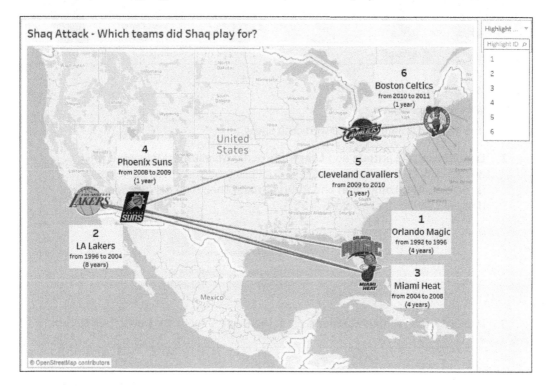

Getting ready

To follow this recipe, open B05527_05 - STARTER.twbx. Use the worksheet called Using Path, and connect to the Player Stats (NBA Players Regular Season 2009) data source:

You will also need to download the team logos you would like to use (and, of course, check the term agreements to using these logos if you need to use these in public dashboards). Create a folder called NBA in the **Shapes** folder, and place the icons in this folder:

How to do it...

Here are the steps to create the map with path lines:

1. Double-click on **Latitude** and **Longitude** under **Measures**. Make sure you double-click on the data source fields, not the Tableau-generated fields. By default, **AVG(Longitude)** and **AVG(Latitude)** should be the aggregations that are used for these fields:

2. Use *Ctrl* + drag with the **Latitude** pill in the **Rows** shelf to the **Rows** shelf to copy it:

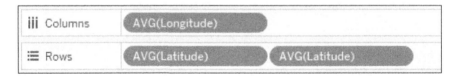

3. Click on the first **AVG(Latitude)** pill to activate the first **Marks** card.
4. Change the mark of the first **AVG(Latitude)** on **Marks** card to **Line**.
5. Drag the **ID** field from **Dimensions** to **Path** of the first **Marks** card.
6. Select the second **AVG(Latitude)** on **Marks** card and change the mark type to **Shape**.
7. From **Dimensions**, drag **Team Name** to **Shape** in the second **AVG(Latitude)** on **Marks** card.

8. Click on **Shape** and assign the icons to the correct team:

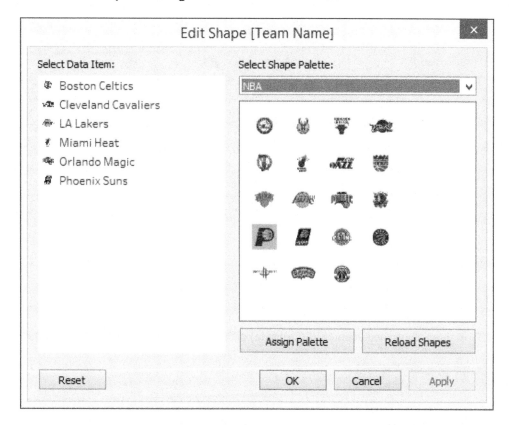

9. Adjust the size of the team icons. Click on the **Size** property in the **Marks** card and slide a little bit to the right to increase the size of the team icons.

10. While the second **Marks** card is still selected, drag the following dimension fields to Label: ID, Team Name, From-To, and # Years Label.

11. Adjust the label formatting to look similar to the following screenshot:

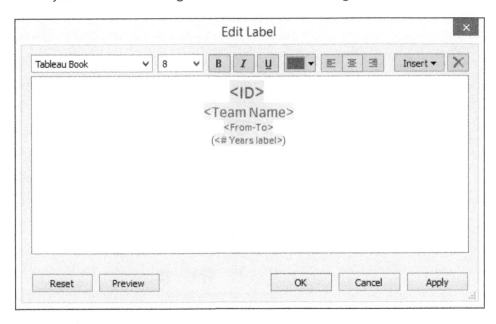

12. Right-click on the second **AVG(Latitude)** pill in the **Rows** shelf and click on **Dual Axis**.

How it works...

In this recipe, we visualized which teams Shaquille O'Neal played for. We represented the teams with the team logo, and drew lines between teams he moved from and to. These are two different marks; therefore, we needed to use a dual axis graph.

To show the teams using the team logo, we simply need to use the **Shape** mark type. Before this, we need to load the team logos into Tableau Repository's **Shape** folder:

If you create the folder and copy the icons while you have Tableau open, you will need to click **Reload Shapes** in the **Edit Shapes** window first before you can see it:

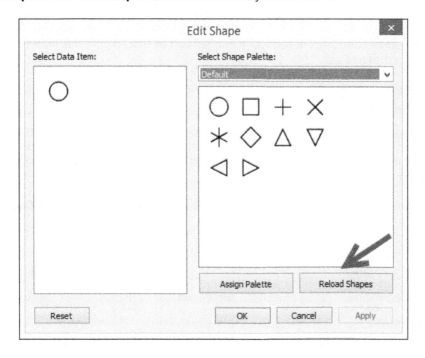

To draw the lines between the teams, we first need to change the mark type to **Line**. When we change the mark type to **Line**, a new property appears in the **Marks** card, which is **Path**:

To better understand what this **Path** property is for, we can start by understanding what the term path means. One of the definitions of path in `www.dictionary.com` is as follows:

A route, course, or track along which something moves

This is exactly what **Path** helps with—we are trying to visualize a route. In our recipe, we are trying to picture Shaq's movement from team to team. Since we want the movement to be influenced by when Shaq moved, we place the **Year** field onto **Path**. This, together with the **Line** mark type, draws the lines, in sequence, between the teams Shaq played for. For other use cases, a date, date/time, or sequence number can be placed onto this **Path** property to control where the lines go.

There's more...

It is possible to calculate distance between locations in Tableau. To calculate distance, we need to have the source and destination latitude and longitude values in the same row. We can achieve this by either manipulating the data source so it already has it, or by performing a self join (that is, a table being joined to itself).

If the data source is Excel, we can do a self join if we connect to it using **Legacy Connection**:

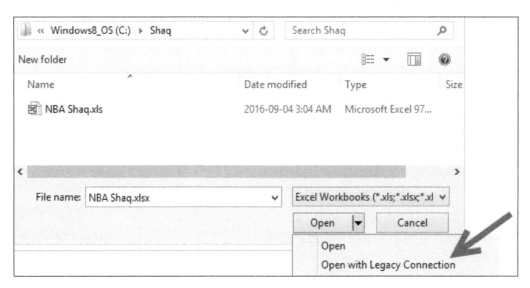

Legacy Connection uses the Microsoft Jet Data Engine driver, which has since been replaced by Tableau.

> The **Legacy Connection** option was introduced in Tableau 8.2. You can learn more about this in the Tableau KB article *Differences between Legacy and Default Excel and Text File Connections*, which can be found at `http://bit.ly/tableau-legacy-jet`.

Choosing **Legacy Connection** enables us to have a new option called **New Custom SQL**:

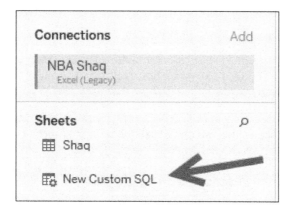

The self join query will look like the following code:

```
SELECT

    [Shaq$].[ID] AS [ID1],
    [Shaq$].[Team Name] AS [Team Name1],
    [Shaq$].[Latitude] AS [Latitude1],
    [Shaq$].[Longitude] AS [Longitude1],

    [Shaq2$].[ID] AS [ID2],
    [Shaq2$].[Team Name] AS [Team Name2],
    [Shaq2$].[Latitude] AS [Latitude2],
    [Shaq2$].[Longitude] AS [Longitude2]

FROM
    [Shaq$]
    LEFT JOIN [Shaq$] [Shaq2$]
    ON ([Shaq$].[ID] = [Shaq2$].[ID] - 1)
```

Once the latitude and longitude values of the previous and next teams are in the same row, we can use the great-circle distance formula to calculate the distance. The great-circle distance has been defined in Wikipedia (https://en.wikipedia.org/wiki/Great-circle_distance) as follows:

> *The shortest distance between two points on the surface of a sphere, measured along the surface of the sphere (as opposed to a straight line through the sphere's interior)*

The procedure for calculating the distance in Tableau is documented here - `http://bit. ly/tableau-distance`. The formula for the Tableau calculated field will look like this:

```
3959 * ACOS
(
SIN(RADIANS([Latitude1])) * SIN(RADIANS([Latitude2])) +
COS(RADIANS([Latitude1])) * COS(RADIANS([Latitude2])) *
COS(RADIANS([Longitude2]) - RADIANS([Longitude1]))
)
```

Once we have the distance values, we can utilize them on the maps:

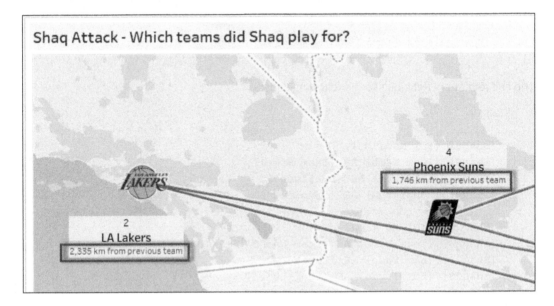

One more tidbit about Tableau maps. If you zoom in enough and use the Radial Selection tool (the dashed circle icon) from the View Toolbar, you will be able to see the distance between two points. The limitation is this is fairly visual in nature and currently cannot be annotated or saved like a calculated field:

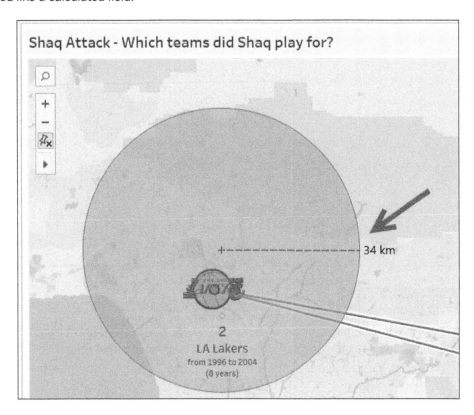

See also

Please refer to the recipes in *Chapter 7, Data Preparation*

Mapping custom polygons

Tableau supports not only using geographic map tiles, but also drawing and display custom polygons (or closed shapes). This can be helpful when visualizing or emphasizing certain areas in a map or background image.

In this recipe, we will draw custom polygons around two points of interest in Vancouver, Canada:

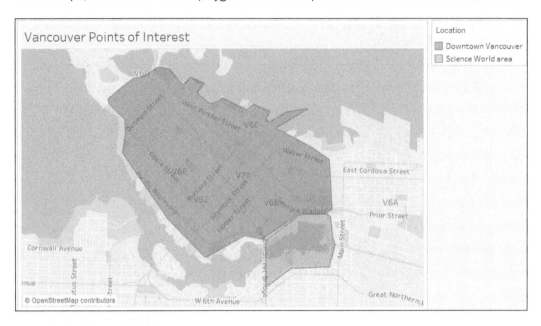

Getting ready

To follow this recipe, open B05527_05 – STARTER.twbx. Use the worksheet called Custom Polygon, and connect to the Vancouver Points of Interest data source:

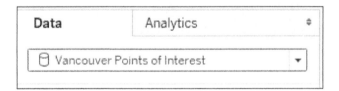

How to do it...

Here are the steps to create the custom polygon areas:

1. Change the mark type in the **Marks** card dropdown to **Polygon.**

2. Double-click on the **Latitude** and **Longitude** appearing under **Measures**. Make sure you double-click the **Latitude** and **Longitude** fields from the data source, not the ones that have the (generated) suffix.

3. From **Dimensions**, drag **Shape Id** to **Detail.**

4. From **Measures**, drag **Point** to **Path** in the **Marks** card.

5. Go to the **Analysis** menu, and uncheck **Aggregate.**

6. From **Dimensions**, drag **Location** to **Color** in the **Marks** card.

How it works...

A polygon is a series of points that are connected together to form an enclosed space. To create custom polygons in Tableau, there needs to be a series of points – pairs of *x* and *y* coordinates—and a sequence that indicates in which order to walk these points.

In our recipe, I created the points using Interworks' Drawing Power Tool (`http://powertoolsfortableau.com/tools/drawing-tool`). This is a great online tool that allows you to draw your custom shape on a map or a custom image:

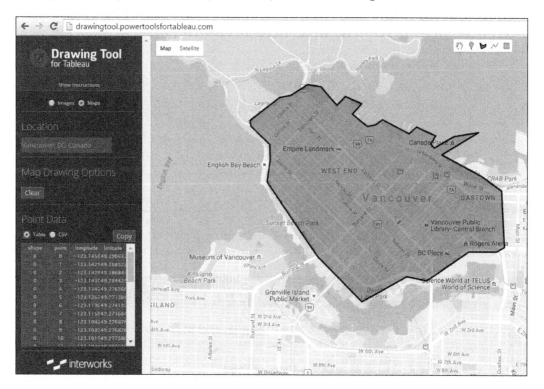

I've produced my point data using the Table format, which can be seen on the website's left-hand section. I copied these points to Excel. The original points look like this:

	A	B	C	D
1	shape	point	longitude	latitude
2	0	0	-123.146	49.29054
3	0	1	-123.143	49.28852
4	0	2	-123.142	49.28684
5	0	3	-123.143	49.28444

To help more easily draw this in Tableau, I added another field, called **location**. I also changed the **shape** column header to **shape id**, so that Tableau will interpret this as a dimension by default instead of a measure:

	A	B	C	D	E
1	location	shape id	point	longitude	latitude
2	Downtown Vancouver	0	0	-123.145838	49.290538
3	Downtown Vancouver	0	1	-123.142576	49.2885226
4	Downtown Vancouver	0	2	-123.14249	49.2868431
5	Downtown Vancouver	0	3	-123.143005	49.2844357

Once this is set up, we simply need to connect to this data source. The **latitude** and **longitude** represent the x and y coordinates, respectively. When you double-click these, **latitude** will be assigned to **Rows** and **longitude** to **Columns**. The **shape id** will identify each enclosed shape, and the point will specify the path to walk (or the sequence of points to connect).

Importing custom geocoding

While Tableau can map most geographic locations, you may still encounter locations that are unrecognizable in Tableau, and therefore do not show up on your map. It is still possible to visualize this. One way to make this happen is by importing your location information along with its latitude and longitude coordinates into Tableau.

In this recipe, we will import custom geocoding to visualize where the busiest airports were in 2015:

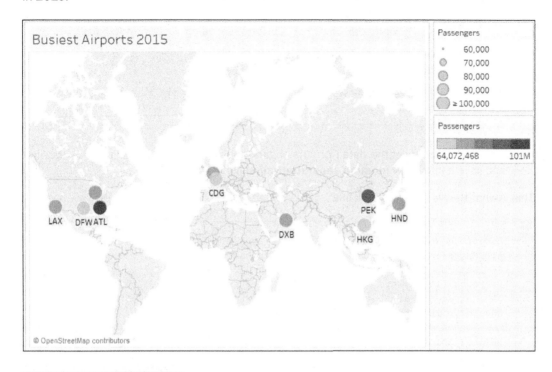

Getting ready

To follow this recipe, open `B05527_05 - STARTER.twbx`. Use the worksheet called Import Geocoding, and connect to the Busiest Airports data source:

In addition, take the file called `Busiest Airports.csv` that comes with the downloadable files for this chapter and place it in a local folder by itself:

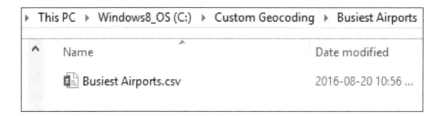

Alternatively, you could get the data from the original source, `www.world-airport-codes.com`, and save it into a **csv** (**comma separated value**) file.

This is what the file contents look like:

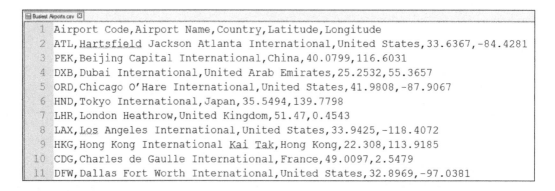

How to do it...

Here are the steps to import custom geocoding:

1. Go to the **Map** menu, and select **Import Custom Geocoding**.

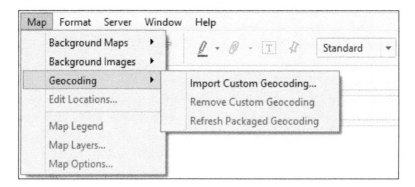

2. In the **Import Custom Geocoding** window, select the folder that contains the `Busiest Airports.csv` file. Note your folder path may be different from what is shown in the following screenshot:

3. Click on **Import**. This will load the custom geocoding, and depending on how fast your machine is, may take a few minutes.

4. After the custom geocoding is imported, right-click on the **Airport** dimension field and change the **Geographic Role** to **Busiest Airports**, and then **Airport Code**:

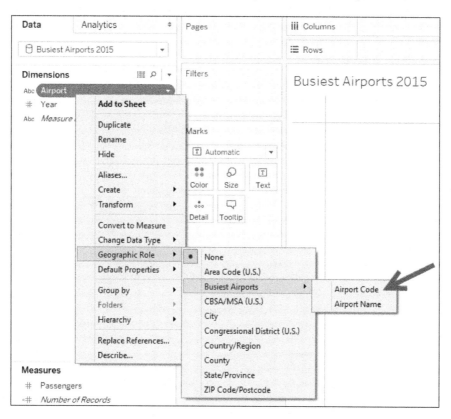

5. Double-click on the **Airport** field in the **Dimensions** section of the sidebar. This will create a map in your view.

6. Click on the indicator shown on the bottom-right corner of your view:

7. In the **Special Values for [Airport]** window, select **Edit Locations...**:

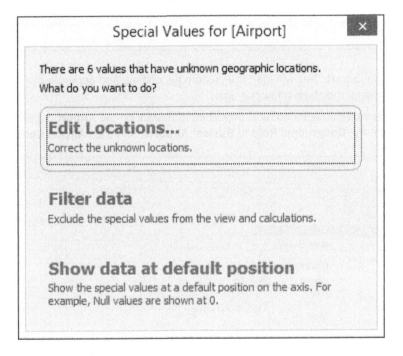

8. Select **None** for **Country/Region** field. Click **OK** when done:

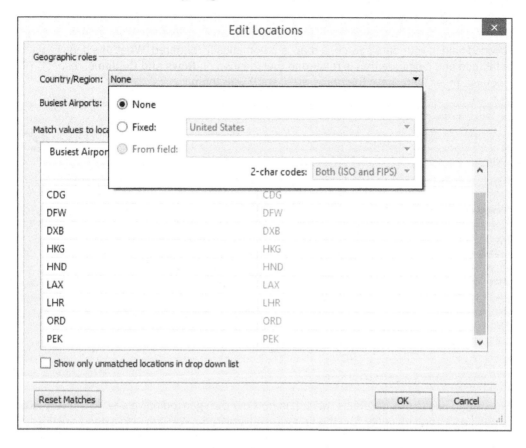

9. From **Measures**, drag **Passengers** to **Color**.

10. Right-click on the **Passengers** pill in the **Color** property in the **Marks** card and select **Measure**, and then **Average**.

11. From **Measures**, drag **Passengers** to **Size**.

12. Right-click on the **Passengers** pill in the **Size** property in the **Marks** card and select **Measure**, and then **Average**.

How it works...

Tableau is installed with its own geocoding database, which is why when you double-click on a geocoded field in your data source, a map is automatically rendered. What this does is place the latitude and longitude that is related to that location on **Rows** and **Columns**, respectively. By default, these fields have the *(generated)* suffix with them.

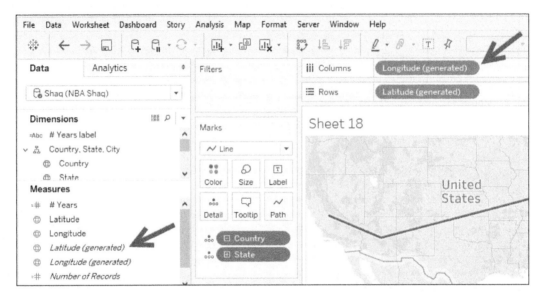

If we want to add to this database, we can import our own geocoding values. At the very least, you need a location identifier and the latitude and longitude. You can also extend existing geographic roles (or a hierarchy of roles) by providing those role names in the CSV (comma separated value) file, as well as the corresponding latitude and longitude.

The requirements for custom geocoding are fully documented in Tableau's website, which you can access using this URL: `http://bit.ly/custom-geocode`.

Before you import custom geocoding, you need to close other instances of the Tableau application. There needs to be just a single instance running.

To import the custom geocoding, the CSV file(s) must be placed in a directory. In Tableau, under the **Maps** menu, there is an option to **Import Custom Geocoding**. When you select this, you will get a window asking for the directory path of the CSV file(s):

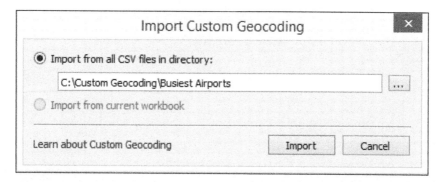

Depending on how fast your machine is, the import may take a few seconds to a few minutes. Once the geocoding is imported, you should be able to see the new role under **Geographic Role**. The new, main role name is based on the directory name you imported from. The additional roles you see in the following screenshot—**Airport Code** and **Airport Name**—are derived from the field names in the CSV file:

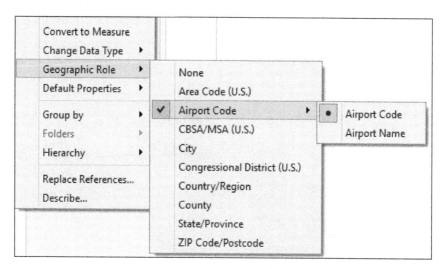

When you assign a field to these new roles, the fields will be assigned a new icon – a globe with a paperclip beside it:

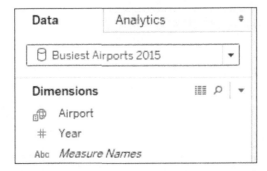

Using a custom image background

It is possible to use custom backgrounds in Tableau. This is useful when we are visualizing data that can be mapped onto a custom image, such as a floor plan or points of interest in a specific venue or conference.

In this recipe, we will use a custom background with Tableau, showing some sushi-related names for beginners:

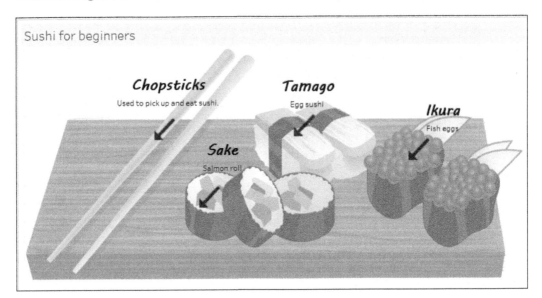

Getting ready

To follow this recipe, open `B05527_05 - STARTER.twbx`. Use the worksheet called `Custom Background Image`, and connect to the `Custom Image (Eating Sushi)` data source:

For this recipe, you also need to save the image, `sushionaboard-800px.png`, to a local folder. Remember the location of this image, as we will need to refer to it in the steps.

How to do it...

Here are the steps to create the view:

1. While connected to the **Custom Image (Eating Sushi)...** data source, create a new worksheet.

2. Go to the **Map Menu**, and under **Background** Images, click on **Custom Image (Eating Sushi)...**:

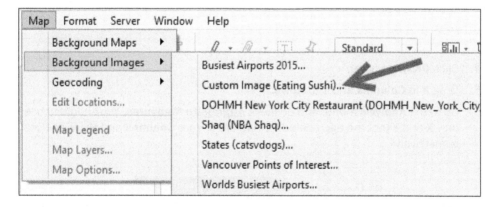

3. In the **Add Background Image** window, do the following:

    ❑   For **File or URL**, use the `sushionaboard-800px.png` image

    ❑   For the **X Field**, select **X** and set **Left** to 0 and **Right** to 100

    ❑   For the **Y Field**, select **Y** and set **Bottom** to 0 and **Top** to 100:

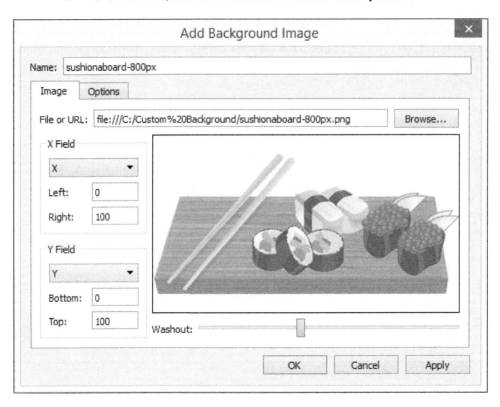

4. Click **OK** when done.

5. Drag **X** to **Columns** and **Y** to **Rows.**

6. Go to the **Analysis** menu, and uncheck **Aggregate Measures**. You should notice that only **X** and **Y** (not the aggregated format) are in your **Columns** and **Rows** shelves, respectively:

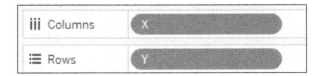

7. Change the **X** and **Y** axes so they are each fixed from 0 to 100. To do this, you can right-click on each of the axes and select **Edit Axis**:

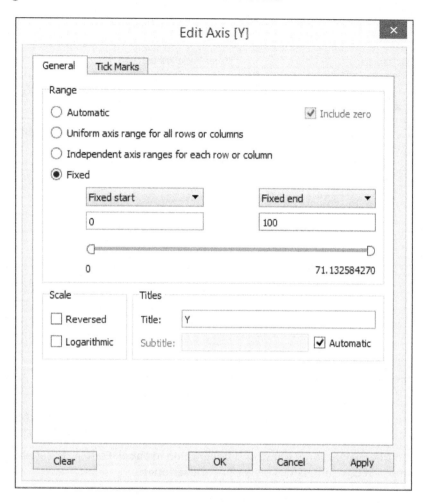

8. In the **Marks** card, change mark to **Shape**.

9. Click on **Shape** in the **Marks** card, and change the **Shape Palette** to thin arrows. Select a diagonal left-downward pointing thin arrow:

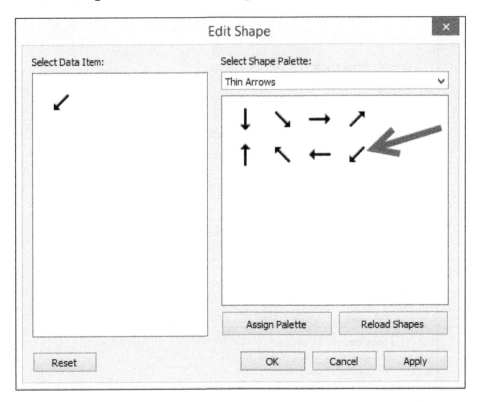

10. Increase the size of the marks so that the arrows appear bigger and more visible. To do this, click on **Size** in the **Marks** card, and move the slider a little bit to the right.

11. From **Dimensions**, drag **Name** and **Description** to **Label**. Format the label so that **Name** is in bold font, and is bigger than **Description**.

How it works...

There are cases when we still want to map our points, but we need to map them on our own custom map or our own custom images. For example, if we needed to plot some measures against a floor plan or a park map, we cannot take advantage of Tableau's built-in geocoding database because we need to map coordinates that are specific to our floor plan or park map.

To use a background image, we can use the **Background Images** option under the **Map** menu to load a background image for a specific data source.

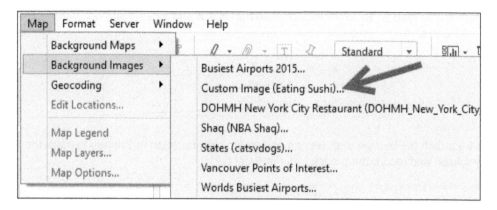

Once the image is loaded, we are also going to need to identify the fields in the data source that correspond to the **X** and **Y** coordinates:

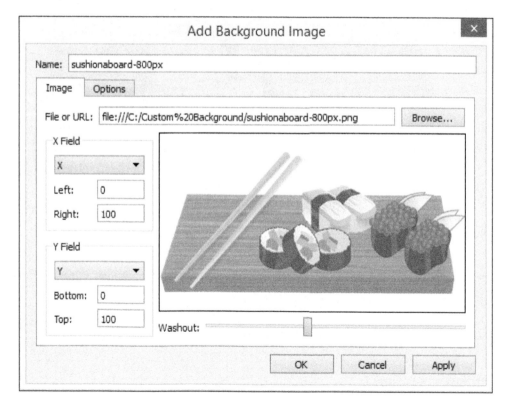

In this recipe, we needed to figure out ahead of time what our x and y coordinates are relative to our custom sushi image. There are a few ways to do this.

One option is to load an Excel file into Tableau that has **X** and **Y** fields and one sample row of data, as follows:

	A	B	C	D
1	Name	Description	X	Y
2	Something	Something	0	0

Once we attach the background, we can use the point annotation in Tableau to mark the x and y values, and record them back into the Excel file:

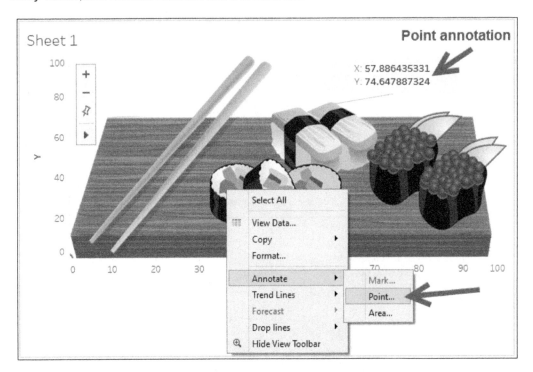

Another way is to use the drawing tool for Tableau to get the coordinates, similar to what we did in the *Mapping custom polygons* recipe in this chapter. Instead of the **Maps** option, we can use the **Images** option and provide the **URL** to the image. As we select points, the *x* and *y* coordinates are recorded in the bottom section of the page:

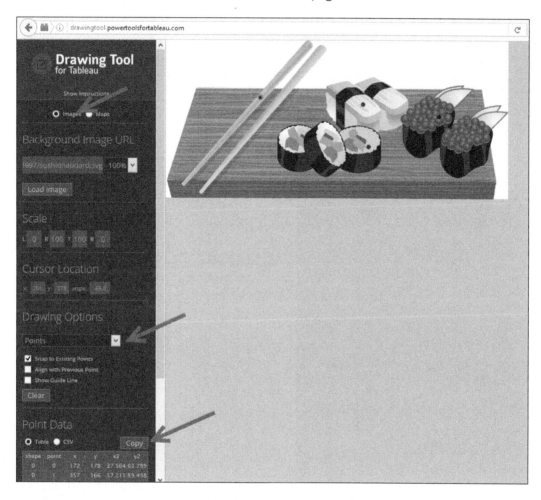

Yet another alternative is to use your preferred photo editor. You can get the dimensions of the image there, and record the *x* and *y* coordinates from there.

There's more...

Credit for the image used in this book goes to Open Clipart. This image was provided by *j4p4n*, and can be found at the following URL:

```
https://openclipart.org/detail/218997/sushi-on-a-boards
```

6
Analytics

In this chapter, we will cover the following topics:

- ▸ Adding a constant line
- ▸ Adding a trend line
- ▸ Adding a reference line
- ▸ Adding a reference band
- ▸ Performing cluster analysis
- ▸ Adding forecasting
- ▸ Performing linear regression with R

Introduction

There are times when it is useful to add additional points of reference to a chart to provide more context for the visualization. Tableau makes it easy to add reference lines, trend lines, box plots, and clusters from the analytics tab in the sidebar. The analytics tab was introduced in Tableau 9.

Appendix C, Working with Tableau 10 introduces the different types of reference components supported in Tableau - line, band, distribution, and box plot. You can also check out the Tableau online documentation, found at `http://bit.ly/tableau-reference-types`, for more details.

Adding a constant line

A constant line is simply a line we add to a graph that has a value that doesn't change. This value is typically hardcoded (or set) and is not determined by other values in the graph. For example, if we wanted to show the value of pi (3.1415927 – depending on the precision you want to show), we can use a constant line.

In this recipe, we will add constant reference lines to visualize players who, relatively, are earning less in salary but getting more in endorsements:

Getting ready

To follow this recipe, open `B05527_06 – STARTER.twbx`. Use the worksheet called **Constant Line**, and connect to the **Top Athlete Salaries (Global Sport Finances)** data source:

How to do it...

Here are the steps to create the graph:

1. Click on the dropdown in the **Marks** card and change the mark to **Circle**.

2. From **Measures**, drag **Salary/Winnings $** to **Columns**.

3. From **Measures**, drag **Endorsements $** to **Rows**.

4. From **Dimensions**, drag **Sport** to **Color**.

5. From **Dimensions**, drag **Athlete** to **Detail**.

6. On the side bar, click on the **Analytics** tab to activate it.

7. Under **Summarize**, drag **Constant Line** from the **Analytics** tab and drop it on the **SUM(Salary/Winnings $)** placeholder:

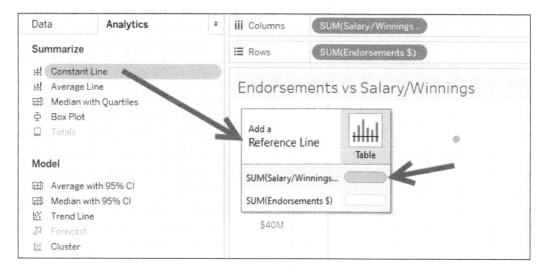

8. Enter the value 20:

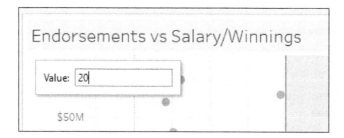

9. Right-click on the constant line that was added and select **Edit**.

10. Set the **Fill Above:** color to **None** and the **Fill Below:** color to a light gray color:

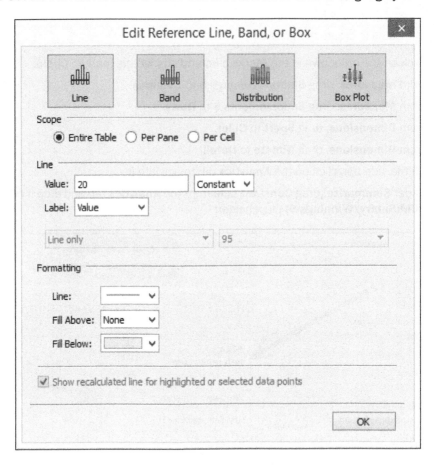

11. Right-click on the constant line again and select **Format**.

12. On the **Format** side bar, under the **Reference Line Label** section, select alignment. Set the **Vertical** alignment to **Top**.

13. From the **Analytics** tab, drag the **Constant Line** again, this time placing it on **SUM(Endorsements $)** placeholder.

14. Set the constant value to 40.

15. Right-click on the new constant line and select **Edit**.

16. Under **Formatting**, set the **Fill Above** color to a light gray color and the **Fill Below** color to **None**.

17. Right-click on the constant line again and select **Format**.

18. On the **Format** side bar, under the **Reference Line Label** section, select **Alignment**. Set the **Vertical** alignment to **Bottom**.

How it works...

A constant line is simply a reference line with a value that does not change. Reference lines are great at showing where values in a view are relative to that point of reference. In Tableau, adding a constant line simply requires dragging the **Constant Line** option from the **Analytics** pane onto your view. If your view has groups, you will be presented the **Pane** and **Cell** options as scope for the reference line, in addition to **Table**.

To edit a constant line, you can right-click on the constant line and choose **Edit**. Alternatively, you can right-click on the axis the reference line refers to, and choose **Edit Reference Line**:

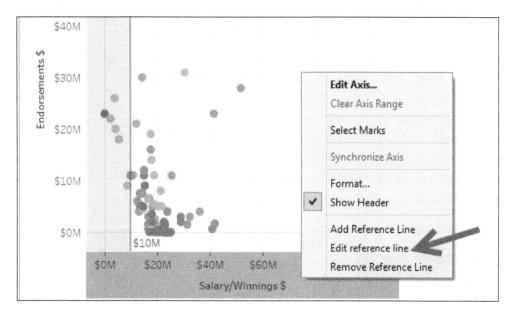

See also

▶ Please refer to the *Adding a reference line* recipe in this chapter

Adding a trend line

Trend lines are typically added to charts to visualize general patterns or movement. An upward trend suggests the two variables being used on the axes are directly proportional, meaning as one value goes up, the other one tends to go up. A downward trend may suggest an inverse relationship between the variables, meaning as one value goes up, the other one goes down.

In this recipe, we will add trend lines for the CO2 emissions of **Canada**, **China**, and **United States**:

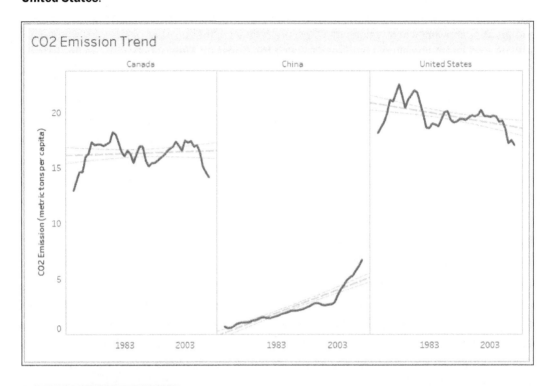

Getting ready

To follow this recipe, open B05527_06 – STARTER.twbx. Use the worksheet called **Trend Line**, and connect to the **CO2 (Worldbank)** data source:

How to do it...

Here are the steps to create the CO2 emission trends lines:

1. From **Dimensions**, drag **Country Name** to the **Filters** shelf.

2. In the **Filters** window, choose **Canada**, **China** and **United States**.

3. From **Dimensions**, drag **Country Name** to **Columns**.

4. From **Dimensions**, right-click and drag **Year DT** to the **Columns** shelf, to the right of **Country Name**. Choose continuous month (that is, **MONTH(Year DT)**, which has a green calendar icon beside it).

5. From **Measures**, drag **CO2 Emission** to **Rows**.

6. Click on the null indicator that appears on the bottom-right of the view, and select **Filter data**:

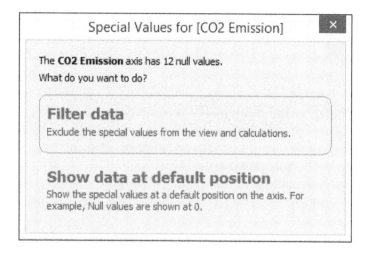

7. On the side bar, click on the **Analytics** tab to activate it.

8. Under **Model**, drag **Trend Line** from the **Analytics** tab and drop it on the **Linear** placeholder:

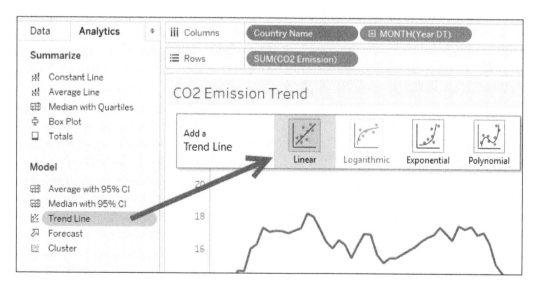

9. Hover over one of the trend lines to see additional information on the trend line **R-Squared** and **P-value**:

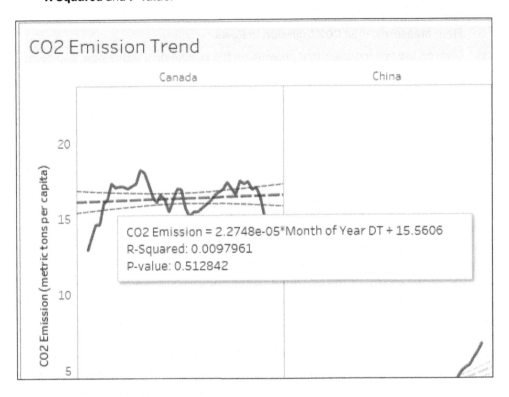

How it works...

Tableau's **Analytics** pane provides a quick way to add trend lines to your view. When you drag the **Trend Line** from the **Analytics** pane, you will be prompted for the type of trend line: **Linear**, **Logarithmic**, **Exponential**, or **Polynomial**:

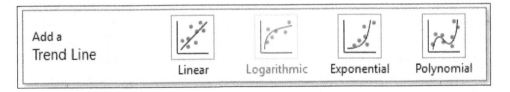

To be able to add trend lines, you need to have two axes that can be interpreted as numeric. Otherwise, the **Trend Line** option is disabled. Dates can be interpreted as numeric so trend lines are generally available for time series graphs.

Once the trend line is in place, you can right-click on the trend line to further edit it, or to describe the trend line or the model:

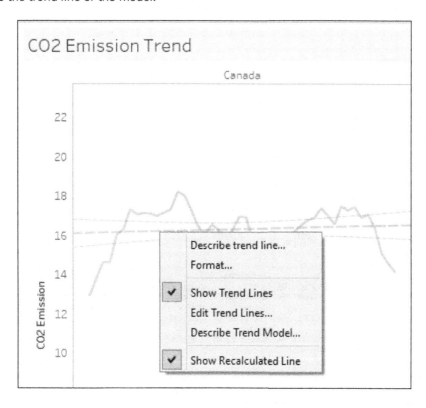

The trend line description shows the **P-value**, the **Equation**, and the **Coefficients**:

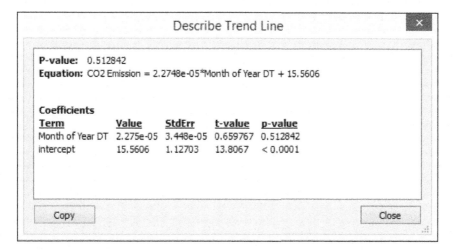

The trend model description box shows the values that were considered for the trend line, and also the significance of the trend model via the p-value:

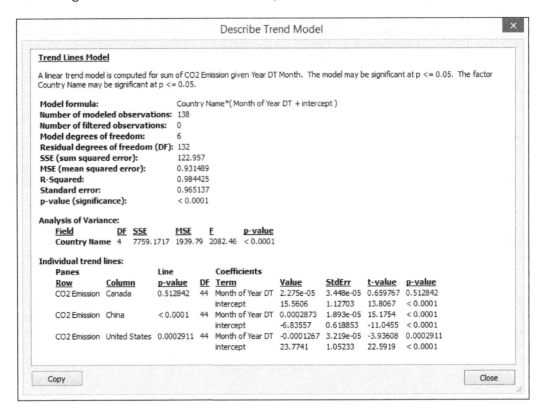

More detailed descriptions of the terms and values can be found in the Tableau online documentation at `http://bit.ly/tableau-trendline-model`.

When you edit the trend line, you can change the model type, as well as add/remove trend line colors, confidence bands, and recalculated fields for highlighted/selected data points:

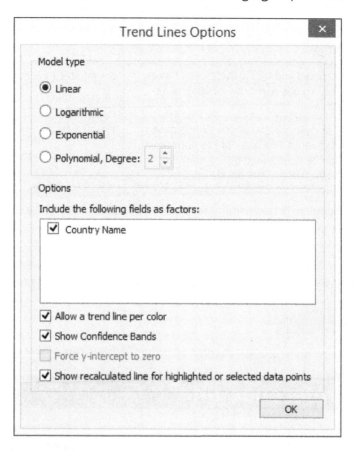

There's more...

The different types of trend lines supported by Tableau are tabulated here. Descriptions of different trend lines are based on a Microsoft Office article about choosing the best trend lines (http://bit.ly/msoffice-choosing-trendlines) and the formulas are from Tableau's online documentation (http://bit.ly/tableau-trendlines):

Type	Description	Formula
Linear	Used with simple linear data sets, and typically shows values are increasing or decreasing at a steady rate.	$Y = b0 + b1 * X + e$

Type	Description	Formula
Logarithmic	A best-fit curved line that is most useful when the rate of change in the data increases or decreases quickly and then levels out.	$Y = b0 + b1 * ln(X) + e$
Exponential	A curved line that is most useful when data values rise or fall at increasing rates.	$Y = e \char`\^ (b0 + b1 * X + e)$
Polynomial	A curved line that is used when data fluctuates. The order of the polynomial can be determined by the number of fluctuations in the data.	$Y = b0 + b1 * X + b2 * X\char`\^2 + ... + e$

The preceding description is taken from *Microsoft Office: Choosing the Best Trendline for your Data*.

According to the Tableau online documentation, regardless of the type you choose:

> *Each trend line in the view visually represents a linear regression statistical model*

See also

Please refer to the *Performing linear regression with R* recipe in this chapter.

Using a reference line

A reference line is simply a line that gets drawn on a chart that represents another measure or point of reference. Reference lines can be useful in providing context to the related chart. For example, a line showing the median will visually show the difference of each mark in the chart relative to the median.

In this recipe, we will show some of the top movie genres from 2007-2011 based on worldwide gross amount and add reference lines to show the average overall and average per year:

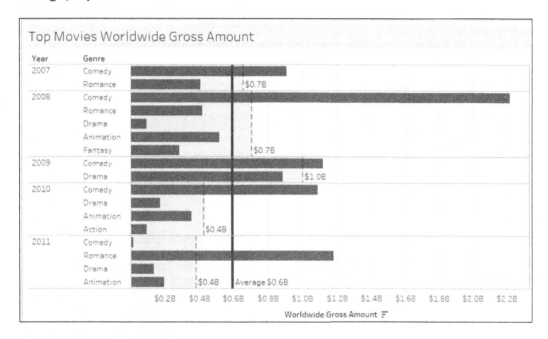

Getting ready

To follow this recipe, open `B05527_06 - STARTER.twbx`. Use the worksheet called **Reference Line**, and connect to the **HollywoodsMostProfitableStories** data source:

How to do it...

Here are the steps to create the bar graph with reference lines:

1. From **Dimensions**, drag **Year** to **Rows**.
2. From **Dimensions**, drag **Genre** to **Rows** to the right of the **Year** pill.

3. From **Measures**, drag **Worldwide Gross Amount** to **Columns**.

4. Hover over the **Worldwide Gross Amount** axis, and click on the sort icon once to sort the bars in descending order.

5. On the side bar, click on the **Analytics** tab to activate it.

6. Under **Custom**, drag **Reference Line** from the **Analytics** tab and drop it onto the **Table** placeholder:

7. Set the following for this reference line:

   ❑ **Scope** as **Entire Table**

   ❑ Under **Line**, set**Value**, set the aggregation to **Average** of the **SUM(Worldwide Gross Amount)**

   ❑ Under **Line Label**, set it to **Custom** with **Average <Value>** as text; note you can use the **>** button to insert values

   ❑ Under **Formatting**, set **Line** to a thick, dark red line

   ❑ Under **Formatting**, set **Fill Above:** to **None**

❑ Under **Formatting**, set **Fill Below:** to **None**:

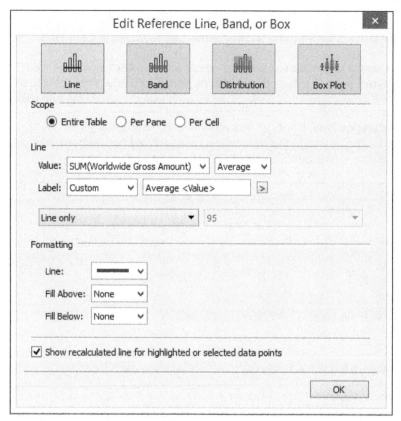

8. Click **OK** when done.

9. Under **Custom**, drag **Reference Line** again from the **Analytics** tab and this time drop it onto **Pane**.

10. Set the following for this reference line:

   ❑ **Scope** is **Per Pane**

   ❑ Under **Line Value**, set the aggregation to **Average** of the **SUM(Worldwide Gross Amount)**

   ❑ Under **Line Label**, set it to **Value**

   ❑ Under **Formatting**, set **Line** to a thick gray line

   ❑ Under **Formatting**, set **Fill Above** to **None**

   ❑ Under **Formatting**, set **Fill Below** to a light yellow color

11. Click **OK** when done.

How it works...

Reference lines can provide additional context to our visualizations, by adding a visual cue that identifies where a reference is relative to the values we are looking at.

In Tableau, adding a reference line is made easier with the **Analytics** pane. With a single drag from the **Analytics** pane, a reference line can be added to a view. Alternatively, the reference line can also be added by right-clicking on an existing axis and choosing **Add Reference Line**.

In the **Edit Reference Line, Band, or Box** window, additional settings can be applied, such as scope, fill, and a choice to add the confidence interval. From this window, the type of reference can also be chosen – line, band, distribution, or box plot:

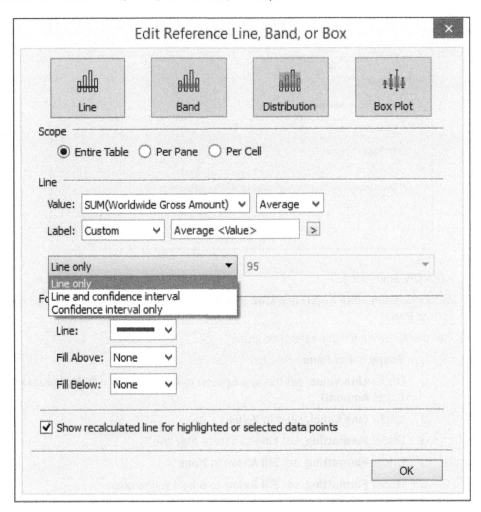

There's more...

When adding a reference line, it is important to remember that the field you want to use as a reference line must be in the view already. If it is not in the view, and if it is not a parameter, the value must be added first to the **Details** property in the **Marks** card before it can be used in the **Reference** line window.

Using parameters for reference lines also add interactivity to your views. This allows the consumers of your dashboards to try out different values and see the visualization change instantly.

See also

> ▸ Please refer to the *Adding a constant line* recipe in this chapter
> ▸ Please refer to the *Adding a reference band* recipe in this chapter

Adding a reference band

A reference band creates a *banded* or shaded area in a chart, and can show if other points fall within a range or interest or not.

In this recipe, will highlight the time range when water quality complaints are filed using a reference band:

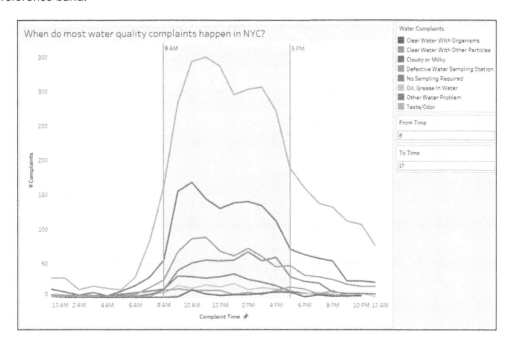

Getting ready

To follow this recipe, open B05527_06 - STARTER.twbx. Use the worksheet called **Reference Band** and connect to the **NYC Water Quality Complaints** data source:

How to do it...

The following are the steps to create the time series graph with reference band in this recipe:

1. From **Dimensions**, right-click and drag **Created Date DT** to **Columns** and select **Discrete Hour**:

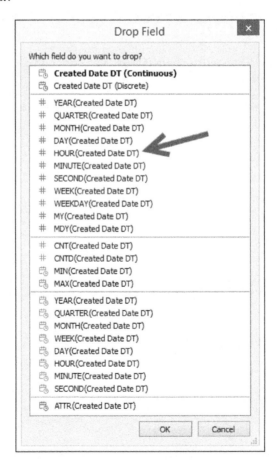

2. Right-click on the **HOUR(Created Date DT)** field in **Columns** and select **Continuous.**

3. Right-click on the **HOUR(Created Date DT)** field in **Columns**, and select **Format**. On the side bar, under **Scale**, choose **12-Hour** format for **Dates**:

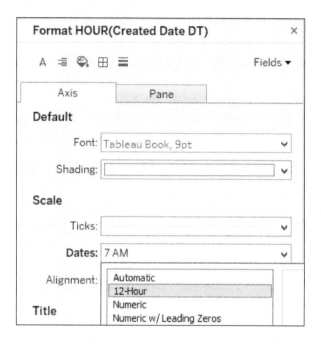

4. Right-click on the **Created Date DT** axis to edit axis. Change the axis title to **# Complaints**.

5. From **Measures**, drag **Number of Records** to **Rows**.

6. Edit the **Number of Records** axis and change the axis title to **Complaint Time**.

7. From **Dimensions**, drag **Descriptor (group)** to **Color** in the **Marks** card.

8. On the side bar, click on the **Analytics** tab to activate it.

9. Under **Custom**, drag **Reference Band** from the **Analytics** tab and drop it onto **Table** in the **HOUR(Created Date DT)** placeholder:

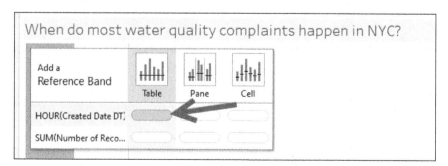

10. In the **Edit Reference Line, Band, or Box** window, use the following settings:
    - ❏ **Scope** is **Entire Table**
    - ❏ **Band From Value** is **From Time**
    - ❏ **Band From Label** is **Custom**, and type in **8 AM**
    - ❏ **Band To Value** is **To Time**
    - ❏ **Band To Label** is **Custom**, and type in 5 PM:

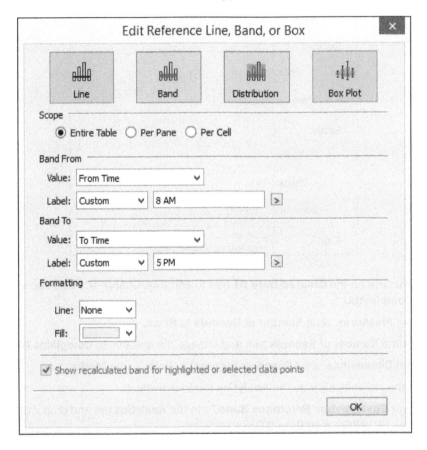

11. Click **OK** when done.
12. Right-click on the **Reference Band** and select **Format**.
13. Set the **Alignment** for the **Reference Line Label** to top.

How it works...

A reference band is essentially two reference lines where the range between the lines are typically shaded. Reference bands help draw the eyes to the range that may be important to highlight or emphasize.

In Tableau, we can drag **Reference Band** from the **Analytics** pane and drop it onto our view. If we have different groups in the view, we will be presented with the scope options **Tableau**, **Pane**, and **Cell**. If there is more than one axis, we also have the option of creating the band on one of the axes or both.

With a reference band, we need to supply the range – the **Band From** and the **Band To** value. Before we can select this in the **Edit Reference Line, Band, or Box** window, we need to make sure the fields for the boundary values are already in the view. If it is not yet there, and it does not need to be placed in a way that affects the overall view, we can place these fields in the **Details** property in the **Marks** card.

For a reference band, we typically also need to change the fill so that the range between the values are shaded.

See also

- ▸ Please refer to the *Adding a constant line* recipe in this chapter
- ▸ Please refer to the *Adding a reference line* recipe in this chapter

Performing cluster analysis

Borrowing from the Wikipedia definition:

> *"cluster analysis or clustering is the task of grouping a set of objects in such a way that objects in the same group (called a cluster) are more similar (in some sense or another) to each other than to those in other groups (clusters)."*

In this recipe, we will try out the new clustering feature introduced in Tableau 10 to group athletes based on endorsements and salary/winnings:

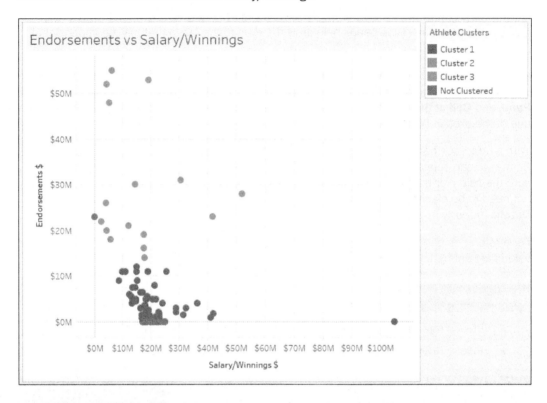

Getting ready

To follow this recipe, open *B05527_06 – STARTER.twbx*. Use the worksheet called **Cluster** and connect to the **Top Athlete Salaries (Global Sport Finances)** data source:

How to do it...

Here are the steps to create the scatter plot with clusters:

1. Click on the dropdown in the **Marks** card and change the mark to **Circle**.

2. From **Measures**, drag **Salary/Winnings $** to **Columns**.

3. From **Measures**, drag **Endorsements $** to **Rows**.

4. From **Dimensions**, drag **Athlete** to **Detail**.

5. On the side bar, click on the **Analytics** tab to activate it.

6. Under **Model**, drag **Cluster** to your view:

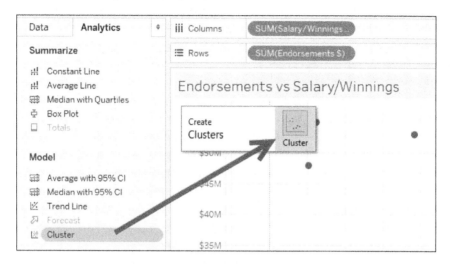

7. In the **Clusters** window, set the number of clusters to 3:

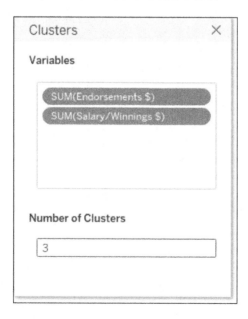

8. Close the **Clusters** window when done.

How it works...

Tableau 10 makes it easier to do cluster analysis. Under the **Analytics** pane in the side bar, there is a new option to add clusters to your view. You simply drag **Cluster** onto your view, and the clusters will be automatically computed. You will also be presented with a window that asks you which variables need to be considered in the cluster, and how many clusters need to be created:

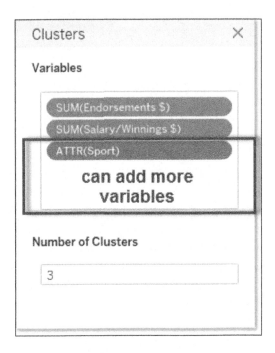

If you need to consider additional measures and/or dimensions when computing the clusters, you can drag them onto the variables pane.

By default, the cluster is placed on **Color** in the **Marks** card. When you right-click on this pill, you will see new options to edit or describe the cluster:

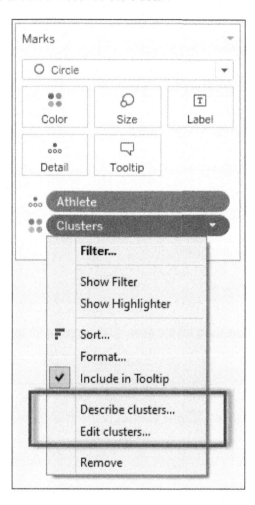

When you choose **Describe clusters...**, you can show the **Summary** values computed for the cluster:

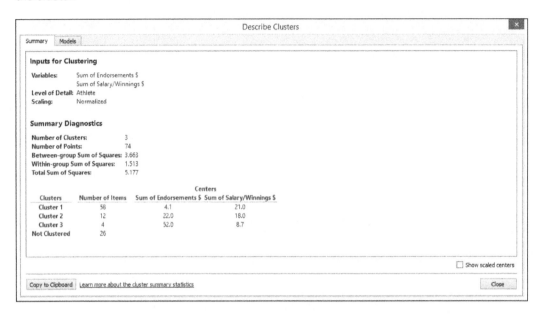

You can also show the model used for the analysis of variance for the cluster:

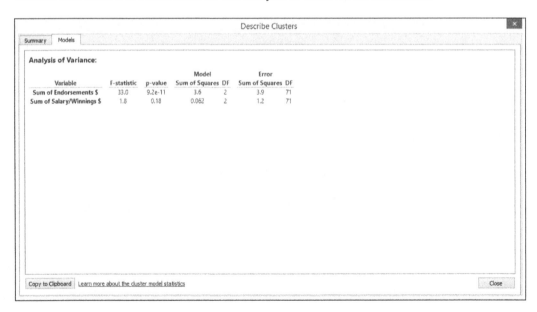

There's more...

Clusters can also be saved back to your Tableau data source. When you drag the cluster pill from the **Color** property in the **Marks** card back to the side bar, the cluster gets saved in the form of a group:

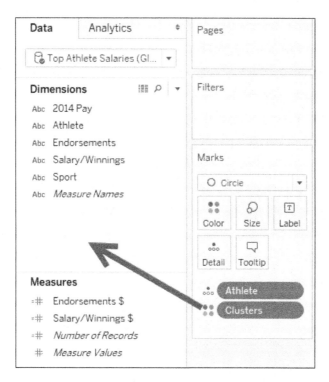

If you would like to take advantage of existing software applications such as R, SPSS, or SAS for your clustering calculations, you can connect to these data sources in Tableau. Tableau also supports R integration, which allows you to write R code from within Tableau.

See also

Please refer to the *Performing linear regression with R* recipe in this chapter

Visualizing forecast

Forecasting is the process of trying to predict what might happen in the future based on historical data and trends.

In this recipe, we will use Tableau's forecasting feature to forecast upcoming floods using flood data from 1985 to 2014:

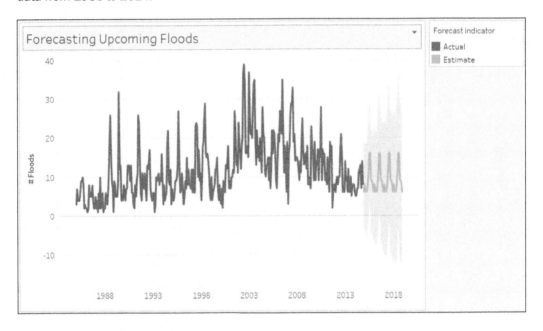

Getting ready

To follow this recipe, open *BO5527_06 – STARTER.twbx*. Use the worksheet called **Forecasting** and connect to the **MasterTable (FlooddataMasterListrev)** data source:

How to do it...

Here are the steps to create the view in this recipe:

1. From **Dimensions**, right-click and drag the **Began** field to the **Columns** shelf. Choose continuous **MONTH(Began)**:

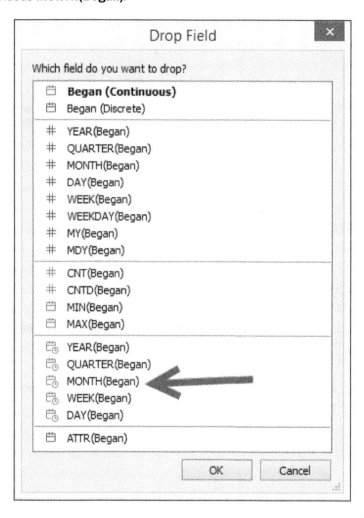

2. From **Measures**, drag **Number of Records** to the **Rows** shelf.
3. Right-click anywhere in the view to show additional options.

4. Under **Forecast**, select **Show Forecast**:

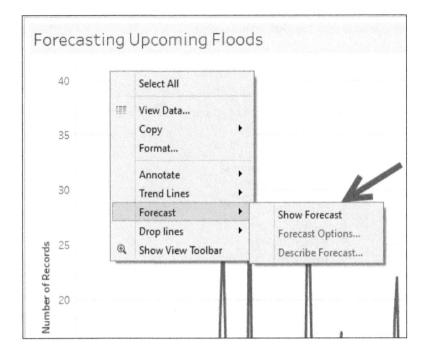

How it works...

Tableau's forecasting feature uses a technique called **exponential smoothing**, as described in the online documentation at `http://bit.ly/tableau-forecasting`. Typically, when forecasting, one of the axes needs to be temporal (or date-related).

To add a forecast, we simply need to right-click on the view and, under **Forecast**, select **Show Forecast**. Alternatively, this can be added from the **Analysis** menu.

To describe the forecast, we can also right-click on the view, and under **Forecast**, select **Describe Forecast**. The window that pops up has two panes: one for **Summary** and another for **Models**. Here is an example of the **Summary** window for a forecast:

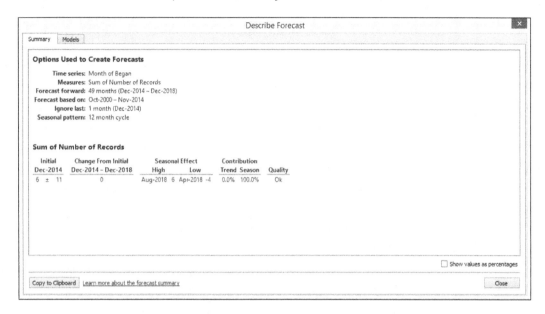

The **Forecast Model** provides additional information on the model used, including the model trend, seasonality, quality metrics, and smoothing coefficients:

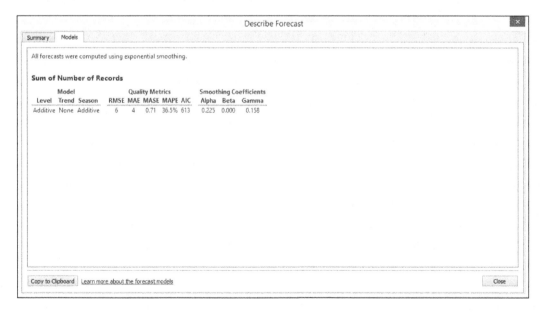

There are not many options to change or set in Tableau's forecasting functionality. The limited options that can be changed include the forecast length, seasonality, and prediction intervals:

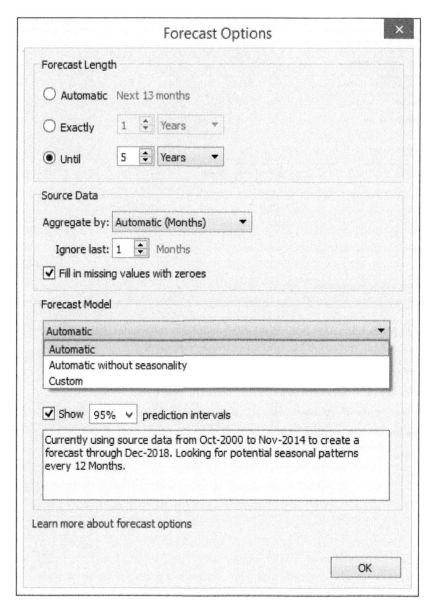

There's more...

Additional forecast results, as shown in the following screenshot, are made available through the measure in the **Rows** or **Columns** shelf that is being forecasted:

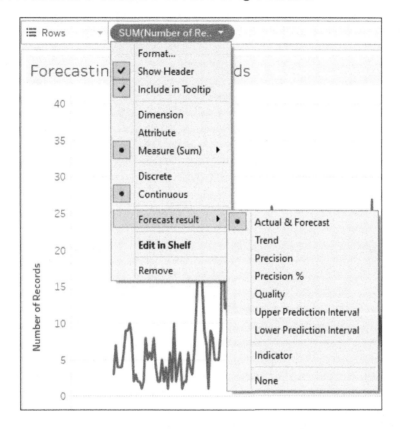

If you want to use more complex models for your forecast, you can take advantage of R integration with Tableau.

See also

Please refer to the *Performing linear regression with R* recipe in this chapter

Performing linear regression with R

Linear regression is a common technique to find the best fit straight line in a scatter plot. The resulting line can help in predictive analysis.

In this recipe, we will add trend lines to CO2 Emission graphs using R:

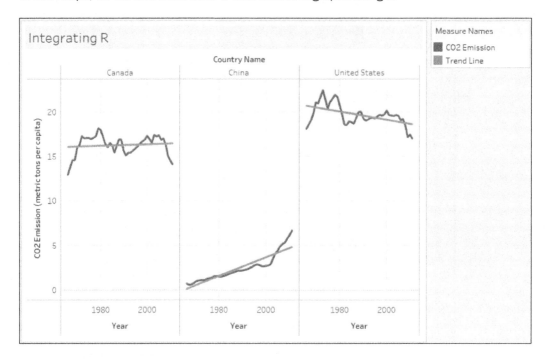

Getting ready

This recipe has a few prerequisites before it can be followed:

1. Install R. The R Project for Statistical Computing website is `https://www.r-project.org/`.

2. Optionally, install RStudio from `https://www.rstudio.com/`, which is an integrated environment for R.

3. Install the Rserve package by running the following in R:

    ```
    install.packages("Rserve");
    library(Rserve);
    run.Rserve();
    ```

4. You will get a message that says the connection is blocked:

```
> install.packages("Rserve");
Installing package into 'C:/Users/Donabel/Documents/R/win-library/3.3'
(as 'lib' is unspecified)
trying URL 'https://cran.rstudio.com/bin/windows/contrib/3.3/Rserve_1.7-3.zip'
Content type 'application/zip' length 631808 bytes (617 KB)
downloaded 617 KB

package 'Rserve' successfully unpacked and MD5 sums checked

The downloaded binary packages are in
        C:\Users\Donabel\AppData\Local\Temp\RtmpATCtNd\downloaded_packages
> library(Rserve);
> run.Rserve()
-- running Rserve in this R session (pid=3944), 1 server(s) --
(This session will block until Rserve is shut down)
```

5. Go to **Help**, and under **Settings and Performance**, select **Manage External Service Connection...**:

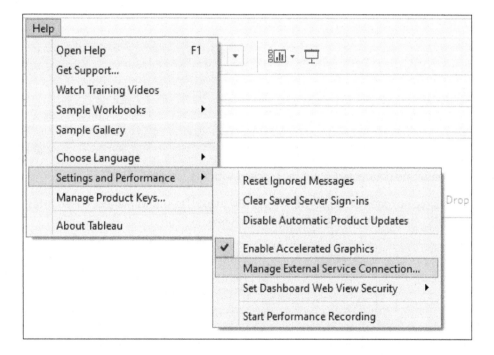

6. Type `localhost` for the **Server:**, and leave the **Port/API Key:** to **6311**. Test the connection, and ensure you get a successful connection message before proceeding:

Once R is ready and connected, you may proceed with the recipe.

To follow this recipe, open *B05527_06 – STARTER.twbx*. Use the worksheet called **Integrating R**, and connect to the **CO2 (Worldbank)** data source:

How to do it...

Here are the steps to create the view with R-generated trend lines:

1. From **Dimensions**, drag **Country Name** to the **Filters** shelf.

2. In the **Filters** window, choose **Canada**, **China**, and **United States**.

3. From **Dimensions**, drag **Country Name** to **Columns**.

4. From **Dimensions**, drag **Year** to **Columns**.

5. Right-click on the **Year** pill in **Columns** and choose **Continuous**.

6. From **Measures**, drag **CO2 Emission** to **Rows**.

7. Click on the null indicator that appears on the bottom right of the view and select **Filter data**:

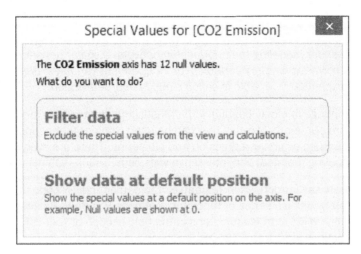

8. Create a new calculated field called **Trend Line** with the following R formula:

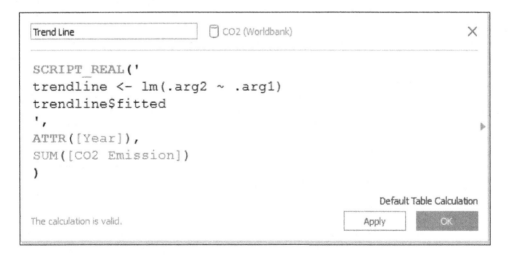

9. Drag the new calculated field **Trend Line** from **Measures** to **Rows**, to the right of **CO2 Emission**.

10. Right-click on the **Trend Line** pill and set **Compute Using** to **Pane across**.

11. Right-click on the **Trend Line** pill and select **Dual Axis**.

12. Right-click on the **Trend Line** axis and select **Synchronize Axis**.

13. Right-click on the **Trend Line** axis and uncheck **Show Header**.

How it works...

Linear regression, according to Wikipedia, is defined as follows:

> *"... an approach for modeling the relationship between a scalar dependent variable y and one or more explanatory variables (or independent variables) denoted x. The case of one explanatory variable is called simple linear regression."*

The R scripting language is widely popular with statisticians, data miners, and data scientists. There are numerous libraries that can be used within R that support various statistical analyses, such as linear regression and clustering. There are even libraries for high performance computing (Pandas) and interactive web visualizations (Shiny).

R support in Tableau was introduced in Tableau 8. Tableau enables R code to be executed from within Tableau by using a series of functions that pass R code to R using the `Rserve` package. You can find a list of these functions in the help section of your calculated field window. All the functions start with `SCRIPT`:

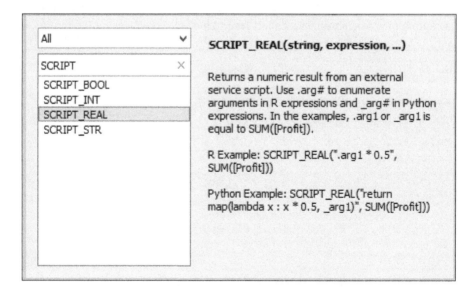

These `SCRIPT` functions will accept R code in the form of a string. In our recipe, we are using the R function `lm`, which is used to fit linear models:

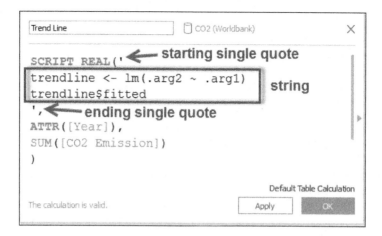

The string expression is followed by the arguments, or the Tableau-supplied values that will be used to replace the arguments in the R code:

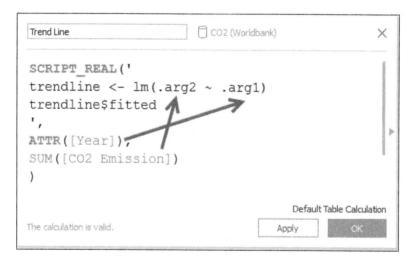

The SCRIPT functions expect aggregated arguments. In the case of dimensions, you may need to resort to using aggregated functions such as MIN, MAX, and ATTR to pass them as arguments. This is why we had to enclose the Year field in ATTR when we passed this field in our **Trend Line** calculated field:

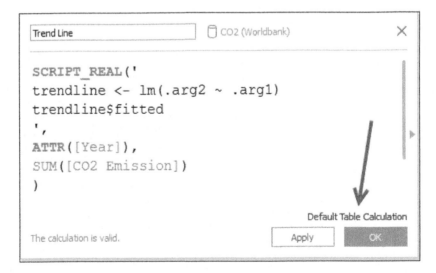

These functions return scalar values back. To be more exact, they return a single column (or vector) of values back. Tableau also treats the resulting values as table calculations:

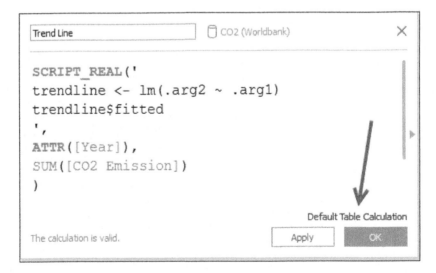

This is why, when you use calculated fields with R expressions, you may need to adjust the addressing and partitioning of the fields depending on the data and layout in your view.

If you need a refresher on table calculations, there is a section on table calculations in *Appendix A, Calculated Fields Primer*.

Before R code can be executed, it is also important to set up your environment so that R is installed, and so that the RServe package is also installed and running.

It is important to filter out the null values before you add the calculated trend line field from R. Otherwise, you will get an error that says there is a mismatch in the number of values in your view and the ones returned by the SCRIPT function:

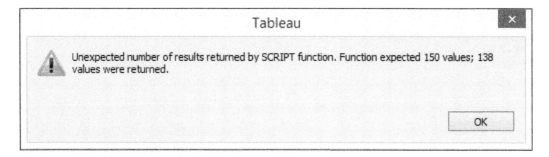

See also

Please refer to the *Adding a trend line* recipe in this chapter

7
Data Preparation

In this chapter, we will cover the following topics:

- Using the Data Interpreter and pivot
- Using the legacy Jet driver
- Using schema.ini to resolve data type issues
- Pivoting columns
- Using union
- Using join
- Using blend

Introduction

In a perfect world, we wouldn't even need to have this chapter. In a perfect world, we would have perfect, clean data that we could easily analyze in Tableau. But, alas, in reality, the data that we need to use will most likely need to be cleaned, transformed, and managed before we can effectively use it in Tableau.

There are tools that exclusively help clean and re-shape data. Many refer to these as **ETL** (**Extract, Transform, and Load**) tools. While Tableau is not an ETL tool, it has the ability to help clean or prepare data if it is not possible to clean or prepare it at the data source. Calculated fields, discussed in *Appendix A, Calculated Fields Primer*, are also invaluable in the data cleaning process.

Using the Data Interpreter and pivot

In this recipe, we will clean up the following spreadsheet on Canada international student permits and ready it for Tableau:

	A	B	C	D	E	F	G	H	I	J	K	L	M	N
1	Canada - International students by destination and year in which permit(s) became effective, Q1 2014 - Q2 2016*													
2														
3				2014						2015				2016
4	Destination	Q1	Q2	Q3	Q4	Total unique** persons	Q1	Q2	Q3	Q4	Total unique** persons	Q1	Q2	Total unique** persons
5	Newfoundland and Labrador	234	227	664	253	1,322	212	212	920	352	1,649	348	352	694
6	Prince Edward Island	111	115	323	73	610	98	168	428	227	908	204	214	413
7	Nova Scotia	1,006	1,049	2,610	852	5,302	862	865	3,672	1,086	6,306	1,241	1,416	2,627
8	New Brunswick	389	417	1,010	385	2,146	316	341	1,272	433	2,302	481	480	952
9	Quebec	4,930	4,270	16,846	4,387	29,240	4,192	3,457	18,832	4,981	30,416	5,046	5,673	10,566
10	Ontario	14,526	19,362	40,968	17,628	88,923	12,069	15,262	51,875	21,358	97,061	17,727	25,774	42,822
11	Manitoba	824	1,050	2,033	1,022	4,729	821	1,051	3,604	1,633	6,863	1,642	1,866	3,436
12	Saskatchewan	536	644	1,210	536	2,833	474	651	2,112	756	3,879	810	931	1,704
13	Alberta	2,486	2,749	4,910	2,249	11,859	1,970	2,596	7,493	2,956	14,383	3,131	4,070	7,064
14	British Columbia	10,865	12,570	28,504	9,367	59,116	9,156	9,994	29,837	11,243	58,085	12,091	15,530	27,097
15	Northwest Territories	--	--	9	--	16	--	--	7	--	14	7	--	10
16	Nunavut	--	0	0	--	--	0	--	0	--	--	0	0	0
17	Yukon	7	6	10	--	23	--	5	17	8	34	9	21	29
18	Province/Territory not stated	2	7	16	9	34	3	9	39	28	79	12	30	42
19	Total unique** persons	35,909	42,439	99,064	36,747	205,428	30,167	34,602	120,086	45,062	221,279	42,737	56,329	97,320
20														
21	* Data for 2015 and 2016 are preliminary estimates and are subject to change. For 2014, these are updated numbers and different from those of Facts and Figures 2014.													
22	** The total unique count may not equal to the sum of permit holders in each destination as an individual may hold more than one type of permit over a given period.													
23														
24	Notes:													
25	- Due to privacy considerations, some cells in this table have been suppressed and replaced with the notation "--". As a result, components may not sum to the total indicated. In general we have suppressed cells containing less than five cases except in circumstances where, in our judgment, we are not releasing personal information on an identifiable individual.													
26	- The table on Temporary Residents (TR) has been revised to reflect the June 20, 2014 overhaul of the Temporary Foreign Worker Program (TFWP). The reporting methodology has also been revised to count TRs, which includes Foreign Workers and International Students, based on the type of permit held by a TR (effective from the date that the permit was signed, or a valid permit at the end of a given year). As a result of the changes above, the reports for each permit holder type has been separated in order to enhance clarity.													
27														
28	For further information, please refer to the Facts and figures 2014 – Immigration overview: Temporary residents overview, and the glossary of terms and concepts.													
29														
30	Source: IRCC, June 30, 2016 Data													
31														

Getting ready

To follow this recipe, download the file from the Citizenship and Immigration Canada website using the following URL:

```
http://www.cic.gc.ca/opendata-donneesouvertes/data/IRCC_IS_0004_E.xls
```

How to do it...

Here are the steps to clean up the file:

1. Connect to the Excel file in this recipe. Make sure you choose **Excel** from the **To a File** section:

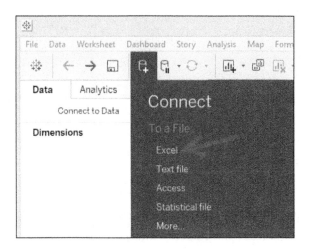

2. Check the checkbox beside **Use Data Interpreter**. Note that when this checkbox is checked, the label changes to **Cleaned with Data Interpreter**:

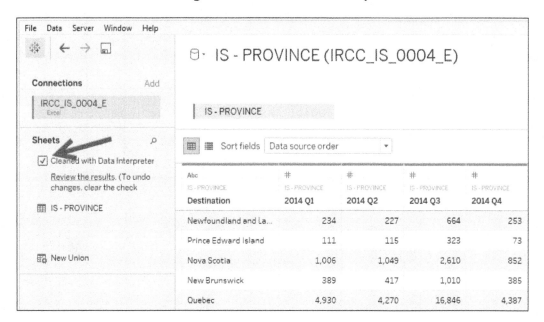

3. Select all fields except for **Destination**.

4. While the fields are selected, right-click and choose **Pivot**:

5. Right-click the new fields to rename them:

    ❑   Change **Pivot Field Names** to **Period**

    ❑   Change **Pivot Field Values** to **International Students**

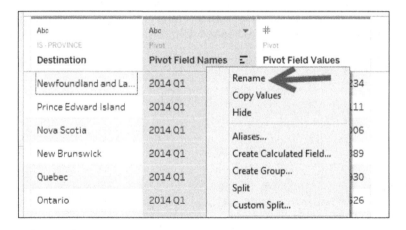

6. Click on **Add** underneath **Filters**:

7. In the **Select a field:** option, choose **Period**:

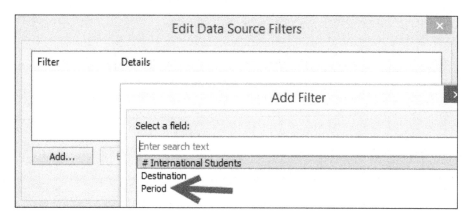

8. In the filter window for **Period**, under the **Wildcard** tab, type Total and check the **Exclude** checkbox:

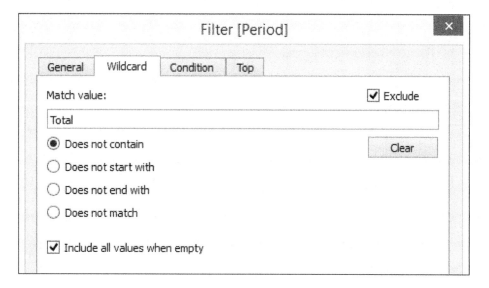

9. Once you click **OK**, you should see the following in the **Edit Data Source Filters** box:

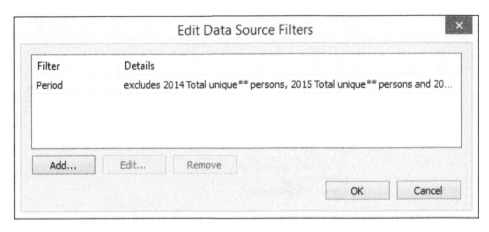

10. Click on **OK** when done.

11. Under the **Filters**, click on **Edit** to add one more filter:

12. This time, choose the **Destination** field:

13. In the filter window for **Destination**, under the **Wildcard** tab, type `Total` and check the **Exclude** checkbox.

14. Once you click **OK**, you should see the following in the **Edit Data Source Filters** box:

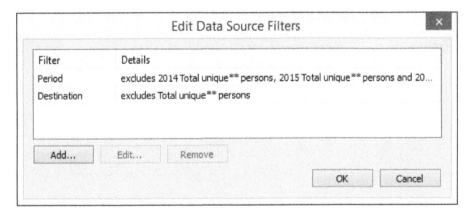

15. Click **OK** when done.

16. In the preview pane, click on the **Abc** symbol above **Destination** and change the **Geographic Role** to **State/Province**:

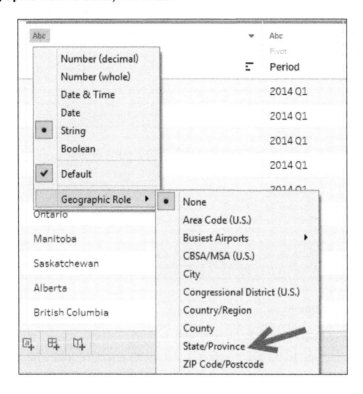

17. Create a new sheet and create your visualization.

How it works...

Tableau works best with clean, tall, and narrow data instead of short and wide data. The same measures should ideally be provided in a single column instead of spread out.

The original Excel file is a common type of file that many data professionals have to work with. The Excel file has a header, a footer, and the measures are spread across the columns. The number of international students—a measure—is spread out across 13 columns.

When you first connect to this Excel file, this is what you will see:

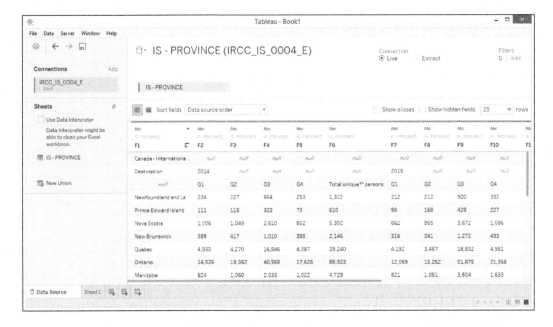

This file needs to be cleaned up:

▸ Header and footer needs to be removed

▸ Year values need to be a dimension, since these are descriptors for the measure

▸ The measure, which is the number of international students, need to be placed in a single column

When we use the Tableau Data Interpreter, it will clean up the headers and footers, but will not clean up the year dimension and the measure for number of international students. When we run the Data Interpreter, we can also choose to review the results by clicking on the provided link. The first tab, presented here, provides the key to what the Data Interpreter does:

	A	B	C	D	E	F	G	H	I	J	K	L
2		**Key for Understanding the Data Interpreter Results**										
3												
4												
5		Use the key to understand how your data source has been interpreted.										
6		To view the results, click a worksheet tab.										
7		Note: Tableau never makes changes to your underlying data source.										
8												
9												
10												
11		**Key:**										
12			Data is interpreted as column headers (field names).									
13			Data is interpreted as values in your data source.									
14			Data derived from a merged cell is interpreted as value in your data source.									
15			Data is ignored and not included as part of your data source.									
16			Data has been excluded from your data source.									
17			Note: To search for all excluded data, use CRTL +F on Windows									
18			or Command F on the Mac, and then type '***DATA REMOVED***'.									
19												
20												
21		If the Data Interpreter has interpreted the Tableau data source incorrectly, close the spreadsheet,										
22		and then clear the Cleaned with Data Interpreter check box from the Data Source page.										
23		If the Tableau data source continues to be interpreted incorrectly or for general information										
24		about why some data was removed by the Data Interpreter, refer to										
25		Resolving Common Issues with Data Interpreter Results										
26		Help Tableau improve the Data Interpreter by emailing your file to support@tableau.com										
27		or filing a support request with an attached file at:										
28												
29		http://tableau.com/support/request										

To further clean our data source, we need to pivot the remaining year so the values and number of international students are stored in single columns.

The original Excel file has some total fields, which we excluded, so that we can keep the granularity of the measure consistent:

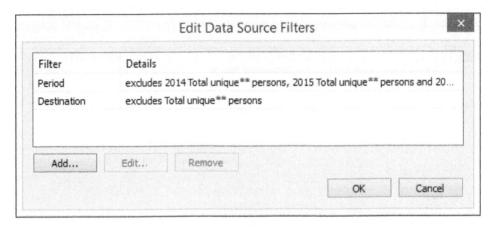

For example, we would not want to sum all the measures and the field for total unique persons.

From here, we can create visualizations that are easier to work with in Tableau. The following screenshot depicts the number of students per period:

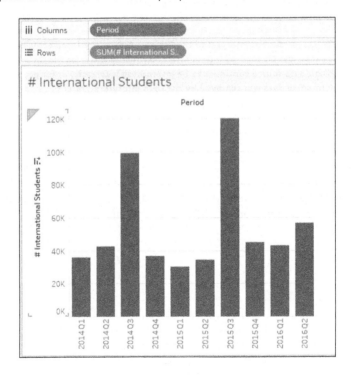

Since we have geocoded the **Destination** and assigned it the **State/Province** geographic role, we can also create a filled map to see where students are going:

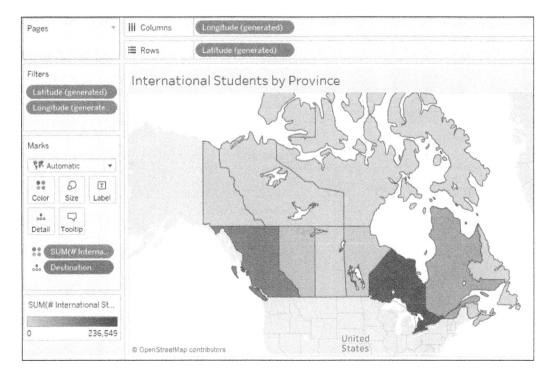

Although the **Destination** field is geocoded to **State/Province**, we will still need the **Country** information before we can successfully create a map. For this data set, we can simply set the country manually by going to the **Map** menu item, and selecting **Edit Locations**. We can set this to **Canada**:

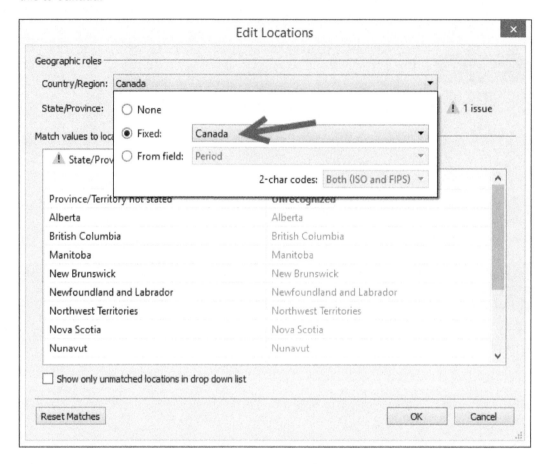

Alternatively, we can create a field for **Country** and use that in the geocoding.

There's more...

You can probably see that there is additional cleanup and transformation that can be done. **Period**, for example, can be split further into year and quarter. We can even go as far as creating a date for the start of the period. This can be done using a calculated field:

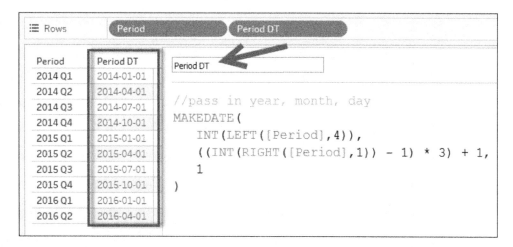

See also

Please refer to the *Creating a bar chart* recipe in *Chapter 1, Basic Charts*.

Please refer to the *Adding data layers to default map* recipe in *Chapter 5, Maps and Geospatial Visualization*.

Using the legacy Jet driver

In this recipe, we will use the New York Restaurant Inspections Excel file and use the legacy Jet driver to shape the file so we can have both the inspection date and grade date in the same column. This will allow us to visualize how many restaurants were inspected and graded for a specific date:

	H CUISINE DESCRIPTION	I INSPECTION DATE	K VIOLATION CODE	N SCORE	O GRADE	P GRADE DATE
1	CUISINE DESCRIPTION	INSPECTION DATE	VIOLATION CODE	SCORE	GRADE	GRADE DATE
2	Indian	02-18-2016	10B	13	A	02-18-2016
3	American	05-19-2016	02G	13	A	05-19-2016
4	Chinese	04-09-2015	04L	26	B	04-09-2015
5	Tex-Mex	08-07-2014	10F	10	A	08-07-2014
6	Caribbean	12-18-2014	04L	6		
7	Japanese	07-23-2013	08A	32		
8	Bakery	01-06-2016	04N	20	B	01-06-2016
9	Bakery	05-28-2015	04L	9	A	05-28-2015
10	Russian	04-30-2015	08A	27		
11	Hotdogs	12-07-2015	08A	13		
12	Latin (Cuban, Dominican, Puerto R	06-09-2014	06C	11		
13	Chinese	05-14-2015	10F	7	A	05-14-2015
14	American	03-14-2014	10F	12	A	03-14-2014
15	Asian	01-28-2014	06E	22		
16	Seafood	12-11-2014	04H	13	A	12-11-2014
17	CafÃ©/Coffee/Tea	10-16-2015	10F	9	A	10-16-2015
18	Bakery	10-04-2014				
19	CafÃ©/Coffee/Tea	08-06-2014	10F	8	A	08-06-2014

Getting ready

To follow this recipe, download the file from the New York City Open Data website using the following URL:

```
https://nycopendata.socrata.com/Health/DOHMH-New-York-City-
Restaurant-Inspection-Results/xx67-kt59/data
```

Once you have downloaded the data, save the file as `DOHMH_New_York_City_Restaurant_Inspection_Results.xls` (Microsoft Excel 97-2003 Worksheet). Note that the records may have been updated between the time of writing and the time of your download.

How to do it...

Here are the steps to prepare the Excel file:

1. Click on **New Data Source** icon, and choose **Excel**:

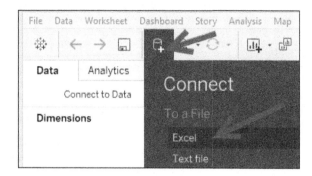

2. Choose DOHMH_New_York_City_Restaurant_Inspection_Results.xls, and select **Open with Legacy Connection**:

3. In the **Connection** window, remove the existing connection to the one sheet in the Excel file:

4. Drag **New Custom SQL** to the main connection pane:

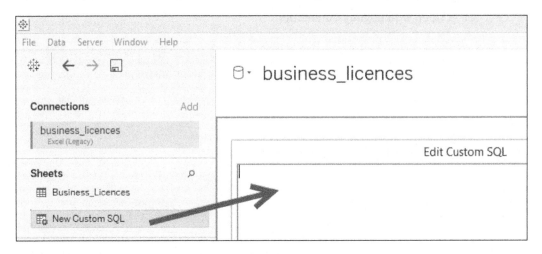

5. Add the following code to the **Edit Custom SQL** window:

```
SELECT
[DBA],
[CAMIS],
[CUISINE DESCRIPTION],
[INSPECTION DATE],
[GRADE DATE],
[INSPCTION DATE] AS [Date],
'Inspected' AS [Type]
```

```
FROM [DOHMH New York City Restaurant$]


UNION ALL


SELECT
[DBA],
[CAMIS],
[CUISINE DESCRIPTION],
[INSPECTION DATE],
[GRADE DATE],
[GRADE DATE] AS [Date],
'Graded' AS [Type]
FROM [DOHMH New York City Restaurant$]
```

6. In the preview window, click on the **Abc** symbol above the **Date** field and select **Date** to change the data type to **Date**:

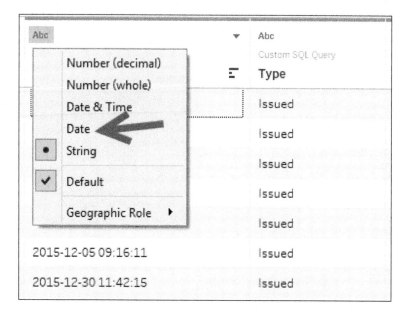

7. Add a new sheet and create your visualization using this data set.

How it works...

The challenge in this recipe is that we often have a universal notion of date, that is, a date is a day that isn't specific to any events. We may want to summarize or aggregate measures based on this universal notion of dates. However, in reality, dates may exist in different fields with different contexts, and this can limit our ability to work on them as a single unit.

In the Excel file for this recipe, we want to count how many restaurants were inspected and how many were graded for a specific date. The Excel file does not have a generic date field that allows us to count how many were inspected or graded. Thus, we need to re-shape our data so that the **Inspection Date** and **Grade Date** exist in one column instead of two.

If we are using an Excel file as our data source, we can potentially use the legacy Jet connection, which allows custom SQL statements against the Excel file.

 The legacy Connection option was introduced in Tableau 8.2. You can learn more about this in the Tableau KB article *Differences between Legacy and Default Excel and Text File Connections*, which can be found at http://onlinehelp.tableau.com/current/pro/desktop/en-us/help.htm#upgrading_connection.html.

In our recipe, we used the following custom SQL statement against our Excel file:

```
Edit Custom SQL                                    ×

SELECT
[DBA],
[CAMIS],
[CUISINE DESCRIPTION],
[INSPECTION DATE],
[GRADE DATE],
[INSPECTION DATE] AS [Date],
'Inspected' AS [Type]
FROM [DOHMH New York City Restaurant$]

UNION ALL

SELECT
[DBA],
[CAMIS],
[CUISINE DESCRIPTION],
[INSPECTION DATE],
[GRADE DATE],
[GRADE DATE] AS [Date],
'Graded' AS [Type]
FROM [DOHMH New York City Restaurant$]


  Preview Results...    Insert Parameter ▼              OK        Cancel
```

When we query our Excel spreadsheet, each tab will be treated as a table and referenced as the worksheet name with a $ symbol at the end and enclosed in square brackets, like so `[DOHMH New York City Restaurant$]`.

 QuerySurge has a good short tutorial on using SQL against Excel spreadsheets here: `http://bit.ly/QuerySurge-SQL-against-Excel`.

What we are doing in this query is stacking two copies of the original data set on top of each other using the `UNION ALL` set operator, and introducing two new fields—**Date** and **Type**. This forces one field to contain the two dates we are interested in.

The first set uses the **INSPECTION DATE** as the value for **Date**, and **Inspected** as the value for **Type**. The second set uses **GRADE DATE** as the value for **Date**, and **Graded** as the value for **Type**. If you need to add additional fields for your analysis, you can simply add the field names to both `SELECT` statements.

Once we have the fields in place, we can analyze and visualize our data. For example, we can create a time series graph with trend lines. Since we have a single date field to consider, we can simply drag that **Date** field and create a continuous axis. Since we also have a single field to differentiate what event that date was related to, we can use that in **Color** in the **Marks** card to create two separate lines for the **Graded** and **Inspected** events:

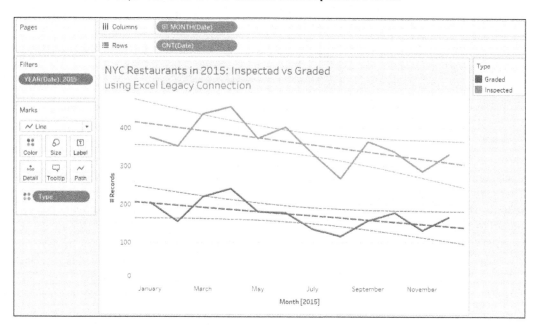

The measure in this example is **CNT(Date)** because **Date** will have a value if it is related to the event, and null (and will not be counted) if it is not.

Be careful when doing other kinds of analysis. Since we stacked two copies of our data set, we essentially doubled our record count.

There's more...

We are only using the legacy connection because our data source in this recipe is an Excel file. If your data source is different, for example if you are using a relational data source, you can re-shape the data using those data sources's query mechanisms. In a relational data source, you may be able to do a union or a self-join at the data source level before the data is consumed by Tableau.

Tableau 10 introduces a new feature called cross database join, which we can also consider. The cross database join allows you to connect to multiple data sources and join them from within the Tableau connection interface. In the following example, we have essentially connected to the same Excel worksheet three times:

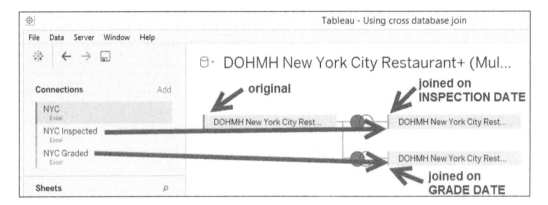

Each connection is a left join. The first one connects mainly based on the **INSPECTION DATE**. There are other fields being considered in the join to ensure we are only matching the correct records. Otherwise, we will end up with something called a cross join and may match one record to all other records of restaurants that were inspected on the same date:

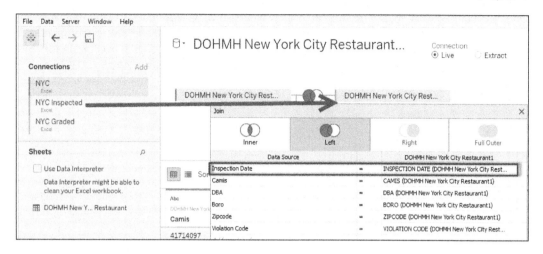

The second one connects mainly based on the **GRADE DATE**. As with the previous join, we also still need to consider other fields in the join to avoid mismatching records:

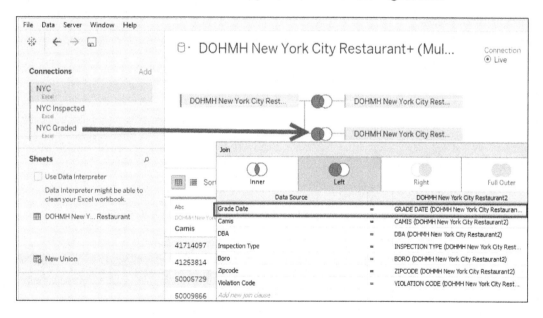

Once the connections are set up, we can create a similar visualization to the one we created using the legacy connection. The following visualization uses a slightly different approach. Since our measures come from different data sources, we are using a dual axis graph for the **COUNT of INSPECTION DATE** from one data source, and **COUNT of GRADE DATE** from another data source:

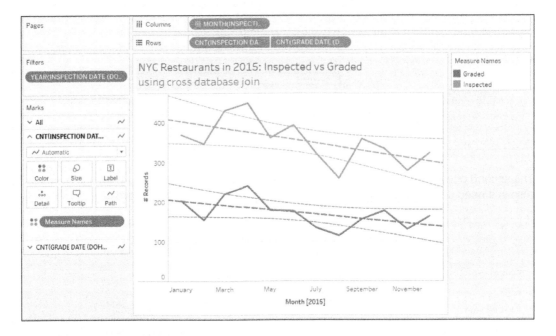

Please refer to the *Creating a line chart* recipe in *Chapter 1, Basic Charts*

Please refer to the *Creating a combo chart (dual axis chart)* recipe in *Chapter 2, Advanced Charts*

Using schema.ini to resolve data type issues

In this recipe, we will use a `schema.ini` file to resolve the data types when we connect to a fixed width text file data source with four columns.

Getting ready

To follow this recipe, download this chapter's files from the Packt website and use the file called `Fixed Width Sample.txt`.

This is what the file looks like when opened in a text editor showing special characters:

```
Fixed Width Sample.txt
 95  150        20020801        Christie        2002-08-01CRLF
 96  151        20020901        Brian           2002-09-01CRLF
 97  154        20030901        Carlisle        2003-09-01CRLF
 98  155        20010901        Castellucio     2001-09-01CRLF
 99  156        20010901        Bowman          2001-09-01CRLF
100  160        20020901        Cavendish       2002-09-01CRLF
101  C160       20150901        Miyamoto        2015-09-01
```

Note that this file does not have any column headers. In addition, note the following:

▸ The first column should be text

▸ The second column should be integers

▸ The third column should be text

▸ The fourth column should be dates

How to do it...

Here are the steps to use the `.ini` file with the fixed width text file:

1. Create a text file with the following contents:

```
schema.ini
 1  [Fixed Width Sample.txt]
 2  ColNameHeader=False
 3  Format=FixedLength
 4  CharacterSet=ANSI
 5  DateTimeFormat=yyyy-mm-dd
 6  Col1="Row Number" Text Width 11
 7  Col2="ID" Integer Width 16
 8  Col3="Name" Text Width 16
 9  Col4="Opened" DateTime Width 10
10
```

2. Save the file as `schema.ini` and save it in the same directory as the `Fixed Width Sample.txt` file.

3. Connect to the text file in Tableau:

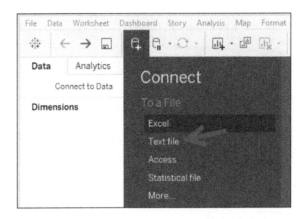

4. Confirm that there are four fields in the Tableau preview window, with the same configuration as specified in the `schema.ini` file:

  ❑ First field is text

  ❑ Second field is number

  ❑ Third field is text

  ❑ Fourth field is date

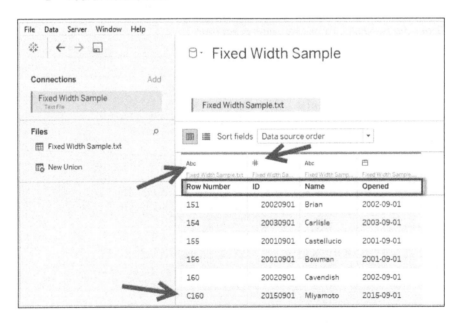

5. Add a new sheet and create your visualization using this data set.

How it works...

Connecting to text files can sometimes be more challenging than connecting to a database or server-based data source. Relational databases will typically have the data types and constraints built in. Tableau can read this metadata and interpret the correct types and settings for the data set.

Text files can be tricky. We usually need to identify delimiters (that is, how is one field separated from another). If we want headers, we will need to either manually assign them from within Tableau, or override them in a configuration file.

If we connect to the file in this recipe from Tableau without a configuration (or `schema.ini`) file, this is what we will get:

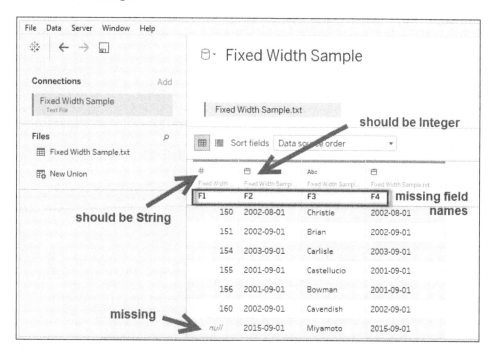

There are a few things that are incorrect or missing:

▸ The field names are missing.

▸ The first field contains a **null** value for the very last record, because Tableau assumes this field is numeric based on the first few rows. The last record has an alphanumeric value of C160, which is invalid for a numeric field. Show how to change with just default text driver properties clicking on the dropdown.

▸ The second field is interpreted as a date because the values, while numeric, can assume the format of yyyymmdd.

Tableau does allow us some flexibility when working with text files. When you click on the dropdown for the text file, there is an option for **Text File Properties**:

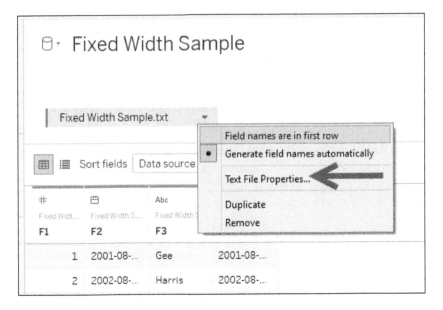

This provides another window that allows us to specify the field separators, text qualifiers (that is, characters that enclose text values), character set, and locale:

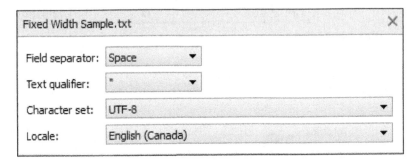

This still makes working with fixed width files without column headers a challenge. Microsoft recommends using `schema.ini` for all fixed length files. `schema.ini` provides a way to specify the data types and other configurations for the text file that Tableau can read. It does not solve all cases, but it can help with some.

The format, supported fields, and options for schema.ini are documented in the MSDN page called the schema.ini File (Text File Driver), which can be found at http://bit.ly/msdn-schema-ini.

Tableau also has a KB article called _Resolving Incorrect Data Type Issues Related to Jet_, which can be found at the following URL: http://bit.ly/tableau-jet-engine.

There's more...

What we used in this recipe is one of the simpler text files that can be cleaned up using a schema.ini file. In reality, there are many limitations.

If we had spaces in the third column, for example, if record #2's name is _Harris Jr_, this is what we will get in Tableau even if we specified the width of the string in the schema.ini file:

Abc	#	Abc ▾	📅	📅
Fixed Width Sample.txt	Fixed Width ...	Fixed Width Samp...	Fixed Width Sample...	Fixed Width S...
Row Number	ID	Name Ξ	Opened	F5
1	200108...	Gee	2001-08-01	_null_
2	200208...	Harris	_null_	2002-08-...
3	200109...	Carreras	2001-09-01	_null_

What if the date format was yyyy-dd-mm and we specified it in the schema.ini like this:

```
schema.ini ☒
1 ⊟[Fixed Width Sample.txt]
2  ColNameHeader=False
3  Format=FixedLength
4  CharacterSet=ANSI
5  DateTimeFormat=yyyy-dd-mm
6  Col1="Row Number" Text Width 11
7  Col2="ID" Integer Width 16
8  Col3="Name" Text Width 16
9  Col4="Opened" DateTime Width 10
```

Tableau still uses the date format `yyyy-mm-dd` and ignores the specification in the `schema.ini` file:

There are other variations that demonstrate the limitations of `schema.ini`. Sometimes, the best way to approach data wrangling problems is to either export to another format that Tableau can more easily read, or to resort to other tools, or even scripting. For example, Python, R, or even PowerShell are great, powerful scripting tools that can give you much more flexibility with how to shape your data.

Pivoting columns

In this recipe, we will prepare the data set that we used in the *Creating a population pyramid* recipe of *Chapter 2, Advanced Charts*. The original file, which is a comma separated value (CSV) file, looks like the following:

```
Population_Projections.csv
 1  "","Local Health
    Area","Year","Gender","<1","1-4","5-9","10-14","15-19","20-24","25-29",
    "30-34","35-39","40-44","45-49","50-54","55-59","60-64","65-69","70-74"
    ,"75-79","80-84","85-89","90+","Total"
 2  "0","British
    Columbia","1986","T","41594","167812","199209","196176","218240","25464
    1","273286","266181","248264","195669","156688","143634","144835","1392
    94","120433","100193","66845","40099","19669","10859","3003621"
 3  "0","British
    Columbia","1987","T","42094","169356","203820","196497","217006","24578
    3","275003","270902","250563","210829","163396","144435","145743","1399
    36","126336","102649","70449","42028","20698","11128","3048651"
 4  "0","British
    Columbia","1988","T","41941","172538","210669","199175","217883","23786
    5","279202","277893","257289","224097","173461","146619","147392","1418
    40","131991","103583","74296","44196","21624","11207","3114761"
```

Getting ready

To follow this recipe, download the file from BCStats using the following URL:

```
http://www.bcstats.gov.bc.ca/StatisticsBySubject/Demography/
PopulationProjections.aspx.
```

When you download, make the following selections and click on **Generate Output**:

- ▸ Select British Columbia for Region
- ▸ Select all the years
- ▸ Select totals
- ▸ Select 5-Year Age Groups

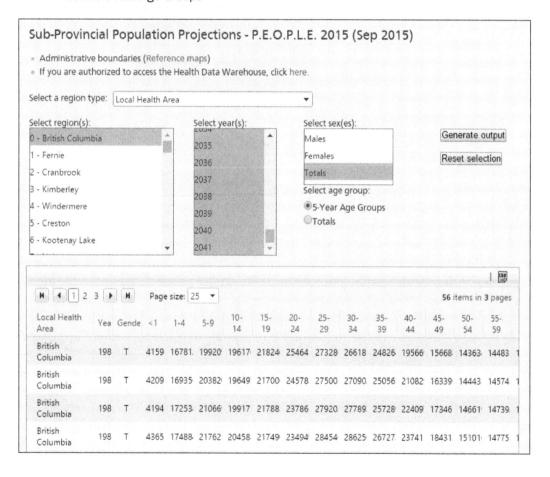

Beside the result pane, click on the CSV icon at the top-right corner of the result pane to download the `.csv` file. Save the file as `Population_Projections.csv`.

How to do it...

Here are the steps to prepare the `.csv` file:

1. Click on **New Data Source** icon and connect to the text file in this recipe:

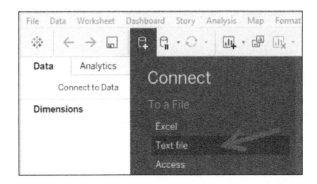

2. Select all the age groups that are presented as individual columns.

3. While all the age group columns are selected, right-click on one of the selected fields and choose **Pivot**:

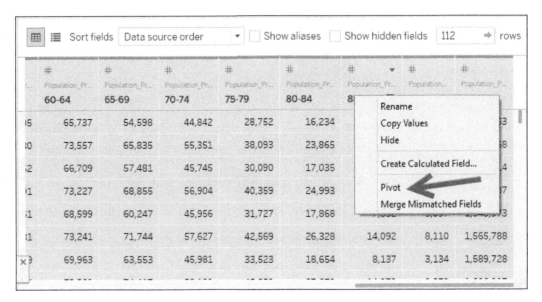

4. Right-click on the newly created **Pivot Field Names** field and choose **Rename**. Rename this field **Age Group**.

5. Right-click on the newly created **Pivot Field Values** field and choose **Rename**. Rename this field **Population**:

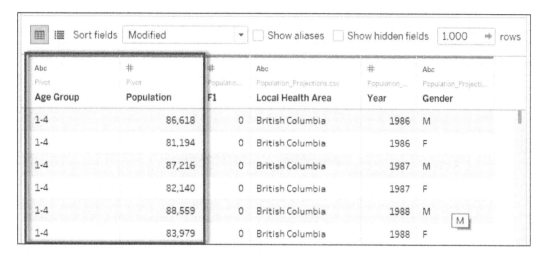

6. Under **Filters**, click on **Add**.

7. In the **Edit Data Source Filters** window, click on **Add**.

8. In the **Age Group filter** window, select the **Wildcard** tab.

9. Type Total under **Match value** and check the **Exclude** checkbox:

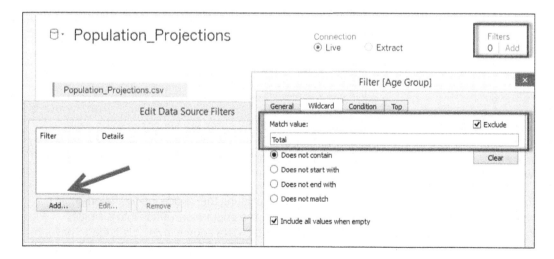

10. Click **OK** when done.

11. Add a new sheet and create your visualization using this data set.

How it works...

Tableau works best with data sets that are tall and narrow instead of short and wide. In the file that we are using in this recipe, the measure field—population—is split by age group. Each population value for an age group is provided as a column, so we end up with multiple measures:

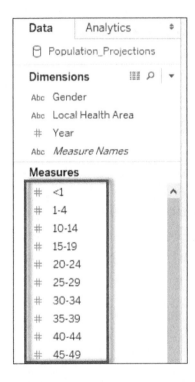

This format is hard to work with, because all these measures are supposed to be a single measure. If we had a single measure for population values, and have another dimension for age group, the analysis will be more flexible. We can slice and dice population by age group if we need to.

Tableau provides a way for us to shape this file by pivoting the values, using the original measure names as a dimension, and collecting all the population values into a single column. Although you may also be able to pivot at the data source level, it is great to have this capability within Tableau.

See also

Please refer to the *Creating a population pyramid* recipe in *Chapter 2, Advanced Charts*

Using union

In this recipe, we will combine a number of comma separated value (CSV) files into a single data set in Tableau.

Getting ready

To follow this recipe, download the business license files from the City of Vancouver's website from `http://data.vancouver.ca/datacatalogue/businessLicence.htm`:

```
Data set details          Current Year

                            1. Business licence (XML)
                            2. Business licence (XLS) 🗎  ⬅
                            3. Business licence (CSV) 🗎  ⬅
                            4. Business licence (JSON)

                          Year 2015

                            1. Business licence (XML)
                            2. Business licence (XLS) 🗎  ⬅
                            3. Business licence (CSV) 🗎  ⬅
                            4. Business licence (JSON)

                          Year 2014

                            1. Business licence (XML)
                            2. Business licence (XLS) 🗎  ⬅
                            3. Business licence (CSV) 🗎  ⬅
                            4. Business licence (JSON)
```

Download the CSV version, and save all the files in a local directory in your computer:

Windows8_OS (C:) ▸ Tableau ▸ BC Open Data ▸ Business License

Name	Type
business_licences.csv	Microsoft Excel Comma Separated Values File
2015business_licences.csv	Microsoft Excel Comma Separated Values File
2014business_licences.csv	Microsoft Excel Comma Separated Values File
2013business_licences.csv	Microsoft Excel Comma Separated Values File
2012business_licences.csv	Microsoft Excel Comma Separated Values File
2011business_licences.csv	Microsoft Excel Comma Separated Values File
2010business_licences.csv	Microsoft Excel Comma Separated Values File
2009business_licences.csv	Microsoft Excel Comma Separated Values File
2008business_licences.csv	Microsoft Excel Comma Separated Values File
2007business_licences.csv	Microsoft Excel Comma Separated Values File
2006business_licences.csv	Microsoft Excel Comma Separated Values File
2005business_licences.csv	Microsoft Excel Comma Separated Values File
2004business_licences.csv	Microsoft Excel Comma Separated Values File
2003business_licences.csv	Microsoft Excel Comma Separated Values File
2002business_licences.csv	Microsoft Excel Comma Separated Values File
2001business_licences.csv	Microsoft Excel Comma Separated Values File
2000business_licences.csv	Microsoft Excel Comma Separated Values File
1999business_licences.csv	Microsoft Excel Comma Separated Values File
1998business_licences.csv	Microsoft Excel Comma Separated Values File
1997business_licences.csv	Microsoft Excel Comma Separated Values File

How to do it...

Here are the steps to prepare the data files:

1. Click on **New Data Source** icon and connect to `business_licenses.csv` which contains the most recent year's records:

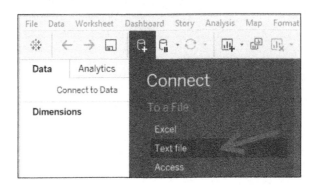

2. Drag **New Union** to just underneath the `business_licenses.csv` until you see the **Drag** table to union message:

3. Select all other CSV files from the **Files** pane and drag them to the **Union** window:

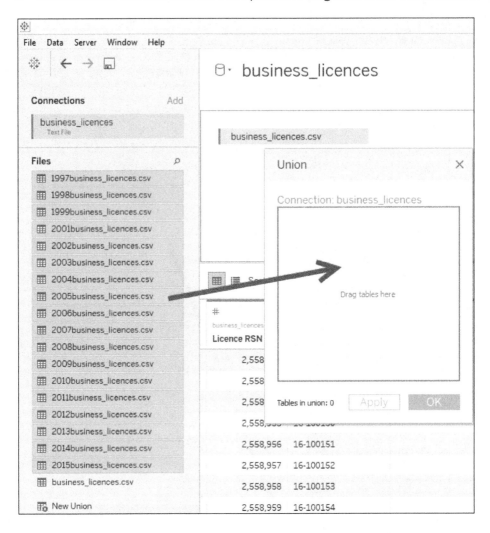

4.   Click on **OK** after you confirm that all the files have been added to the **Union** window:

5.   Add a new sheet and create your visualization using this data set.

How it works...

A union operation allows multiple sets of data to be appended to each other, that is, new records will be added to the end of the existing set of records.

To perform a union, we can simply drag the **New Union** operator to the data connection window and add all the files (or Excel worksheets from the same workbook) to the **Union** window.

Alternatively, we can skip dragging the **New Union** operator and simply drag the files (or worksheets) directly underneath the first text file or worksheet:

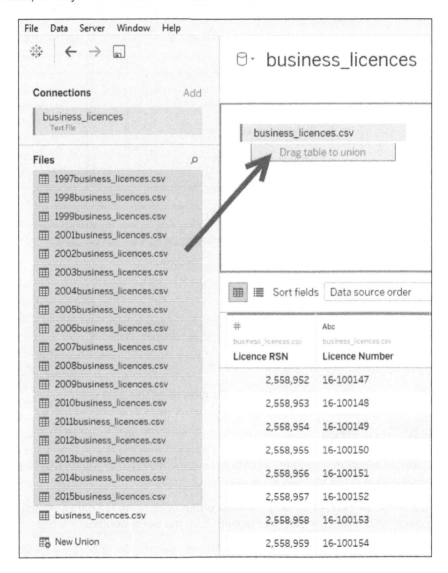

A union in relational databases requires what is called union compatibility. This means the two sets of records need to have the same number of columns and similar data types.

In Tableau, the union operation does not necessarily require union compatibility. If some of the incoming fields do not match the existing fields, the mismatched fields will simply have null values.

For example, if in some of our files the **Business Name** field was called **Business Trade Name** instead, we can use Tableau's **Merge Mismatched Field** operation:

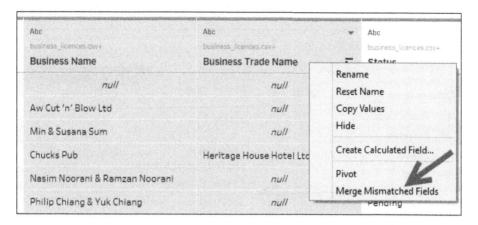

What this operation does is combine the fields into a single field in the resulting data set. It will take the first non-null value for this new combined field. Thus, we have to take care to ensure that the fields are indeed supposed to be the same but just named differently; otherwise, we risk losing information.

Should you need to undo the merge, Tableau also provides a way to remove the merge:

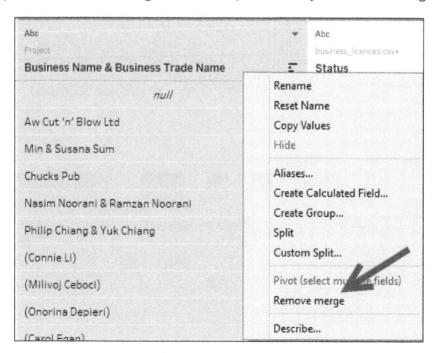

When we union files or worksheets, Tableau adds metadata fields in the resulting data set. Tableau has the **Table Name** dimension for text files, which uses the original file name as the value:

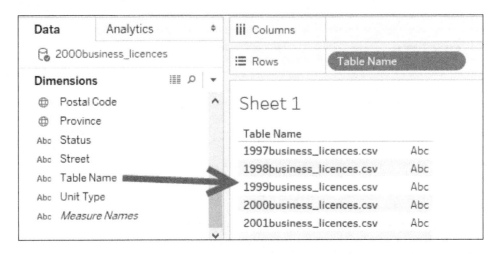

After we union our files, we can do our analysis. One possibility is a heat map. In the view below, we have a heat map of issued business licenses in downtown Vancouver. This type of visualization can indicate how long businesses have been operating:

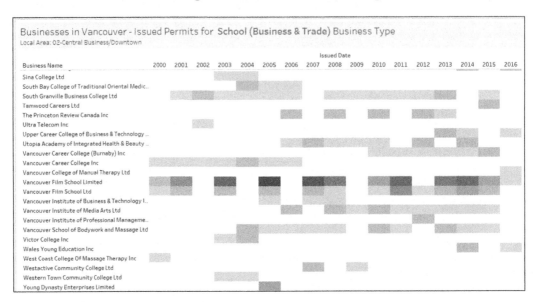

There's more...

In the past, a union with multiple worksheets in the same Excel workbook can be done using a custom SQL in Excel, if using the legacy Jet connection. There is a recipe in this chapter called *Using the legacy Jet driver* that discusses this option.

In Tableau 10, the union operator is baked into the product. In this version, union works with text files (including the `.csv` and `.txt` file extensions) and multiple worksheets in Excel if saved in a single workbook. What if you need to combine multiple Excel files?

One improvement that is being promised in the future, and was showcased in the 2015 Tableau conference, is a wildcard union. This allows the union to operate on multiple files based on specific patterns on the filename. While not available in the initial release of Tableau 10, this will for sure be a much-awaited feature improvement for this operator.

A possible alternative to adding multiple Excel files is using data extracts. When you create an extract, you can append additional records from another file:

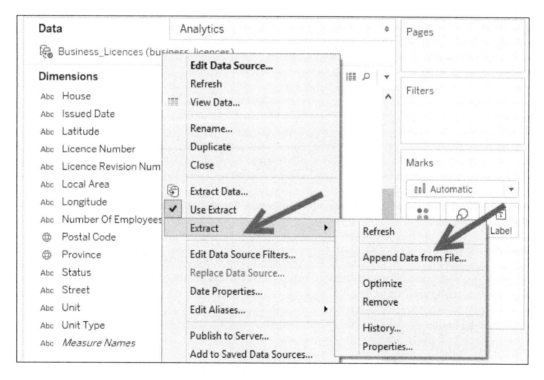

This is more restrictive than the union operator because you need to ensure the worksheet names are the same. You also need to ensure union compatibility; otherwise, you may encounter errors during the extract process. The following error is produced by the field name mismatch between the original file in the extraction and the incoming field names in the file being appended:

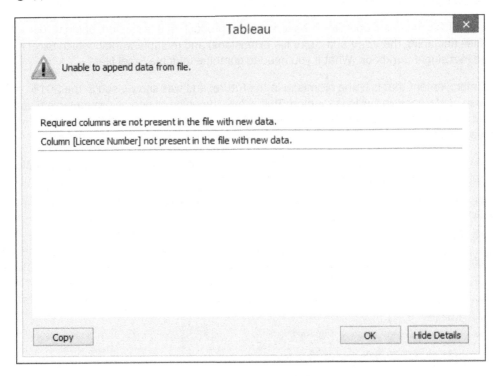

This field mismatch issue can be resolved in the new Tableau 10 **Merge Mismatched Fields** feature.

 Learn more about the union operator from the Tableau online documentation: `https://onlinehelp.tableau.com/current/pro/desktop/en-us/union.html`.

See also

Please refer to the *Creating a heat map* recipe in *Chapter 1, Basic Charts*

Please refer to the *Using the legacy Jet driver* recipe in this chapter

Using join

In this recipe, we will combine the fields in two different Excel worksheets into one:

Getting ready

To follow this recipe, download this chapter's files from the Packt website and use the file called `Worlds Busiest Airports-Join.xls`.

How to do it...

Here are the steps to combine the fields from the two worksheets:

1. Connect to the **Excel** file in this recipe. Make sure you choose Excel from the **To a File** section:

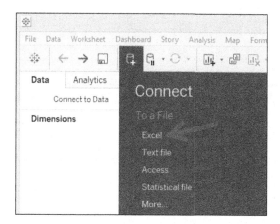

2. Drag **Busiest Airports** 2015 from the **sheets** section to the data connection window:

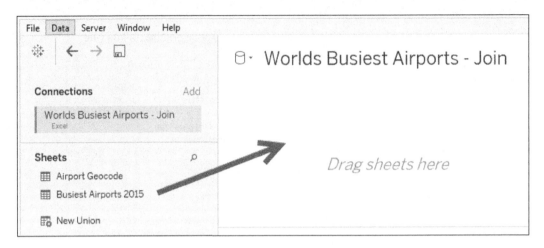

3. Drag **Airport Geocode** to the right of **Busiest Airports** 2015 in the data connection window.

4. In the **Join** window that comes up, choose **Airport** from **Busiest Airports 2015** to match up to the **Airport Code** field from the **Airport Geocode** sheet:

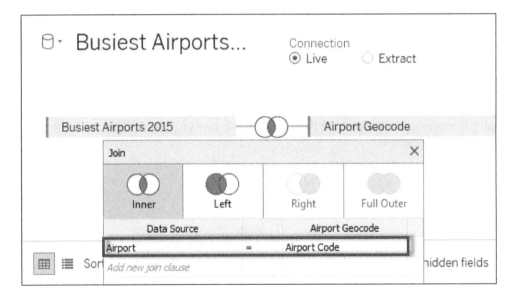

5. Add a new sheet and create your visualization using this data set.

How it works...

A join is primarily a relational database concept that allows you to combine records from different tables using common fields. When data sets are joined, all fields are combined based on the join conditions provided.

In Tableau, joins can be done on file-based data sources as well. For Excel files, each tab or worksheet in an Excel file acts like a table with records. If your data source is text files, each file in a folder is considered a table.

In our recipe, we combined two worksheets from the same Excel workbook. Records in both worksheets will be combined only if the **Airport** field from **Busiest Airports 2015** has the same value as the **Airport Code** field in the **Airport Geocode** worksheet. This join, based on the equality of values, is also called an equi-join:

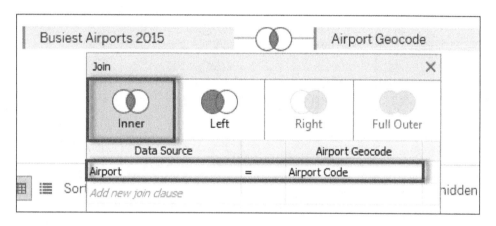

Once the fields are joined, you will find the fields from both worksheets represented in the side bar. Fields are grouped based on their source:

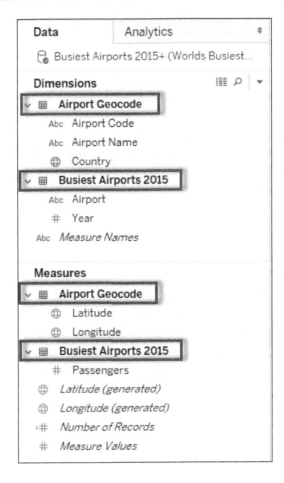

In general, we have two types of join: inner and outer joins.

Inner joins find matching values from both tables based on the join condition. The join condition is not always based on equality. There are cases where you may use other operators such as greater than (>), greater than or equal to (>=), less than (<), less than or equal to (<=) or even not equal to (<>). Depending on the data source, some of these operators may not be supported.

Outer joins, also called preserving joins, preserve one or both sides of the tables as well as matching records. Outer joins can be further classified as left outer, right outer, and full outer. Some data sources do not support certain types of outer joins. Outer joins are positional; the placement of the tables relative to the JOIN operator affects the results.

A `left outer join` preserves the table to the left of the join operator and finds the matching values from the table on the right side of the operator. If a record on left table being preserved does not have a matching value in the right table, that record is preserved but the fields from the other table will show NULL. A NULL value means the absence of value.

Here is an example of a `LEFT OUTER JOIN` using our worksheet in this recipe. The records in the table to the left, **Busiest Airports 2015**, is matched up to the records to the right, **Airport Geocode**, based on **Airport** and **Airport Code** fields respectively:

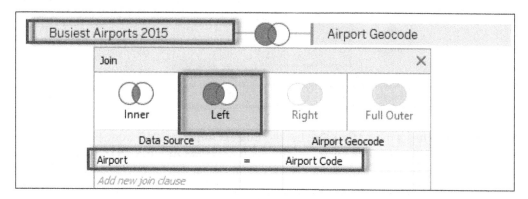

Busiest Airports 2015 has a record for **Airport** value **CDG**, but this **Airport Code** does not exist in the **Airport Geocode** worksheet. Hence, as can be seen in the following screenshot, the corresponding **Airport Geocode** fields are reporting **Null** for the **CDG** airport:

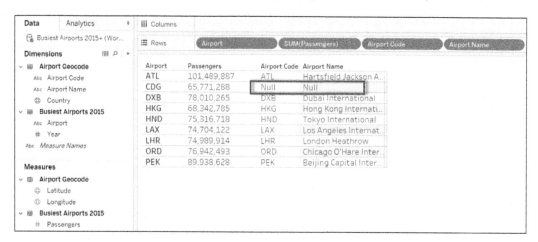

A right outer join is the reverse; it preserves the records from the right table and finds matching values from the left table. Right outer joins are not natively supported in Excel data sources. However, we could simply switch the data sources—putting **Airport Geocode** to the left and **Busiest Airports 2015** to the right—to achieve the same desired result:

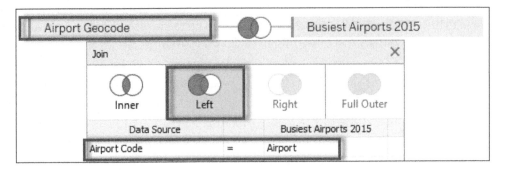

Airport Geocode has a record for **DFW**, but the **Busiest Airports 2015** worksheet does not have this. The resulting records will report **Null** for the **Busiest Airports 2015** columns for the **DFW** record:

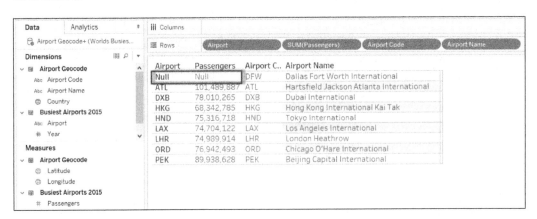

A full outer join preserves both tables being operated on. If the data source driver does not support this, a full outer join result can be derived by getting the result of the left outer join and appending it to the result of the right outer join.

There are a few other types of join—a self-join and a cross join. A self-join simply means that the same table is joined to itself. The actual join type can be inner or outer or even cross join. A cross join gets the cartesian product of the records in the tables being cross joined. When we get a cartesian product, we match up the records from one table to all records in the other table. If we have m of records in one table and n of records in another table, after a cartesian product we will end up with *mxn* records.

In our recipe, once we have combined the fields, we can start visualizing our records. Here is a possibility—creating a map that depicts the busiest airports and ranks them based on the average number of passengers:

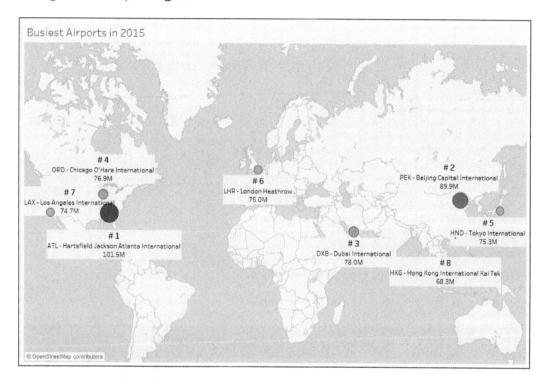

There's more...

A union is another operation that can be used to combine different data sets. Joins are fundamentally different from a union. In a union, the record sets are stacked on top of each other, thus producing a taller result set. A join works by combining records and fields horizontally based on common fields, thus creating wider data sets that have all the combined fields together. A join also does not require union compatibility.

Before Tableau 10, joins were limited to combining tables from the same data source, that is, the tables need to be using a single data connection. Tableau v10 adds flexibility to the join operation by allowing cross-database joins. Tables are no longer restricted to coming from the same data source.

In the following example, we can see that there are two color-coded connections in the left-hand pane. One is an Excel connection, and the other is a text file connection. In the middle connection window, we can see that the join operation was allowed between the two data sources:

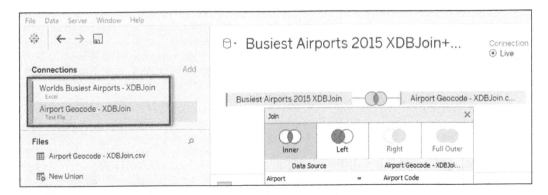

See also

Please refer to the *Using union* recipe in this chapter

Please refer to the *Using blend* recipe in this chapter

Using blend

In this recipe, we will combine the records from a text file and an Excel file using a blend.

Getting ready

To follow this recipe, download this chapter's files from the Packt website and use the following files:

▸ The Airport Geocode–Blend.csv file
▸ The Worlds Busiest Airports–Blend.xlsx file

This is the content of the `Airport Geocode—Blend.csv` file:

```
Airport Geocode - Blend.csv
 1  Airport Code,Airport Name,Country,Latitude,Longitude
 2  ATL,Hartsfield Jackson Atlanta International,United States,33.6367,-84.4281
 3  PEK,Beijing Capital International,China,40.0799,116.6031
 4  DXB,Dubai International,United Arab Emirates,25.2532,55.3657
 5  ORD,Chicago O'Hare International,United States,41.9808,-87.9067
 6  HND,Tokyo International,Japan,35.5494,139.7798
 7  LHR,London Heathrow,United Kingdom,51.47,0.4543
 8  LAX,Los Angeles International,United States,33.9425,-118.4072
 9  HKG,Hong Kong International Kai Tak,Hong Kong,22.308,113.9185
10  DFW,Dallas Fort Worth International,United States,32.8969,-97.0381
```

These are the records in the `Worlds Busiest Airports - Blend.xlsx` file:

	A	B	C
1	Airport	Year	Passengers
2	ATL	2015	101489887
3	PEK	2015	89938628
4	DXB	2015	78010265
5	ORD	2015	76942493
6	HND	2015	75316718
7	LHR	2015	74989914
8	LAX	2015	74704122
9	HKG	2015	68342785
10	CDG	2015	65771288
11	ATL	2014	96,178,899

How to do it...

Here are the steps to blend the two data sources:

1. Connect to the Excel file in this recipe. Make sure you choose **Excel** from the **To a File** section:

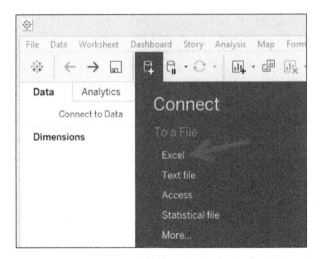

2. Go to new worksheet:

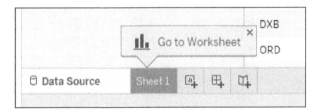

3. Click on the **New Data Source** icon, and this time connect to a **Text file**. Connect to the text file in this recipe:

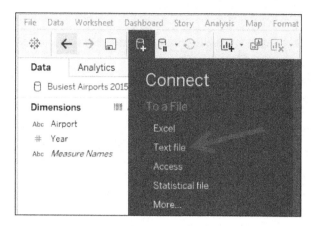

4. If you are directed back to the initial connection screen, go back to sheet 1.

5. Under the **Data** menu, click on **Edit Relationships**:

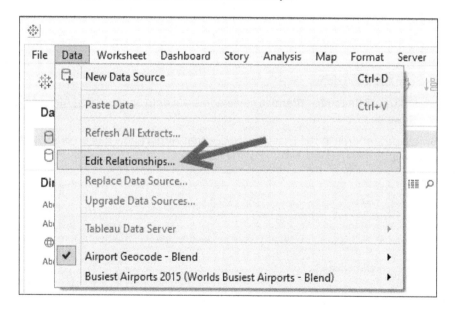

6. While **Airport Geocode—Blend** is selected as the **Primary data source**, click on **Custom** and match up the **Airport Code** field to **Airport**:

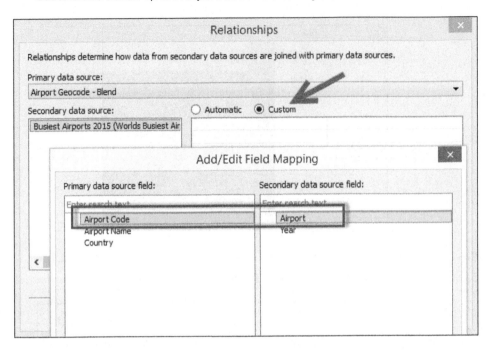

7. Click on **OK** when done.

8. While **Airport Geocode—Blend** is selected as the data source, drag **Airport Code** to the **Rows** shelf.

9. Switch data source to the Excel file. Notice that **Airport** now has an orange link icon beside it:

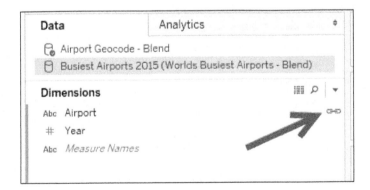

10. Continue to create your visualization using this dataset.

How it works...

Blends are great for data mashups. Blending in Tableau allows multiple data sources to be linked together. The data sources can be of different types—for example, one could be an Excel file while another could be a text file.

 In previous versions of Tableau, a blend was the only way from within Tableau to link multiple data sources together. Starting in Tableau 10, cross-database joins are supported. See *Using Join* recipe in *Chapter 6, Analytics* for more information.

The data sources must have some common fields before they can be blended in Tableau. By default, Tableau looks for the same field names in the data sources and links the sources together based on these fields.

However, if the fields have different names, Tableau will give a warning message indicating that there is no relationship between the data sources. You will also find that when you start using fields from one or both data sources, there will be a broken link icon:

If the field names are different, the relationship needs to be defined. To do this, we can go to the worksheet menu and select **Edit Relationships**. From there, instead of **Automatic**, **Custom** can be chosen as well as identify which fields from both sources should match up:

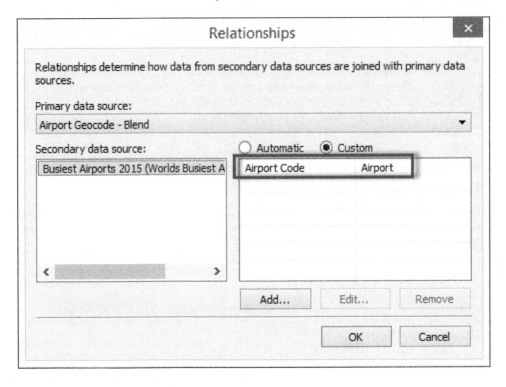

After the relationship is set, you will find that the link will be enabled. This link will only appear after you have dragged one of the blending fields into the view. If none of the blending fields are in the view, the icon will still appear as broken:

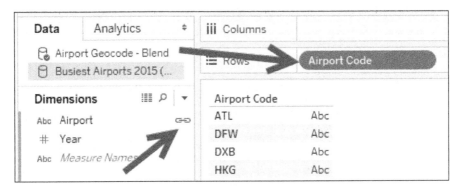

With a blend, there must be only one primary and at least one or multiple secondary data sources. The primary data source is identified by a blue check arrow icon beside it, and the secondary data sources have an orange check arrow icon:

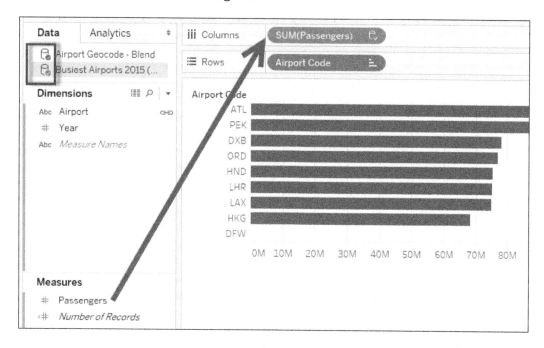

Fields from the secondary data sources will automatically be aggregated when dragged into the view or used in a calculated field. The level of aggregation follows that of the primary:

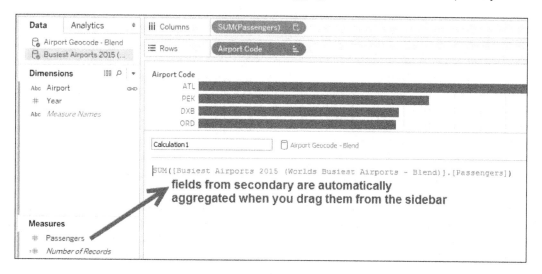

Dimension fields will also be aggregated using the **ATTR** function. If there are many related records in the secondary data source, and if there are multiple values for that field, the **ATTR** function will return an asterisk (*):

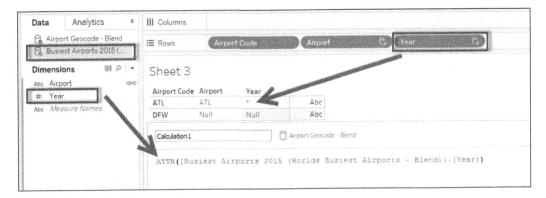

This leads to a common issue faced in blends when creating calculated fields. We need to make sure that we have the primary and secondary data source fields in an aggregated format when we use them in our expressions. Otherwise, we will get the error *Cannot mix aggregate and non-aggregate arguments with this function*:

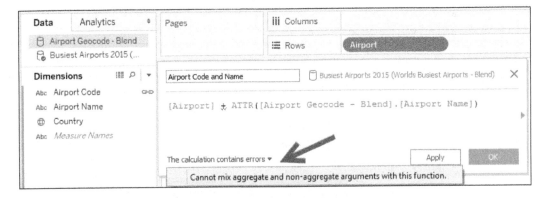

Blend settings are per worksheet. If you create a new worksheet, the data source you drag from the first will be the primary.

There's more...

Now that Tableau 10 supports cross-database joins, why would we still want to consider blending data? There are still some compelling reasons to go with blends. The first is, currently, the cross-database join functionality is not supported in all possible connections. Second, we may want to achieve a level of aggregation first before we want to data sources combined.

To better illustrate this, let's consider the two following data sources:

Data Source 1 - Customer		
Customer ID	Customer Name	Credit Limit
A01	John	500
B02	Miyuki	100
C03	Aisha	300

Data Source 2 - Sales		
Customer ID	Order ID	Amount
A01	S01	100
A01	S02	200
B02	S03	300

If we were to use a join operation (specifically a `left outer join`, with customer on the left side of the join operator so it is preserved), we will get the following result. The **Credit Limit** for **Customer ID A01** is incorrect because the credit limit was doubled—**$1,000** is being reported when it really is only **$500**:

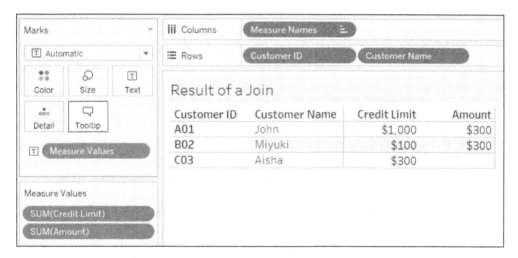

This is the nature of joins, however. The join is working perfectly—it finds the matching values from the other table. Since **Customer ID A01** bought twice, **Customer ID** from the **Customer** table matched twice to the **Sales** table and therefore reported the credit limit twice.

If we were to blend, however, we will get the following result set, reporting some different values:

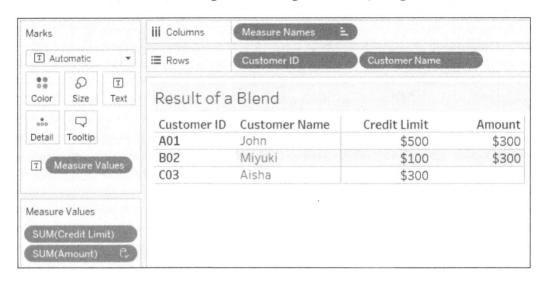

In a blend, the aggregation happens at the data source level first, before the records from the two data sources are combined. Notice in the **Measure Values** card, the pill still says **SUM(Credit Limit)**— the same expression you saw in the previous join operation. This time, though, the **SUM(Credit Limit)** happens at the customer data source only, not at the resulting joined records. The **SUM(Credit Limit)** for **Customer ID A01** in the customer data source is still **$500** because there is only one record for that **Customer ID** in that data source.

One more important thing to know about blends is that after the records in both data sources are aggregated to the same level, the records are combined using an operation akin to a left outer join. This means that if some values in the blending field are absent in the primary, they will not be reported at all.

For example, if our primary is the **Airport Geocode**, and it does not have the airport code **CDG** which our secondary has, **CDG** will not be pulled into any view:

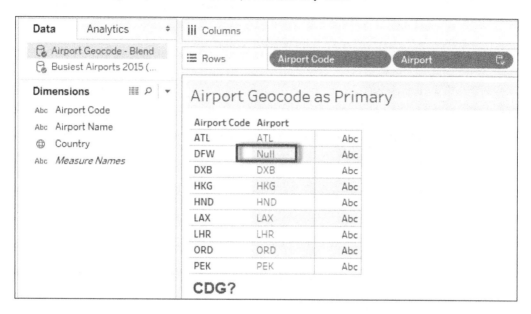

The same issue will occur even if we reverse the primary and secondary data sources, and if the new primary is missing some values that are present in the secondary. The following shows what you would see if we made **Busiest Airports 2015** the new primary data source, but it is missing the code for **DFW**:

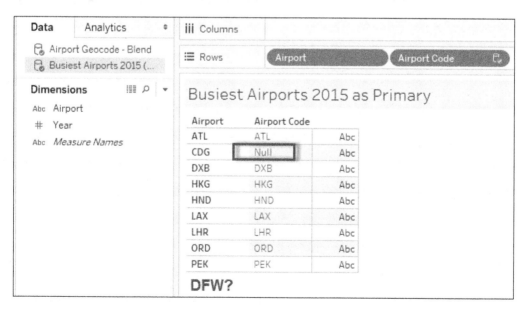

There is no magic bullet solution for this issue, however. What we need to do is have another data source that has the complete set of values, and make that our primary. Or, if this is a data quality issue, this is great way to illustrate why data quality is of utmost importance in data analysis. Remember—good data in, good data (analysis/visualization) out. Not-so-good data in, not-so-good data (analysis/visualization) out.

See also

Please refer to the *Using union* recipe in this chapter

Please refer to the *Using join* recipe in this chapter

Calculated Fields Primer

Often when we analyze or visualize data, we find ourselves needing additional fields, which are not available in the data source. Not to worry! Most of the time, we can derive these fields using some logic within the Tableau scripting language. We can choose to create ad hoc calculations and even save them back in our Tableau data source or workbook so we can reuse them for multiple worksheets.

Different ways to create calculated fields

There are different ways to create calculated fields in Tableau, as follows:

1. From the drop-down arrow beside the **Dimensions** section in the side bar:

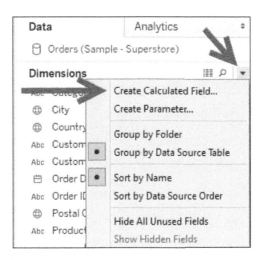

2. From the field you want to use in the calculated field:

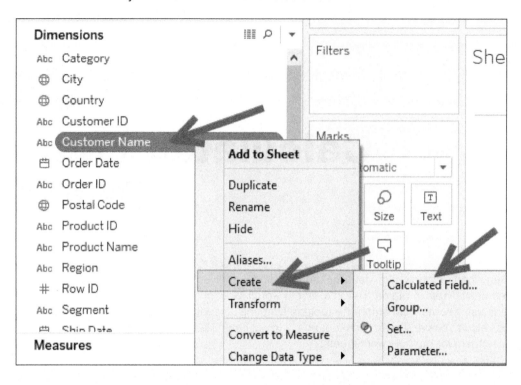

3. From the **Analysis** menu:

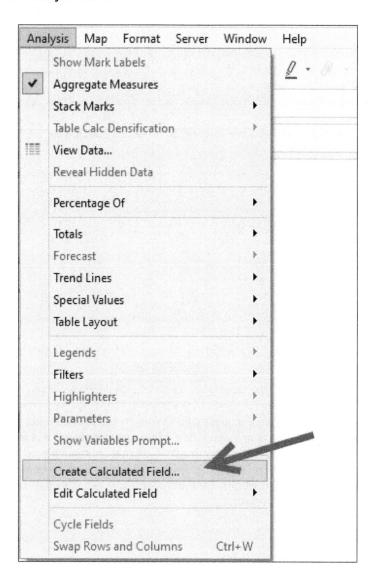

4. From the **Rows** or **Columns** shelf by double-clicking on an empty space. This is called ad hoc calculation:

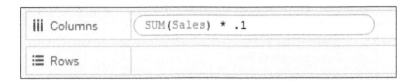

5. From the **Marks** card by double-clicking on an empty space. This is also called an ad hoc calculated field:

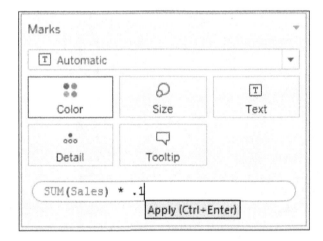

If you create an adhoc calculation, this piece of information can only be used within the worksheet you created it in. This is not viewable in other worksheets in the same workbook. If you need to persist this field, you can simply drag the pill that contains the ad hoc calculation to anywhere in the side bar. You can rename this field once you see it in the side bar. Once the field is saved, you can use this anywhere in the workbook, just like any other calculated fields. This is shown in the following screenshot:

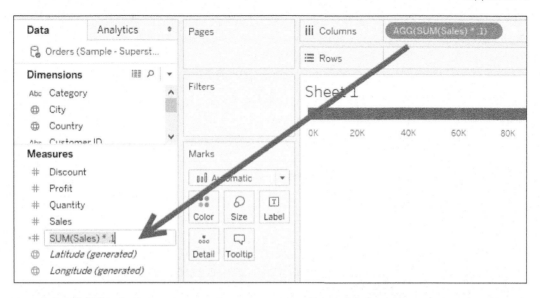

Calculated field window

Starting with Tableau V9, the calculated field window shows up a white, modeless window. Prior to Tableau V9, you needed to close the calculated field window before you could do anything else with Tableau. With the modeless window, you can continue to work on your tasks, such as dragging fields to shelves, while the calculated field editor is open. The modeless window also allows you to drag and drop fields from the sidebar onto the calculated field window.

In the calculated field window, you have to specify the calculated field name and an expression (or formula).This expression can include the following:

- ▸ Data fields from your data source(s)
- ▸ Functions
- ▸ Parameters
- ▸ Comments

Comments are optional but highly recommended. Tableau supports single line comments. Anything that starts with two forward slashes, //, will be considered a single line comment and will not be executed by Tableau, as shown next:

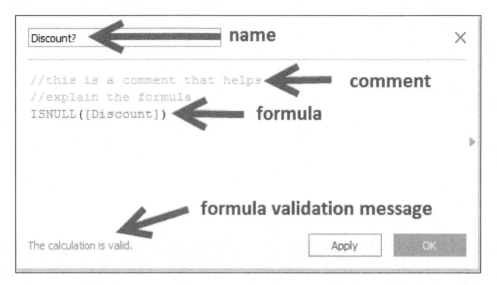

If there are any errors, there will be a message at the bottom of the editor that will show the error message. The formula itself will have a red squiggly underline to signal the error in the syntax. This is shown in the following screenshot:

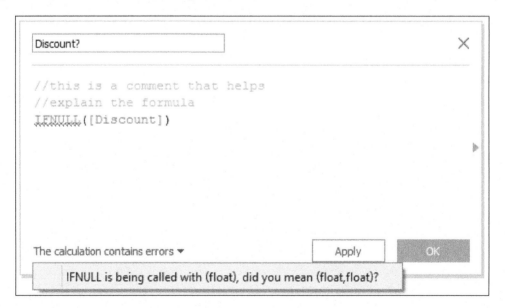

Functions in Tableau

Often, when we need to derive data, we may need to incorporate some built-in functions in Tableau. Functions are reusable, "callable" code that can be used in calculations. Functions also return some kind of value.

In the calculated field editor, there is a faint arrow on the right side of the rectangle. When you click on this, it will expand and show a **Help** box for functions that are supported in Tableau:

When you click on the dropdown of the help window, you will see a list of the function categories available:

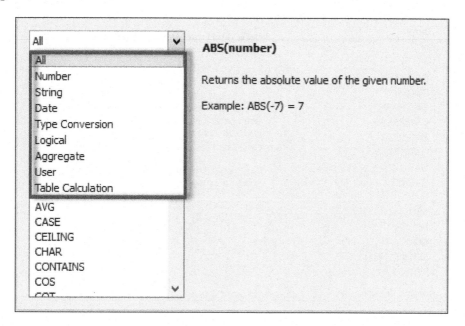

Function syntax

It is very helpful to click through the list of functions even just to see what the syntax is and to see some examples.

In general, functions have to be used with parentheses. The items inside parentheses are the values that the function expects when you use them. These are called arguments.

function name(mandatory argument, [optional argument])

If the syntax for a specific function shows an argument enclosed in square brackets, it means that that specific argument is optional, that is, it is not a syntax error if you do not have to pass the value for it.

 A list of Tableau functions can be found at:
`http://bit.ly/tableau_fxns`

In the following screenshot, you can see the function syntax for DATEDIFF. The first argument, date_part, is a common value you will need to supply for a number of date-related functions:

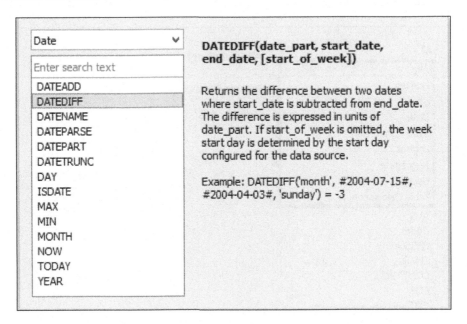

As the DATEDIFF example illustrates in the aforementioned screenshot, if a constant date needs to be used, they need to be enclosed in # (hash or pound) signs.

The Tableau website lists the date_part values. You can also access them from http://bit.ly/date_part.

Word of caution

Although some of the functions supported in Tableau have the same name as the functions you use in other applications or languages (SQL, for example), I caution you against assuming that it works the same way. There are functions that have the same name but will require different arguments, or return a different type, or both.

One example is the ISNULL function. In Tableau, the syntax of ISNULL is as follows:

    ISNULL(expression)

This function in Tableau accepts a single argument and returns a Boolean value.

Transact-SQL (or T-SQL) has a similar function. However, the syntax in T-SQL is as follows:

    ISNULL(check_expression, replacement_value)

In T-SQL, this function accepts two arguments and replaces the expression value if it is null. The return type is not a Boolean value. The function returns the same return type as the check_expression argument.

Support for regular expressions was introduced in Tableau V9. Regular expressions allow searching through patterns. This is quite powerful because sometimes the information is embedded in text, and it would be hard to search or extract otherwise.

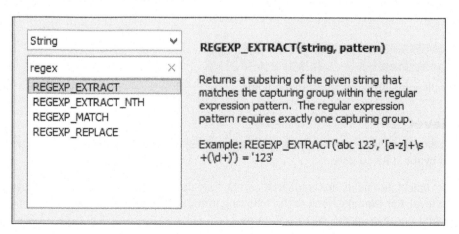

Check out the following URL for some regular expression reference:
`http://www.regular-expressions.info/reference.html`

Tableau also supports R expressions within Tableau calculated fields. The following is a list of functions that accept R expressions:

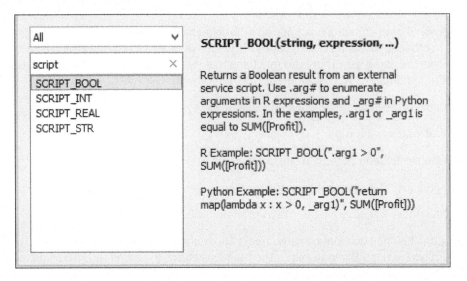

Different types of calculated fields

There are different types of calculated fields. They differ in function and behavior. They also differ in where they are executed and in what order.

Regular calculated fields

Let us look some different levels in the fields:

Row level

Simple calculated fields are fields that include expressions and/or formulas and are typically handled by the data source.

Row-level calculated fields are fields that can be calculated at the row level or the most granular level. For example, look at the following formula for concatenating a series of strings—first name, a space, and a last name:

```
FirstName + " " + LastName
```

The preceding code can derive the full name using only the information within the row itself. It does not need to refer to the result of a group first before it can concatenate the first and last names.

Group level (or aggregation)

An aggregated calculated field involves some calculation after some records are grouped. For example, the expression below checks the total profits of a group:

```
SUM(Profit) > 0
```

The term group seems somewhat vague. However, in Tableau, the group is determined by all other discrete fields present in the view.

In the aforementioned expression, a single record is not sufficient to determine the total profit of the group. All the individual records for the group must be processed to come up with a collective profit amount.

Row level versus aggregations

There is a distinct difference between row-level calculations and aggregations. Row-level calculations are processed first since they occur for each record. Aggregations happen after the row-level calculations are processed.

To illustrate, have a look at the following comparison:

Operation	Formula 1	Formula 2
	`Profit/Sales`	`SUM(Profit)/SUM(Sales)`
1	Each record gets a ratio	All of the profits will be summed up, and all sales will be summed up
2		Total of profit will be divided by total of sales
When dragged to the view	Will be aggregated	Will not be aggregated, since the aggregation is already embedded in the formula
	Default aggregation is `SUM`, so all the individual ratio values will be added together	Will show as `AGG`
	This will produce an incorrect ratio for the group	This will produce a correct ratio for the group

Table calculations

Table calculations, as the name implies, are calculations that happen at the table. Unlike regular calculations, table calculations do not happen at the data source. These happen in Tableau locally and are calculated based on what is in the view and how the data is laid out.

When I present the concept of table calculations in my training sessions, I usually start by asking students for a random number. Let's say they gave me the following numbers:

3	5	1
2	8	5
7	9	4
6	1	5

If we were trying to get the running total of the numbers, and we start with the top left number, what will be our first result? That's easy, it's 3.

But what if I asked you what the next number is? It's not so straightforward, is it? The following points will help answer the question:

1. Which direction is next? Should you go across and add **5**, or go down and add **2**?

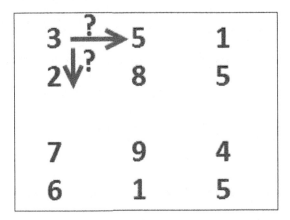

2. What happens when we get to the next group? Do we keep going? Or do we start again?

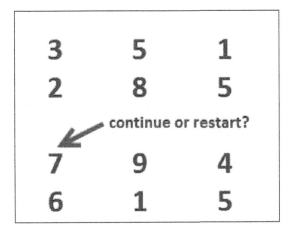

This is the pivotal moment of the discussion. Students start to really understand how table calculations work at this point, and it makes it clear that table calculations are affected by the following factors:

▸ What is in the view and what is filtered out of the view. If we were to take all the 5s out, the running total numbers would change.

▸ How the data is laid out. If we were to swap the rows and columns or move the columns around, the running total numbers would be different.

You can add table calculations from a continuous (green) pill on your view. When you click on the dropdown, you can find some predefined **Quick Table Calculations**:

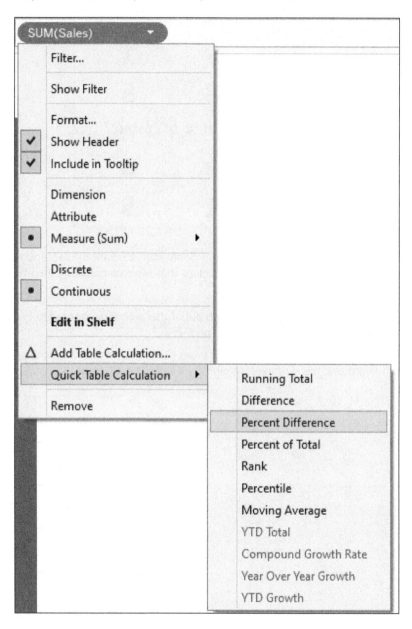

If the fields required to do the quick table calculation are not present, some of the options will be disabled. In the aforementioned case, if date fields are missing, any **YTD (year to date)** or **YOY (year over year)** calculations will be grayed out.

You can also create a customized table right off the bat by selecting the **Add Table Calculations...** option. Here is the window that appears when you click on **Add Table Calculations...**, which looks different from the Tableau V10 version. The window is modeless starting in V10, meaning you don't have to close the window to work on your view. You can still work on your view with this window open:

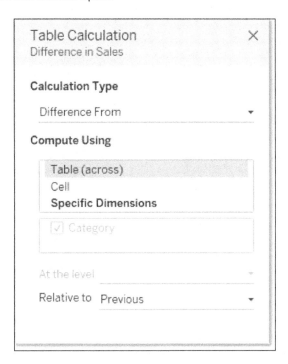

Some table calculations also allow for secondary table calculations, such as `Running Total`. Once you select the option for **Secondary Table Calculation**, a second window opens with additional options:

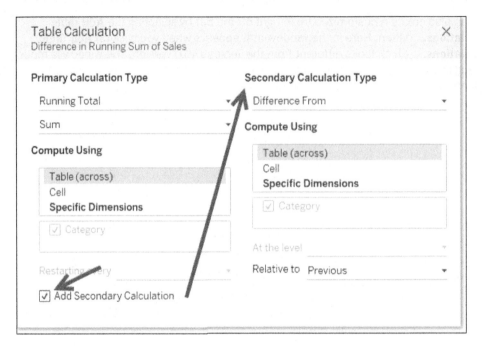

You can also use table calculation functions in your formulas. If you open the help window in the calculated field editor and choose **Table Calculation** from the dropdown, you will see a list of table calculation functions supported in Tableau, as shown in the following screenshot:

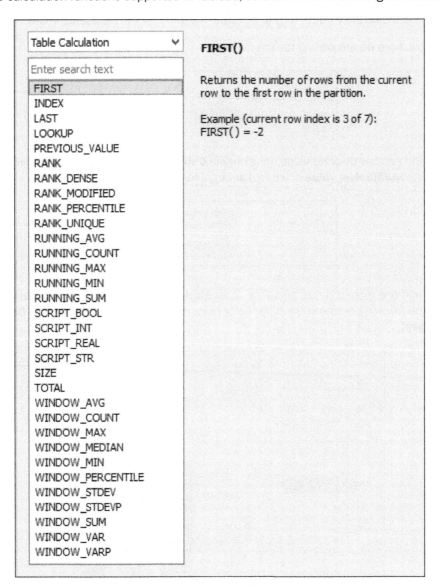

Level of detail expressions

Granularity or level of detail in Tableau, by default, is based on the discrete values you have in your view. Each discrete value is a by or per value—a slicer for the measures in the view.

For example, here we are getting the overall sum:

Once we add another discrete value, for example **Category**, to the **Columns** shelf, we are breaking the **SUM(Sales) value** down to a subtotal for each **Category**:

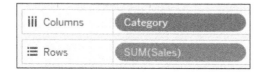

When we add one more discrete pill to the other **Marks** cards, the number is further broken down. In the following example, each bar color represents the **SUM(Sales)** for that **Category** and **Segment**:

But what if we wanted to have different levels of aggregation in one view, such as show a grand total but also the average per customer? A grand total will be more aggregated, and an average per customer will be less aggregated. **Level of detail** (**LOD**) expressions allow us to combine different aggregation levels in the same view.

The main syntax of an LOD expression is as follows:

```
{
    [FIXED | INCLUDE | EXCLUDE] <dimension declaration > : <aggregate expression>
}
```

LOD expressions produce a separate call to the data source and produce a row-level value as far as Tableau is concerned.

Tableau V10 now allows expressions to be used instead of dimension field names. In previous versions, if you needed to derive a dimension based on some logic, you needed to create a new field first and then use it in the LOD expression. In Tableau V10, this step can be eliminated by embedding another expression in place of the dimension name. For example, if you want to fix average sales per the company code, and the company code is the second substring in the **Company** field, you can simply use the corresponding expression that splits the company code in the LOD expression:

```
{FIXED TRIM(SPLIT([Company], "-", 2)): AVG(Sales)}
```

There are three types of LOD expression: FIXED, INCLUDE, and EXCLUDE.

FIXED

A FIXED LOD expression only considers the dimensions or expressions in the dimension declaration in its calculation. It is a fairly static calculation, which is not affected by what is dragged to or off the view. FIXED LOD expressions are not affected by dimension filters, but they respect data source and context filters.

In the following example, the profit values for each of the categories are plotted in individual line graphs. There is also a big, thick line graph that represents the average of the categories. This average is calculated using some FIXED LOD expressions. This means that the average value will not change even if some of the categories are unchecked from the filter. This is shown in the following screenshot:

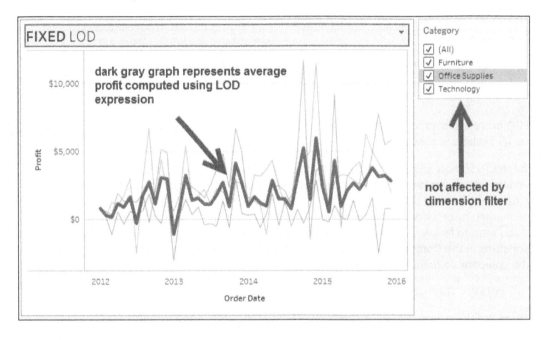

The formula for the average fixes the sum of profit for category, year, and month first. This is then passed to an outer expression, which then calculates the average of the sums based on a time period (year and month):

FIXED Monthly Average Profit   Sample - Superstore

```
{FIXED YEAR([Order Date]), MONTH([Order Date]):
    AVG(
            {FIXED [Category], YEAR([Order Date]), MONTH([Order Date]) :
            SUM([Profit])
            }
        )
}
```

INCLUDE

An INCLUDE LOD expression computes values as if the fields in the dimension declaration have been dragged onto the view. INCLUDE LODs are affected by dimension filters.

INCLUDE LODs will be used when you want a lower level of detail aggregation in the view.

In the following graph, although the view shows only the sum of profit for each category, a finer level of aggregation is introduced, which is the average per customer. This is done using an INCLUDE LOD expression, as shown next:

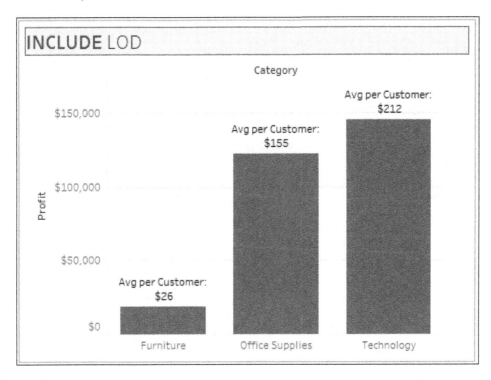

The formula for the **Avg per Customer** calculation is as follows:

Include Customer - Profit   Sample - Superstore

```
AVG({INCLUDE [Customer Name]: SUM([Profit])})
```

This means that the calculation will create an aggregation based on all the dimensions in the view and the **Customer Name**, as if the **Customer Name** was dragged onto the view.

EXCLUDE

An EXCLUDE LOD expression computes values as if the fields in the dimension declaration have been removed from the view. EXCLUDE LODs are affected by dimension filters.

EXCLUDE LODs will be used when you want a higher level of detail aggregation in the view:

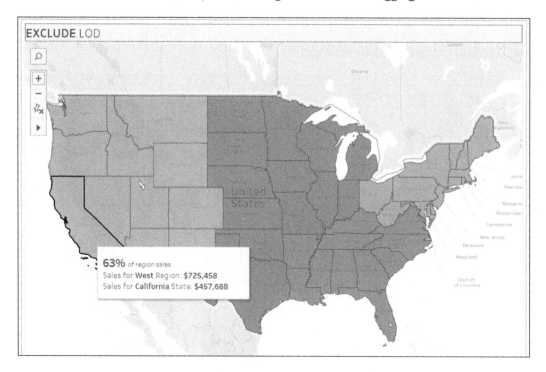

The formula for the **Exclude State for Region Sales** field is as follows:

In the aforementioned example, the view presents a level of detail at the **State** level represented by the map, but the tooltip shows one aggregation by **State** and another by **Region** regardless of **State**.

By default, if we drag **Sales** onto the view, it will be **SUM(Sales)** per **Region** per **State**. However, if we want to display both **SUM(Sales)** per **State** (less aggregated) and **SUM(Sales)** per **Region** (more aggregated), we can use the EXCLUDE LOD expression to ignore the **State** field when calculating **SUM(Sales)** per **Region**.

Significance of LODs

Level of detail (LOD) expressions formed one of the most anticipated features introduced in Tableau v9. LODs add immense flexibility to Tableau and simplify how complex calculations were done in the past versions.

Some of the most common use cases where LODs can be used are listed in Bethany Lyons' article on Top 15 LOD expressions, which can be found at `http://bit.ly/top15LOD`. A few use cases are as follows:

▸ **Cohort analysis**: Depending on the situation, we may need to keep or fix specific data points in order to perform group analysis. For example, we may need to know when customers first ordered, first joined a program, first got paid and so on, and from there perform additional aggregations.

▸ **Aggregating an aggregate**: LODs can be used to calculate the aggregate of aggregates. For example, we may need to know the average of maximum or minimum values and make the calculation immune to dimension filters.

▸ **Comparing to others**: LODs can be used to compare one data point to others. For example, to compare one vendor to other vendors, or one customer to other vendors, we may be required to have certain fields fixed to that customer or vendor. LOD calcs can help with this.

▸ **Relative period filtering**: LOD expressions allow us to find the maximum date in a data set to facilitate performance analysis through relative filtering, for example if we want to compare YTD values of this year with last year's.

▸ **Proportional brushing**: LOD expressions facilitate proportional brushing. This is a technique that allows us to compare one value to another without filtering the "other" values while showing the two values together, relative to the whole.

Despite being quite powerful and flexible, LODs have limitations, and we need to be aware of them. The limitations are listed at `http://bit.ly/lod-overview`, and include the following:

▸ Avoiding using floating point measures in LOD aggregations

▸ Using the linking field from the primary data source in the view before using LOD expressions from the secondary data source

Order of operations

It is important to understand the order of operations in Tableau, especially with the filters. For example, do dimension filters affect LOD expressions? If this is not understood, there will be some unexpected behaviors.

The following is Tableau's updated illustration for order of operations (as of August 2016), as shown in the Tableau official online documentation:

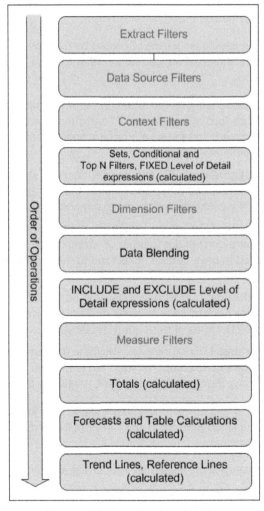

Source - Tableau online documentation

You can find the original at http://bit.ly/tableau-orderofoperations.

Deep dive

What this section has covered is barely the tip of the iceberg, and I encourage you to learn more about calculations in depth. Understanding the types of calculations and when they are appropriate to use can make you really efficient and effective in Tableu.

 Here is a great article by Alan Aldridge on choosing the right calculation type: `https://blog.databender.net/2016/03/06/choosing-the-right-calculation-type/`

Dealing with NULLs

When working with calculated fields, it is important to understand what NULLs are and how to deal with fields that have NULL values.

A NULL is a missing value. It is an indeterminate value. A NULL is *not*:

- a zero
- a space
- an empty string

Whenever there is an operation between a field that has a value and a field that has a NULL, the result is always a NULL. When you add 1 to nothing, what is the result? Indeterminate. When you concatenate a first name to an unknown value, what is the result? Indeterminate—we don't know.

Let's take the following data set:

	A	B	C
1	Order ID	Sales	Discount Percentage
2	A02	100	25
3	B05	200	
4	C10	300	10
5	D55	1000	

Once you connect this Excel file to Tableau, the initial connection screen will look like the following. Notice how the missing values in Excel appear as NULL in the preview screen:

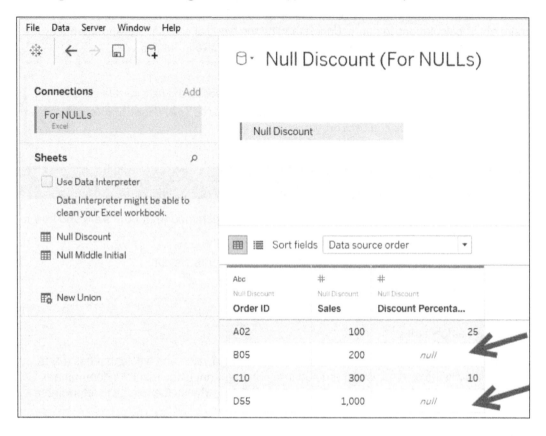

The following formula will calculate the discount amount correctly if there are no NULL values:

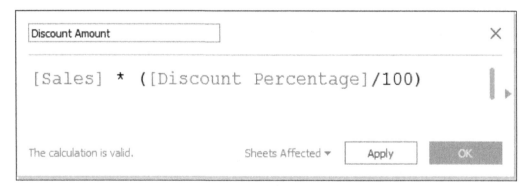

If we try to calculate the total discounted price as normal, using the following formula, we are going to get incorrect results:

Dealing with NULLs - Problem				
Order ID	Sales	Discount Percentage	Discount Amount	Discounted Sales
A02	$100	25%	$25	$75
B05	$200			
C10	$300	10%	$30	$270
D55	$1,000			
Grand Total	$1,600	35%	$55	$345

Here are a few ways to deal with NULL values:

▶ The IFNULL value:

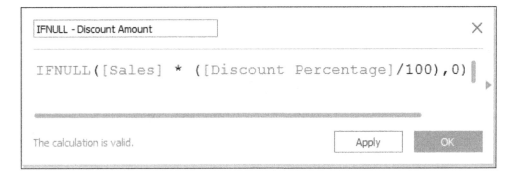

IFNULL - Discount Amount

```
IFNULL([Sales] * ([Discount Percentage]/100),0)
```

The calculation is valid.   Apply   OK

▶ The IIF and ISNULL value:

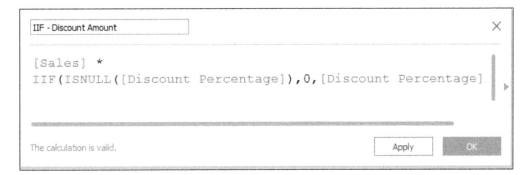

IIF - Discount Amount

```
[Sales] *
IIF(ISNULL([Discount Percentage]),0,[Discount Percentage]
```

The calculation is valid.   Apply   OK

▸ The IF...ELSE and ISNULL value:

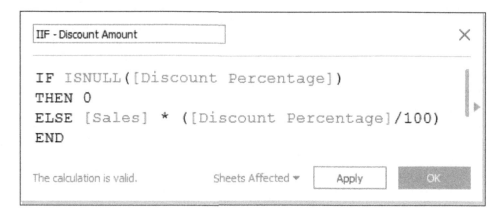

▸ The ZN value:

Note that ZN stands for *Zero if null*, which means this function will only work if the expected return value is numeric.

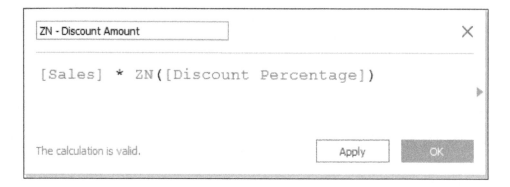

▸ The CASE value:

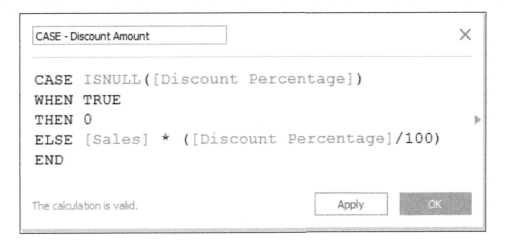

Each of these calculations will produce a 0 for the discount amount if the discount percentage is missing. This will allow the discounted sales amount, that is, sales less discount amount, to be calculated correctly:

Order ID	Sales	Discount Percentage	Discount Amount	Discounted Sales	ZN - Discount Amount	ZN - Discounted Sales
A02	$100	25%	$25	$75	$25	$75
B05	$200				$0	$200
C10	$300	10%	$30	$270	$30	$270
D55	$1,000				$0	$1,000
Grand Total	$1,600	35%	$55	$345	$55	$1,545

original calculation, not handling NULL, incorrect total

updated calculation using ZN, correctly handling NULL

Tidbits

Here are a few tidbits/tricks that you may find helpful as you venture into the world of calculated fields in Tableau (Conversion error):

Cannot mix aggregate and non-aggregate arguments

One of the most common calculation errors you may encounter will be related to mixing aggregate and non-aggregate arguments in functions:

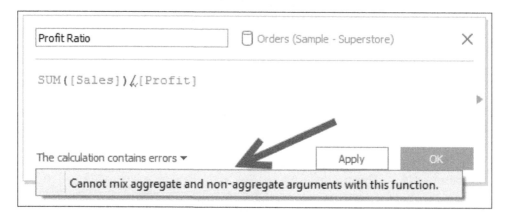

What this simply states is that if one part of the calculation is an aggregation (such as SUM, AVG, MAX, and MIN), all other parts should also be aggregations.

This becomes tricky when working with level of detail calculations. For example, we may have an LOD expression that gets a FIXED sum of sales:

What if we need to use this with another calculated field that is aggregated? In the following example, we are dividing SUM(Quantity) by our fixed LOD calculated field, which is already an aggregated field. However, we are getting the notorious **Cannot mix aggregate and non-aggregate...** error, as shown in the following screenshot:

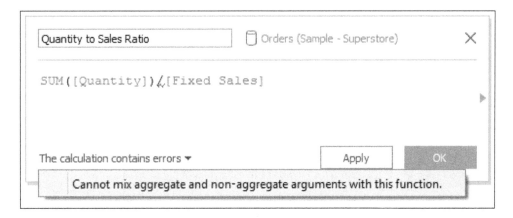

Not to worry. Since LOD expressions are technically treated as row-level values, all we need to do is enclose this field in another aggregation. Putting Fixed Sales in a SUM or MIN or MAX or AVG will not change its value; the SUM of one value is still the same value, but it will help get around the aggregation error:

Discrete fields in measures

When you first open the sample Superstore Excel file that comes with Tableau, you may have noticed that by default, all the blue (discrete) fields are in the **Dimensions** section, and the green (continuous) fields are in the **Measures** section. However, do not assume that only discrete fields can be in **Dimensions** and continuous fields in **Measures**.

Numeric and date fields can be converted into **Continuous** and can still appear in the **Dimensions** section:

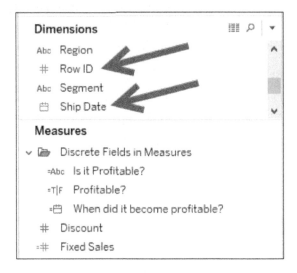

By the same token, measures can be converted to discrete, but they still stay in the **Measures** section.

Calculated fields that include any aggregation will always appear in the **Measures** section regardless of the data type. In the following screenshot, you will see different discrete data types in the **Measures** section as a result of using aggregate functions (such as **SUM(Profit)**) in the underlying formula:

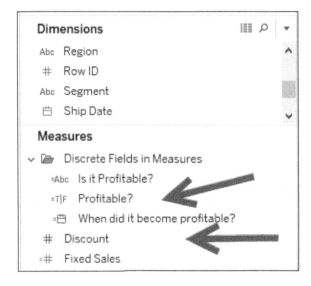

How ATTR works

In Tableau, it is possible to aggregate dimensions too. **MIN** and **MAX** are aggregation functions, which can be applied to dimensions. Tableau also has a function called **ATTR**, which does allow dimension aggregation.

ATTR checks for heterogeneity of values. The ATTR function returns a value if all of that group's values are the same. Otherwise, an asterisk (*) is returned. If we were to convert it to another formula, the ATTR function would be similar to the following expression:

```
IF MIN(dimension) = MAX(dimension)
THEN "dimension"
ELSE "*"
END
```

To illustrate, have a look at the following example:

Category	Sub-Category	ATTR([Sub-Category]
Furniture	Bookcases	Bookcases
	Chairs	Chairs
	Furnishings	Furnishings
	Tables	Tables
Office Supplies	Appliances	Appliances
	Art	Art
	Binders	Binders
	Envelopes	Envelopes
	Fasteners	Fasteners
	Labels	Labels
	Paper	Paper
	Storage	Storage
	Supplies	Supplies
Technology	Accessories	Accessories
	Copiers	Copiers
	Machines	Machines
	Phones	Phones

ATTR ▼

Sub-Category

- ☑ (All)
- ☑ Accessories
- ☑ Appliances
- ☑ Art
- ☑ Binders
- ☑ Bookcases
- ☑ Chairs
- ☑ Copiers
- ☑ Envelopes
- ☑ Fasteners
- ☑ Furnishings
- ☑ Labels
- ☑ Machines
- ☑ Paper
- ☑ Phones
- ☑ Storage
- ☑ Supplies
- ☑ Tables

The **ATTR([Sub-Category])** field was calculated using the formula ATTR([Sub-Category]). At this point, all the **Sub-Category** values in every line are uniform; therefore, the ATTR function returns and displays that single value.

However, once we take the **Sub-Category** field away and aggregate the dimensions to **Category**, **ATTR([Sub-Category])** should have multiple values and therefore report an asterisk.

In the following screenshot, **Bookcases** appear only because all the other values in the **Furniture** group—**Chairs**, **Furnishings**, and **Tables**—have been deselected from the **Filter** shelf, leaving **Bookcases** as the only value under that group:

You may see ATTR used a lot when you have blended data. Fields from the secondary data source need to be aggregated, and this is a way to ensure that the returned values from the secondary data source come back as a single label. You may have noticed it before that when you drag dimension fields that produce multiple values, values are displayed as asterisks instead.

Another possible use case is when we want to check whether something or someone has been consistent in behavior. For example, if I want to quickly check whether a students has taken only courses from the Computer Science department, I can use the ATTR () function on Department. All students who have taken only Computer Science courses should reveal Computer Science, while students who have taken from other departments will yield an asterisk (*).

Conclusion

In this section, we covered different ways to create calculated fields in Tableau as well as different types of calculated fields: basic, table calculations, and level of detail calculations. Our data sources will not have all the possible fields we want to use in our analysis. Calculated fields allow us to derive values based on logic and expressions; they ultimately add more flexibility and drive more insights into our Tableau dashboards.

B

Resources

This is just the start! There are worlds to explore in Tableau, and we are fortunate that there are many resources available to help us explore and learn more.

Data sources for recipes in this book

Here are some of the sample data sets from Tableau Public's Resources page (`https://public.tableau.com/s/resources`):

- Top Baby Names in the US
- Cat vs Dog Popularity in the US
- Startup Venture Funding
- Global Burden of Disease
- Global Sport Finances
- Summer Olympics Medalist Dataset
- NFL stats, 1999-2013
- Hollywood's Most Profitable Stories
- Significant Volcanic Eruptions
- Global Active Archive of Large Flood Events
- Magnitude 6+ Earthquakes

Now let us look at ample data sets from other resources:

- New York Open Data – Restaurant Inspections: `https://data.cityofnewyork.us/Health/DOHMH-New-York-City-Restaurant-Inspection-Results/xx67-kt59/data`

- NBA Basketball Data Set 2009: `http://www.databasebasketball.com/stats_download.htm`

- Open Flights: `http://openflights.org/data.html`

- Our Airports: `http://ourairports.com/data/`

- Spatineo: `http://directory.spatineo.com/`

- Gapminder: `https://www.gapminder.org/data/`

- BC Stats Population Projection: `http://www.bcstats.gov.bc.ca/StatisticsBySubject/Demography/PopulationProjections.aspx`

- World Bank – World Development Indicators: `http://data.worldbank.org/data-catalog/world-development-indicators`

- City of Vancouver Open Data: `http://vancouver.ca/your-government/open-data-catalogue.aspx`

- Canada Open Data: `http://open.canada.ca/en`

- National Water Quality Monitoring Council – Water Quality Data: `http://www.waterqualitydata.us/portal/`

- World Health Organization: `http://apps.who.int/gho/data/node.home`

Articles and white papers

Here are some useful articles and white papers (in no particular order). This is just a partial list of many useful articles about Tableau and visualization in general:

- Five things I wish I knew about Tableau when I started (*This is an older article, but still useful and relevant to the current version.*): `http://bit.ly/5things-tableau`

- Top 10 Tableau Table Calculations: `http://bit.ly/top10tablecalcs`

- Understanding Level of Detail Expressions: `http://bit.ly/UnderstandingLOD`

- Top 15 LOD Expressions `http://bit.ly/top15LOD`

- Tableau and R Integration `http://bit.ly/tableau-and-r`

- Visual Analysis Guide Book `http://bit.ly/vaguidebook`

- Tableau Drive Manual `http://bit.ly/tableaudrivemanual`

- Designing Efficient Workbooks `http://bit.ly/efficientworkbooks`

- A Guide to Creating Dashboards People Love to Use by Juice Analytics `bit.ly/`

DashboardsPeopleLoveToUse

- ▶ Design Tips for Non-Designers by Juice Analytics `http://bit.ly/designtipsfornondesigners`
- ▶ Designing Effective Tables and Graphs by Stephen Few `http://bit.ly/stephenfew-effectivechart`
- ▶ Tapping the Power of Visual Perception by Stephen Few `http://bit.ly/stephenfew-visualperception`
- ▶ Bullet Graph Design Specification by Stephen Few `https://www.perceptualedge.com/articles/misc/Bullet_Graph_Design_Spec.pdf`
- ▶ Implementing Tableau Server: Top 10 Pitfalls `http://bit.ly/tableauserver-top10pitfalls`

Blogs and additional resources

These are some great blogs and sites on visual analytics and Tableau (in no particular order). This is by no means an exhaustive list of valuable blogs and resources about visualization and Tableau:

- ▶ The Information Lab blog: `http://www.theinformationlab.co.uk/category/blog/`
- ▶ Interworks blog: `https://www.interworks.com/blog`
- ▶ DataBlick blog: `http://datablick.com/blog/`
- ▶ Perceptual Edge by Stephen Few: `https://www.perceptualedge.com/`
- ▶ Vizwiz by Andy Kriebel: `http://www.vizwiz.com/`
- ▶ Health Intelligence by Ramon Martinez: `http://www.publichealthintelligence.org/`
- ▶ VizPainter by Joshua Milligan: `http://vizpainter.com/`
- ▶ Data Blender by Alan Eldridge: `https://blog.databender.net`
- ▶ Tableau Picasso by George Gorczynski: `http://tableaupicasso.com/`
- ▶ Drawing with Numbers by Jonathan Drummey: `http://drawingwithnumbers.artisart.org/`
- ▶ Vizcandy by Kelly Martin: `http://www.vizcandy.ca/`
- ▶ Tableau Zen by Mark Jackson: `http://ugamarkj.blogspot.ca/`
- ▶ Data Plus Science by Jeffrey Shaffer: `https://www.dataplusscience.com/`
- ▶ Data Revelations by Steve Wexler: `http://www.datarevelations.com/blog-page`
- ▶ Jewel Loree: `http://www.jewelloree.com/`

- Bora Beran: `https://boraberan.wordpress.com/`
- VizNinja by Paul Banoub: `https://vizninja.com/`
- Data Boss by Tamás Földi: `http://databoss.starschema.net/`
- Paint by Numbers by Peter Gilks: `http://paintbynumbersblog.blogspot.ca/`
- Ryan Sleeper: `http://www.ryansleeper.com/content/`

Index

CPSIA information can be obtained
at www.ICGtesting.com
Printed in the USA
BVOW09s2231270717

490462BV00003B/8/P